Religion as Social Capital

Religion as Social Capital

Producing the Common Good

edited by

Corwin Smidt

Baylor
University
Press
Waco, TX 76798

Library of Congress Cataloging-in-Publication Data

Religion as social capital : producing the common good /
Corwin Smidt,
editor.
     p. cm.
Includes bibliographical references and index.
  ISBN 0-918954-85-1 (pbk. : alk. paper)
  1. United States--Religion. 2. Social capital (Sociology)--
Religious
aspects. 3. United States--Social conditions. 4. Social captial
(Sociology)--United States. I. Smidt, Corwin E., 1946-

BL2525.R458 2003
306.6'0973--dc21

                                        2002154539

Printed in the United States of America on acid-free paper

Contents

Preface and Acknowledgments

This volume addresses the relationship between religion and civil society and how the nature of that relationship can serve to shape democratic life. Many of the chapters are drawn from papers presented at the "Conference of Religion, Social Capital, and Democratic Life" held at Calvin College on 16-17 October 1998, sponsored by the Paul B. Henry Institute for the Study of Christianity and Politics, and funded, in part, by a grant from The Louisville Institute. The aim of the conference was to provide scholars with a forum in which they could examine the interrelationships among religion, social capital, and democratic life more fully. This volume reflects some of the interests, discussions, and analyses evident at that conference, but we also hope that it will serve to stimulate other scholars to examine these relationships more fully and in greater depth.

Chapter 1

Introduction

Corwin Smidt

Culture plays a central role in political life because political institutions do not operate in a vacuum, isolated and cut off from the society of which they are a part. Cultural values and practices influence the tone and style of political life as well as the operation of political institutions, and changes in cultural life have a profound impact on how politics is practiced.

Such an understanding of politics served to undergird Tocqueville's analysis of political life in early Jacksonian America. He contended that democracy requires the presence and vitality of civic associations that are not necessarily political in nature but that serve as sources of meaning and social engagement. Associational life served a double purpose—not only did it function to protect individual liberty against the coercive powers of the state, but it also served to mitigate against the dangers of rampant individualism within the political community. For Tocqueville, associational life actually provided the foundation for democratic life, because democracy could not survive unless citizens continued to participate actively, joining with others of similar mind and interest to address matters of common concern.

Given this alleged importance of civil associations, it is hardly surprising that Putnam's (1995a) contention that "the vibrancy of American civil society . . . has notably declined over the past several decades" has received considerable attention both within and outside the scholarly community. Like Tocqueville, Putnam views the vibrancy of democratic life to be an outgrowth of these associations and the positive attitudes and actions they evoke from their members. Consequently, he finds it alarming that Americans are not only less likely today to interact with one another than three decades ago, but they are less likely to trust either government or others as well. Though other scholars have challenged this contention (e.g., Ladd 1996), Putnam's assertion has helped to place the examination of associational life once again at the heart of scholarly analyses of democratic life. In fact, in recent years, there has been a "growth industry" in studies related to "civil society" and the role that civic associations may play in forging "social capital."[1] For Putnam (1993a), associational life contributes to the formation of social capital, which, in turn, fosters civic engagement. For present purposes, it is sufficient to note simply that the term "social capital" is generally used to denote any facet of social relations that serve to enable members of society to work together to accomplish collective goals. Though he did not coin the term, it has been Putnam's scholarly works that have brought the analysis of social capital into prominence.

In light of this scholarly interest and attention, it is noteworthy that relatively little scholarly attention has been given to the role of religion in social capital formation. In part, this may be due to the fact that religious associations can be viewed, in many ways, to be similar to other kinds of associations that individuals may forge. Yet, there are also aspects of religious life that tend to make religious associations distinctive from other kinds of association. Putnam (2000, 66) himself has recognized that "faith communities in which people worship together are arguably the single most important repository of social capital in America." Yet, despite this recognition, Putnam and others have treated religion primarily as one form, among many such forms, of association. Little attention, as yet, has been devoted to the unique role that religion may play in building social capital.

There are a variety of reasons why the relationship between religion and social capital formation and its consequences should be examined more carefully. Certainly, as noted earlier, congregational life has traditionally been a major component of associational life in the United States. Not only is church affiliation the most common form of association in American life, but these associations provide important services and resources to their members and others in the community—e.g., by providing physical care, social support, and social networks. Likewise, religious beliefs can serve to shape the level, form, and goals of one's associational life. Different religious doctrines may affect the ways in which people may view human nature generally, the extent to which such believers choose to relate to those outside their religious community, and the priorities given to political life generally and personal political agendas specifically. Finally, religious behavior may contribute to social capital formation in that volunteering, charitable contributions, and other distinct acts of mercy can, at least in the short run, help to provide a "safety net" for members of society who are "at risk." Given these characteristics, Miller (1998) has asserted that religion has more potential to contribute to America's social capital than any other institution in American society.

But religion's potential importance with regard to social capital formation is not limited to the extent to which religion likely contributes to social capital formation. Religion is important because of the sectors of society in which this social capital formation may occur. Wood (1997), for example, argues that church-based social organizing in urban settings has proved more successful than other bases for such organizational efforts due, in large part, to the demise of other forms of civic associations in urban areas. According to Wood (1997, 601), religious institutions play a distinctive role within inner-city contexts because "those settings that previously generated trust and sustained broad social networks have deteriorated badly: unions, blue-collar workplaces, cultural associations, families and so forth." In fact, within many inner-city neighborhoods, religious institutions are among the few institutions that still are trusted (Miller 1998, 24).

The present volume seeks to address this lack of attention. It is distinctive in its focus in that it analyzes the role religion plays in social capital formation and how such social capital forged through religion shapes civic engagement in American public life. It addresses how religious social capital is similar to, or different from, the social capital generated through other forms of association. It analyzes how the social capital generated through religion contributes to a greater and richer democratic life. Finally, it examines how the influence of religious associational life in the formation of social capital may vary across different domains or contexts. Thus, the volume focuses on the relationship between social capital and democratic life, but it does so primarily through the lens of religious life.

Because the social capital framework may not be familiar to all, this introductory chapter first provides a brief review of the larger debate about the topic that is currently enjoined within the scholarly community. Second, the chapter provides a discussion of the various concepts and analytical distinctions employed in the volume and identifies some of the major issues associated with the social capital framework of analysis. And, finally, the chapter provides an overview of the volume, indicating how the various chapters are organized and interrelated.

CIVIL SOCIETY AND SOCIAL CAPITAL

While the term "civil society" has had a variety of different meanings, it is generally used to denote "those forms of communal and associational life which are organized neither by self-interest of the market nor by the coercive potential of the state" (Wolfe 1998, 9). Because such associations are not formed on the basis of coercive means, civil society is viewed to be composed of voluntary associations. And because they are not formed purely on the basis of personal self-interest, the motivational basis for forming such associations is viewed as constituting a more civic, rather than self-centered, foundation.

Most civic associations do not fall directly within the public realm in that civic engagement denotes "people's connection with the life of their communities, not merely with politics" (Putnam 1995b, 665). In fact, much of associational life is not explicitly political in nature. Still, while most civic associations do not fall directly within the public realm and while much of associational life may not be explicitly political in nature, such "non-political" civic associations have important political consequences, e.g., with regard to the role that civic associations may play in promoting civic education, fostering civic skills, and bridging social cleavages. Moreover, such associational life may well serve to undergird the public realm by helping to keep the power of governmental coercion at bay. Thus, while much of associational life may not be explicitly political in nature, it is inherently political given its possible ramifications for fostering democratic life.

More recent analyses of associational life, and its impact politically, have focused largely on what has been called "social capital," a framework of analysis that refers to features of social organization (e.g., friendship networks, norms, and social trust) that facilitate working and cooperating together for mutual benefit. Accordingly, social capital can be viewed as a set of "moral resources" that lead to increased cooperation among individuals. In the words of James Coleman (1990, 302-4):

> Like other forms of capital, social capital is productive, making possible the achievement of certain ends that would not be attainable in its absence. . . . For example, a group whose members manifest trustworthiness and place extensive trust in one another will be able to accomplish much more than a comparable group lacking that trustworthiness and trust.

While it is difficult to specify everything that social capital might entail, Coleman does provide us with a starting point. He lists several elements of social relationships that include social capital (1990, 311-13). First, there are social obligations and expectations. Such obligations and expectations help to forge the element of social trust that is inherent in interpersonal relationships where "if A does something for B and trusts B to reciprocate in the future, this establishes an expectation in A and an obligation on the part of B" (Coleman 1988, S102). These obligations and expectations are often enforced by a second element of social capital—norms and sanctions. For Coleman, one important form of social capital found within a collectivity is the "prescriptive norm that . . . one should forgo self-interest to act in the interest of the collectivity" (Coleman 1990, 311). Third, social support reinforces these norms and applies sanctions if the norms are not followed: "This social capital . . . not only facilitates certain actions but also constrains others" (1990, 311). Finally, social capital is tied to voluntary associations because such group involvement tends to generate obligations and expectations as well as foster social trust (Coleman 1990, 311-13).

The concept of civil society is much more encompassing than that of social capital. Social capital originates in, but does not constitute, civil society. The concepts of civil society and social capital are interrelated in that both the current debate over civil society generally and social capital more specifically are concerned both with the extent and quality of social interaction as well as with the kinds of relationships that serve to build and sustain moral commitment and character (Wuthnow 1996a, 2).

Still, the concept of social capital is used more narrowly to denote those features of social organization that facilitate working and cooperating together for mutual benefit (e.g., friendship networks, norms, and social trust). Generally speaking, however, the social capital framework presumes that associational life and interpersonal trust are simply interrelated. According to Putnam (1995b, 665): "the more we connect with other people, the more we trust them, and vice versa."

The importance of social capital is tied to its capacity to bind together autonomous individuals into communal relationships. Social capital serves to transform self-interested individuals exhibiting little social conscience and weak feelings of mutual obligation into members of a community expressing shared interests and a sense of the common good. And, "spontaneous cooperation is facilitated by social capital" (Putnam 1993, 167).

What ingredients provide social capital with such a transforming capacity? Two, in particular, have been frequently cited as crucial aspects of social capital—trust and reciprocity. According to Putnam (1993, 170), trust constitutes "an essential component of social capital." Trust facilitates and "lubricates" cooperation in that increased trust leads to the likelihood of increased cooperation.

Still, not all social trust is likely to be the same; the nature of social trust is likely to vary by the particular social context within which it is expressed. In communities in which face-to-face interactions predominate, "thick" trust is more likely to be evident, a trust that is produced through intensive, highly regular, and relatively frequent contact between and among people (Williams 1988, 8). Not surprisingly, these kinds of communities tend to be ones that are relatively homogeneous socially and isolated geographically, where members can apply the relatively strict sanctions needed to sustain such thick trust (Coleman 1988, 105-8). Modern societies, however, tend to generate a thinner form of social trust, a kind of trust that is tied to "looser, more amorphous, secondary relations" (Newton 1997, 578). In large, more complex, social settings, it is difficult to generate the thick kind of trust produced in more face-to-face communities. In its place, a less personal, more indirect, form of trust tends to be generated. This "thin" form of trust is the result of weak social ties—but even such weak ties can nevertheless serve as a relatively powerful and enduring basis for social integration in these larger, more complex, modern societies (Granovetter 1973).

Just how does the social trust that tends to be generated in more face-to-face settings, where people are relatively well known, become evident in modern, large-scale societies as some form of a more generalized social trust?

Within modern, relatively complex social contexts, social trust is thought to be generated through two different but related means—norms of reciprocity and networks of civic engagement (Putnam 1993, 171). With regard to the first means, the term "reciprocity" is used not to suggest some form of "eye for eye" mentality. Rather, what is suggested here is something akin to the expectation that "good deeds will not go unrewarded." It is the assumption that good deeds, though not necessarily rewarded in the short term, will nevertheless be "repaid" at some, though unknown, point in the future—perhaps even by some stranger who may not have been a recipient of that particular kindness. Thus, there are risks and uncertainties associated with exhibiting good deeds in more impersonalized settings, because one's deeds of kindness may not be rewarded. Such acts of kindness rest, in part, on trust in others that such actions will, at some point, be reciprocated. Moreover, even ordinary daily life entails so many small risks that life would be impossible to handle without placing some trust in one's fellow citizens (e.g., one largely takes for granted, or trusts, that the stranger in the car approaching the stoplight will stop his or her car when the light turns red). Thus, the Hobbesian state of nature in which life is characterized as nasty, brutish, and short is transformed through social trust; it serves to create a social context in which life is more pleasant and less dangerous (Newton 1997, 576).

The second means by which social trust may be generated is through networks of civic engagement. How do voluntary associations help to generate social capital? Generally speaking, it is argued that participation in voluntary associations fosters interactions between people and increases the likelihood that trust between members will be generated. Group activity helps to broaden the scope of an individual's interest, making public matters more relevant. In addition, it is argued that participation in organizations tends to increase members' level of information, trains them in social interaction, fosters leadership skills, and provides resources essential for effective public action (e.g., Verba, Schlozman, & Brady 1995). Collectively, the results of such memberships in voluntary associations is an "increased capacity for collective action, cooperation, and trust within the group, enabling the collective purposes of the group to be more easily achieved" (Stolle & Rochon 1998, 48). Thus, the argument is made that such civic associations (1) help to socialize individuals, teaching them mores with regard to how one should think and behave—mores necessary for maintaining a healthy society and polity, and (2) foster engagement politically through greater public awareness, broadened interests, and enhanced skills.

A CLOSER EXAMINATION OF SOCIAL CAPITAL

Despite the growth in the use of "social capital" in scholarly discussions, there are a variety of issues related to the concept and the theoretical foundation upon which it is based. These issues relate to the adequacy of its theoretical explanatory power, its conceptual clarity, its posited empirical relationships, and its normative perspective.

Theoretical Issues

The social capital framework of analysis stresses the socialization of individuals that occurs through associational life and that such socialization instills shared norms and encourages cooperative societal action. To the extent that it is a causal theory, the social capital approach "embodies a fundamentally social psychological proposition about the roots of efficient government and social institutions, focusing on the socialization of individuals into collective behavior" (Skocpol & Fiorina 1999, 13). The theory that undergirds the social capital approach focuses on the alleged beneficial effects of relationships that occur primarily on the basis of face-to-face interactions. People who regularly interact with each other in such settings supposedly not only learn to work with each other to solve collective problems, but they learn to trust each other and develop norms of reciprocity as well. It is further argued that this forging of interpersonal trust has consequences for the political system in that such personal trust "spills over" into a kind of "generalized trust" in others as well as a trust in government more generally. The net results that flow from this learning of social trust through regular and sustained civic engagement are increased capacities for "wise public policy, robust economic development, and efficient public administration" (Skocpol & Foriona 1999, 13).

In emphasizing the beneficial effects on the political system that are wrought through associational activities, the social capital approach places "the cure" for the ills of American democracy on a different doorstep than those analysts who emphasize structural or procedural changes in American social and political life. For Putnam and others who follow him, reforms related to such issues as term limits, campaign financing, or any proposed constitutional amendment, will not address the deeper, more fundamental, cause of America's problems. Instead, advocates of the social capital framework hold that it is basically associational life that serves to produce the trust, networks, and norms that ultimately issue forth in the kind of social trust and civic engagement that sustain healthy democratic systems (Foley & Edwards 1998, 12).

Those analysts who are skeptical of the relative efficacy of the social capital account of democratic life generally contend that the framework is too simplistic and that it neglects or downplays crucial factors that also serve to shape the nature of democratic life. Critics argue that Putnam and his followers generally ignore the important role that institutional structures, particularly the state, play in the formation and continuation of associational life and that the process of social capital production not only has social, but structural, antecedents (e.g, Walzer 1991). This fact is most clearly evident in those countries that seek to undergo a transition to democracy. Simple constitutional rights enjoyed in the

United States—such as freedom of speech, assembly, and association—that serve to enable associational life to function easily are often a struggle to institutionalize in other contexts. Moreover, voluntary associations may also thrive, in part, because of the state's economic policies. Even in the United States, particular kinds of associations may receive either direct or indirect (e.g., non-profit tax status) state funding.

But, even if one assumes that the social capital theorists are correct in their assessment of the fundamental importance of associational life, the mechanisms by which such affiliations get transformed into social capital are far from being clearly specified. It is not clear, for example, just how the social trust forged in primary, face-to-face, interactions becomes somehow transformed into a more "generalized social trust" (trust in people in general). Nor is it clear how such personal trust moves people to become more trusting in either governmental officials or public institutions. Likewise, even the assumption that healthy democracies need high levels of trust in government can be disputed, particularly given the "distinct possibility that a large dose of distrust in government might sometimes be essential to the defense of democracy" (Foley & Edwards 1998, 13).

Conceptual Issues

In addition to these theoretical issues, there are also several issues related to the concept of social capital itself. One basic issue relates to where social capital resides and, in turn, how it should be differentiated from other forms of capital—specifically, financial, human, and cultural capital (Edwards & Foley 1998, 135). This debate can not be resolved here. But it may be helpful to highlight some of these differences in the conceptualizations in order to better understand their implications.

While Putnam and his followers have drawn upon Coleman's discussion and understanding of social capital, they do not follow fully Coleman's conceptualization of social capital. Coleman understood and treated social capital as a structural variable, something that only exists between and among certain individuals within a particular context. For example, Coleman (1990, 302) states that

> Unlike other forms of capital, social capital inheres in the structure of the relations between persons and among persons. It is lodged neither in individuals nor in physical implements of production.

As such, social capital is not a property or characteristic of an individual, and as such it is not a transportable resource that one takes with oneself in entering a new relationship with some stranger. Rather, for Coleman, social capital is something that is socially embedded in *particular* relationships.

Putnam has also defined social capital as facets of social relations that serve to enable members of society to work together and to accomplish collective goals. For example, in *Making Democracy Work,* Putnam (1993a, 167) defined social capital as "features of social organization . . . that can improve the efficiency of society by facilitating coordinated actions." But, more recently, Putnam (2000, 20) has argued that "Social capital has both an individual and a collective aspect." When he emphasizes this more individual facet of social capital, Putnam focuses either upon attitudes of "generalized social trust" or perceived norms of reciprocity. But when social capital is understood in this fashion, it becomes a resource that is transportable—something that one can take along as one moves from one social relationship to another.

Whether social capital is seen as an individual or structural resource shapes how one might choose to differentiate between and among other forms of capital—particularly, how social capital might relate to human capital. Those who define social capital as a structural variable view it as something different from human capital, which inheres in individuals. Human capital might include one's level of education or one's level of organizational skills. As individuals move in and out of different social contexts, they take their human capital with them, whereas social capital, in contrast, "represents resources that reside in function-specific social relationships in which individuals are embedded" (Teachman, Paasch, & Carver 1997, 1344). On the other hand, those who define social capital as something an individual possesses see it simply as one other form of human capital, along with one's level of education and organizational skills.

How one chooses to define social capital also affects the way in which one chooses to study social capital. If social capital is something an individual possesses, then one might study social capital through survey research that assesses individual involvement in associational life and the attitudes and orientations that may be linked to such life. On the other hand, if social capital is something that inheres in personal relationships that are specific to the particular individuals involved, then questions related to social capital need to be studied through techniques that employ personal observation and that are more ethnographic in their approach.

Empirical Issues

There are also a variety of empirical issues related to the recent attention given to associational life and its alleged effects upon American life. Putnam has argued that Americans are exhibiting declining levels of civic engagement across a spectrum of American social life—in politics, in the workplace, in informal social interactions, and in the neighborhoods in which they reside. In seeking to substantiate this contention, Putnam has presented data on formal membership levels found in long-standing organizations (e.g., the League of Women Voters, the P.T.A., and the Shriners) in which comparable membership statistics could be analyzed over time. But the merits of Putnam's contention have not gone unchallenged (e.g., Brehm & Rahn 1997; Ladd 1996; Tarrow 1996). As his critics have noted, Putnam's focus on change in the formal memberships in these long-standing organizations ignores any growth in membership that has occurred in more newly formed organizations (e.g., the Sierra Club or the American Association of Retired Persons). Thus, according to his critics, Putnam simply has confused change with decline. They cite the possibility of shifting patterns in membership affiliations rather than any overall decline in such memberships.[2]

Whether or not there has been any real decline in American associational life, there remains the issue of just how crucial voluntary associations are in the formation of social capital. For the most part, Putnam seems to hold that associational life is the key to such production. It is life in association with others that serves to inculcate the particular kinds of cooperation and trust, social networks, and norms that, in the end, produce the social trust and civic engagement that healthy democracies require (Foley & Edwards 1998, 12).

Certainly, one would be hard pressed to argue that formal memberships in voluntary organizations serve as the only basis for generating social trust. One can easily argue, as does Levi (1996, 48), that "trust is more likely to emerge in response to experiences and institutions outside the small associations than as a result of membership." In fact, it may well be that the family serves as the most important context for the generation of social capital. For example, Coleman (1988, 109-16) has stressed the importance of the family and school in the development of social capital. And even Putnam (1995a, 73; 1995b, 667) has recognized that the family serves as the most important form of social capital and that education constitutes the strongest correlate of both social trust and associational membership. Thus, the voluntary sector may well serve as only one of several possible sources of social capital.

Likewise, is it formal membership in voluntary organizations *per se* that is likely to produce the social capital that is widely valued, or is it participation in only certain kinds of voluntary organizations? Simply put, it is highly unlikely that all types of associational membership are equal in terms of social capital formation, as "different types of voluntary activity may have very different implications for social capital" (Newton 1997, 581). Not all associations are likely to foster social capital in the same ways or to the same extent (Stolle & Rochon 1998, 49). For example, the particular purposes for which the organization is formed and dedicated are likely to affect social capital formation. The relative inclusiveness of the association is also likely to affect the level and extent of social capital formation.

Putnam (2000, 22) himself recognizes that there are different forms of social capital, as he has begun to differentiate between bonding and bridging forms of social capital. Whereas bonding social capital has beneficial aspects by "undergirding specific reciprocity and mobilizing solidarity," it can have certain negative consequences should it also foster strong "out-group antagonisms." Bridging social capital, on the other hand, serves to "generate broader identities and reciprocity" (Putnam 2000, 23). However, associations cannot be neatly classified simply as "bonding versus bridging" associations, because "many groups simultaneously bond along some social dimensions and bridge across others" (Putnam 2000, 23).

Associations and their social networks may vary along the bonding and bridging dimensions, in part, because of the social composition of their membership. But even all relatively homogenous associations in which face-to-face relationships are evident are not alike. Some homogeneous associations and their structures promote, either directly or indirectly, civic action and cooperation, whereas other such associations do not. Thus, it may not be simply the particular structure of the social relationships that fosters and generates social capital that is bridging in nature. Rather, it may well be the particular ideas that are associated with the ideology or worldview of such relatively homogeneous groups that serve to differentiate between the types of social capital they generate. Stated somewhat differently, similar social structures can function differently—it depends, in part, on the ideas that "fill" or are associated with those social structures that serve to differentiate between their varied by-products.

In the end, it is likely that there are few social analysts who would dispute the contention that involvement in civic associations serves to generate interpersonal trust, foster habits of cooperation and norms of reciprocity, and forge expanded social networks. Rather, the issue really centers more on the question: "Which kinds of associations do so, under what circumstances, and with what effects for the polity?" (Foley & Edwards 1998, 15). In exploring these questions we are, in effect, raising empirical questions concerning the "nature, causes, and consequences of social capital" (Newton 1997, 584).

Thus, it is important that we begin to specify just what types of religious cultures, structures, and values foster and promote what type of social capital. Some facets of different religious traditions or organizations may be relatively similar in nature (e.g., emphasizing norms of honesty and compassion), but other facets may be highly variable (e.g., organizational structures of authority). Not all religious structures, for example, necessarily foster the same levels of social capital; opportunities to develop civic skills are likely to vary across religious bodies with regard to such factors as congregational size, liturgical practice, and forms of church polity. Participation in highly formal, bureaucratically organized religious bodies and "checkbook" participation in voluntary organizations (by giving money but not one's time) are likely to have different implications for the development of civic skills and virtues that differ from active participation in more horizontally organized, decentralized associations or congregations. Even among the latter forms of social organization, there are likely to be differences evident among those associations that comprise loose-knit, relatively weak-obligation support groups than other forms of face-to-face, horizontally organized, voluntary organizations.

Participation in different sectors of social life may well result in different social consequences. Accordingly, one could argue that participation in religious life is likely to have disproportionate benefits with regard to social capital formation. First, participation in religious life tends to promote certain beliefs, values, and norms that could contribute to the formation of social capital. Generally speaking, a variety of religious norms call upon religious adherents to exhibit honesty, truthfulness, compassion, and mercy. Such qualities are likely to be those that would foster social trust. Moreover, religious values and involvement with religious institutions have been found to promote civic behavior in other arenas: volunteering (Dynes & Quarantelli 1980; Wuthnow 1991, 199-200) and charitable contributions (Hodgkinson, Weitzman, & Kirsh 1990, 107-9). Religious structures have been found to generate social capital not only for their own voluntary efforts but for many other kinds of voluntary efforts as well; thus, "the social capital generated by religious structures supports not only formally religious volunteering but 'secular' volunteering as well" (Greeley 1997a, 592).

Normative Issues

Finally, though they are not directly addressed in this volume, there are also some important normative issues related to the social capital framework and its emphasis upon associational life and civic society. As Putnam (2000, 22) has noted, "social capital . . . can be directed toward malevolent, antisocial purposes, just like any other form of capital."

Given that not all civic associations are necessarily alike in their social effects, one can question whether civic renewal without moral renewal is sufficient to foster the renewal of democratic life (Eberly, 1998). Scholars are divided with regard to this issue, with one stream being primarily concerned with the civil life of the nation and the other with its cultural and moral underpinnings. Civic revivalists are more interested in promoting public work by individuals. Adherents of this perspective want civic recovery, among other things, to temper the public's recent repudiation of government activism by splicing in an emphasis on civic localism. The overriding objective is the promotion of civic works, not necessarily the promotion of some moral or cultural renewal; what is sufficient for democracy, they say, is civic character—or, in other words, a quickness to join.

On the other hand, others contend that America's civic crisis is primarily philosophical and moral in nature because the moral ideas that formed and sustained our civic institutions no longer exert the same power they once did to shape our behavior and unite us. For example, why would anyone choose to participate in civil life? And, why should one seek to work to relieve suffering or achieve justice? Once one moves beyond arguments rooted in self-interest alone, moral arguments come to the fore. Thus, those who argue for cultural renewal contend that the motive for democracy is, at its very basis, fundamentally moral in nature—as "the qualities necessary for self-governance are the results of certain moral ideas about the human person and the nature of the good life" (Eberly 1998, 47). When we ignore the moral grounds of human existence, only power is left as a basis for structuring human behavior.

While religion may well serve as an integrative force in society or as a major agent in the formation of social capital, it is also true that religion can serve to deepen social cleavages in civil society. Over the past decade, there has been increased discussion within religious communities that they may be engaged in a cultural war. Such an interpretative frame does not move those who accept such imagery to exhibit political civility towards those with whom they disagree. While religious language should not be removed from the public square, it can nevertheless be used inappropriately or unadvisedly in such public settings. As a result, in order to renew civic and democratic life, greater attention needs to be given to the manner in which religious beliefs, values, and speech *should* be expressed in the public arena. What imagery should guide religious thinking about civic life, what standards of social behavior or civility should be utilized by believers in their relationships with others in civil society, and what guidelines should be followed in the expression of religious beliefs and values within the public square. These types of issues need also to be more fully addressed when examining the role of religion in civil society.[3]

OVERVIEW OF THE VOLUME

The various theoretical, conceptual, and empirical issues discussed above are embedded in the chapters of this volume. Given scholarly differences on these issues, it is not surprising that the authors of these chapters adopt different conceptual approaches to social capital, with some treating social capital as something possessed by an individual, and others treating social capital more as a relational quality. Similarly, the chapters of this volume exhibit different methodological approaches to the study of social capital—with some authors employing survey research methodology and others employing more qualitative, ethnographic approaches. But, regardless of the particular framework and methodology adopted, each chapter points to the important role that religion plays in social capital formation and democratic life within the American political system.

Still, while all the authors contend that religious social capital plays an important role in American democratic life, not all argue that every religious factor is necessarily distinctive or similar in terms of its importance socially and politically. For example, some chapters suggest that the social capital produced through religious means has certain distinctive qualities, while other chapters suggest that religious social capital mirrors social capital produced through other means. Likewise, some chapters suggest that it is religious attendance with its patterns of social interaction, and not the specific religious faith tradition wherein which interactions occur, that is of particular importance in terms of social capital's consequences. But other chapters indicate that the social capital produced within certain religious traditions has particularly important, and distinctive, consequences.

Since little systematic attention has previously been given to the relationship between religion and social capital formation, it is not clear the extent to which these differences may be a function of the different frameworks, the different methodologies, the different contexts, or the different data employed. Nevertheless, such differences in findings are characteristic of any effort to investigate a new, but relatively complex area of study. In this sense, many of the chapters in this volume may be viewed as studies that are as much "hypothesis generating" as "hypothesis testing" in nature.

The chapters in this volume fall into three broad sections. The chapters of the first section, Chapters 2 and 3, focus on the nature and limits of religious social capital. Chapters 4 through 7 examine the contributions of religious social capital to civic engagement and the development of civic virtues. Chapters 8, 9, and 10 focus on contextual factors that serve to identify the circumstances under which religious social capital is more fully generated and its effects more fully evident. The final section, Chapters 11 and 12, suggests further avenues by which to analyze and assess religion's role in fostering a healthy civil society that, in turn, is productive for democratic ends.

The Nature and Limits of Religious Social Capital

What kinds of associations foster social capital? Are religious associations particularly distinctive in the amount of social capital they produce? Is the United States distinctive in terms of the role religion plays in social capital formation? And, is the social capital forged through religious means different from social capital forged through nonreligious means? These are questions addressed by Chapters 2 and 3.

Ram Cnaan, Stephanie Broddie, and Gaynor Yancey argue in Chapter 2 that the United States is distinctive in the extent to which social capital is generated through the religious, particularly congregational, life within American society. According to the authors, the United States is relatively unique in the way in which congregations are actively involved in community life, and they identify certain features of American congregations that contribute to religion's high level of human and social capital production in American society. As a result, the authors argue, congregational life serves as the key producer of social capital in American life.

While the United States may be distinctive in the amount of social capital generated through its congregational life, are congregations the only vehicles by which religion generates social capital in American society? In recent years, there has been a major growth in para-church organizations within American religious life. Do such structures add to or diminish the social capital generated in congregational settings? And, is the social capital generated through religious life similar to, or different from, the social capital generated outside of religious life? These are the questions that John Coleman addresses in Chapter 3. Coleman contends that para-church organizations both depend on and add to the social capital they find in congregational settings and that religious structures can generate a kind of social capital that is qualitatively different from that generated through other means. On the other hand,

Coleman also argues that there are certain limits to social capital generated through religious means, and, as a result, any effort to renew American social capital solely, or even primarily, on the basis of religious social capital is likely to be inadequate.

The Benefits of Religious Social Capital

Religious social capital may have distinctive qualities, but are the beneficial consequences tied to religious social capital different from the consequences associated with social capital generated through other means? And, while religion may generate social capital, is it "self-serving" in nature, benefiting only the members of the religious group to which one belongs? In other words, does religious social capital have any social benefits outside the church? Does it foster civic, as well as religious, values? Chapters 4 and 5 focus on religious social capital, community organizing, and democratic participation across different religious traditions and organizational strategies. In Chapter 4, Mark Warren examines faith-based efforts at community organizing for democratic action—particularly how differences across faith traditions may affect the efforts and success of such organizing endeavors. Specifically, Warren compares how differences in theology and institutional structures associated with Mexican-American Catholic communities and those of African-American Protestant communities shaped the efforts and success of the Industrial Area Foundations (IAF)—the largest faith-based community organizing network in the U.S.—among some of its affiliates in Texas. In this enthographic study, Warren reveals how differences in religious institutional structures and cultures affected IAF's faith-based organizing efforts to expand the basis of participation in Hispanic and African-American communities. The study suggests that "the specific institutional setting in which social capital is embedded affects its ability to be translated into the political arena."

In Chapter 5, Richard Wood examines whether religiously generated social capital differs from racially generated social capital. In so doing, he focuses on two models of grassroots political participation: faith-based community organizing versus "race-based" community organizing. Based on a three-year, ethnographic study of community organizing efforts, Wood analyzes two different organizations that embody these different strategies as they engaged in such organizing in identical neighborhoods in Oakland, California. By holding "constant" the wider social environment of these two organizations, Wood is able to assess the role of social capital in their organizing efforts. The greater success that the faith-based organizing effort enjoyed was due to its "unhindered access to the networks and trust . . . embedded in church congregations."

In Chapter 6, David Campbell and Steven Yonish address the issue of whether religious life contributes to, or detracts from, Americans' engagement in volunteer activity in America. Using data from the Giving and Volunteer Surveys, the authors find that the churched volunteer more than the unchurched, and that one's level of church attendance, rather than one's particular religious tradition, more fully accounts for differential levels of volunteer efforts. Increased levels of church attendance are associated with increased levels of volunteering—both with regard to religious and nonreligious endeavors. In fact, church attendance rivals education as a predictor of the extent to which one engages in volunteering. In addition, Campbell and Yonish find that there are important similarities between the social capital formed within religious and secular communities, at least with regard to effects related to volunteerism.

In Chapter 7, Roger Nemeth and Donald Luidens analyze the role that religion plays in charitable giving—both religious and nonreligious in nature. These authors also draw on data from the Giving and Volunteering Surveys and find that church members are more likely than nonmembers to contribute to charitable causes—both religious and nonreligious in nature. Not only do they contribute more broadly, they contribute more generously. Regardless of income level, church members contribute more than nonmembers to religious as well as nonreligious charities. While Nemeth and Luidens do not report the particular religious affiliations of the respondents they analyzed, the authors also find that it is the impact of church attendance that affects such differential giving—with those who attend church most frequently exhibiting the highest charitable giving.

CONTEXTUAL FACTORS, RELIGIOUS SOCIAL CAPITAL AND DEMOCRATIC LIFE

While the initial chapters focus on the nature and benefits of religious social capital generally, the three chapters in the third section examine the nature, level, and impact of religious social capital within different social contexts. These chapters analyze religious social capital and democratic life within the contexts of different racial groups, different rural communities, and different national settings.

In Chapter 8, Frederick Harris examines the way in which religion promotes the formation of social capital among African Americans and argues that a unique feature of religion's contribution to the formation of social capital is its ability to nurture and sustain reciprocity within its social networks. Harris analyzes the extent to which black, Latino, and white churchgoers practice civic skills within their congregational settings. Given the history of blacks in American political life and the particular institutional structure of black churches, Harris argues that religious tradition, through its institutional structure, can affect the extent to which religion shapes the learning of civic skills. And, he presents evidence that black churchgoers benefit more from developing civic skills than do other churchgoers. Thus, for Harris, it is not just one's level of church attendance, but one's institutional affiliation (with its particular structures of authority) that is important.

In Chapter 9, Jan Curry examines the relationship between religious world-views and social capital, both bonding and bridging in nature, within small, relatively homogeneous, Iowa communities in which high levels of face-to-face interaction occur. The study reveals that not all small communities are alike with regard to bonding social capital. Even in such rather "intimate" communities, face-to-face social interactions with familiar people did not necessarily lead to high levels of bonding social capital. Nor did associational involvement necessarily lead within each of these communities to the social trust that is linked to social capital. It was only those communities that combined bridging social capital with sufficient bonding social capital that were likely to be healthy communities exhibiting sustainable institutions. And whether sufficient bonding social capital is present depends, according to Curry, on the particular religious worldviews held by those within such communities.

In Chapter 10, Corwin Smidt, John Green, James Guth, and Lyman Kellstedt examine the interrelationships between and among religious involvement, civic engagement (in terms of associational involvement and level of volunteer activity), and political participation from a comparative, cross-cultural perspective. Using data from the 1996 Angus Reid Survey of Religion, Politics, and Social Involvement in Canada and the United States, the authors find that both religious tradition and, more importantly, church attendance play an important role in fostering civic engagement in both Canada and the United States, and that civic engagement is strongly tied to political participation in both contexts as well. However, once religion's role in fostering civic engagement is taken into account, religion appears to have little additional direct impact on political participation beyond its indirect effects through civic engagement. Thus, in both settings, it appears that religious involvement fosters civic engagement which, in turn, spurs political participation.

Additional Avenues of Study

Most chapters in this volume address different ways in which religion is related to social capital, and they reveal the breadth of studies that can be conducted when examining the relationship between religion and democratic life through the lens of the social capital framework of analysis. However, if social capital relates to any facet of the social relations that enable members of society to work together to accomplish collective goals, then the focus on the socialization effects of participation in voluntary associations may be too narrow in scope. There are also other features of social relations that can serve to accomplish collective goals—e.g., language and institutional structures. The final two chapters of the volume suggest that to fully capture religion's role in fostering democratic life, one must also take into account these broader features of social relations.

In Chapter 11, Rhys Williams suggests that greater attention should be given to religious language as a form of "social capital" that can foster a democratic public politics. Williams suggests that we think of religious language as a cultural resource that, if rightly used, can facilitate or contribute to doing public, collective activity. Williams notes that religious language has several characteristics that distinguish it from other forms of political discourse: religious language is democratically available; it can serve as a motivating force; and it resonates widely among a variety of populations within American society. Thus, there are both "production" reasons (its availability and its ability to serve as a motivating and mobilizing force) and "reception" reasons (its resonance across a variety of publics) for political actors to adopt religious language. Still, not all kinds of religious language facilitate the expansion of political space or foster collective action. As a result, Williams assesses what kinds of religious language either opens or closes such political or cultural space within a democratic polity.

In Chapter 12, Robert Wuthnow examines the question of whether religion has the capacity to revitalize civil society, and, in so doing, he provides an analytical overview of religion's role in civil society. Wuthnow argues that scholars need to give greater attention to the institutional role of religion within civil society. While Wuthnow recognizes the importance of interpersonal relations, social networks, and voluntary associations, he argues that to concentrate solely on such matters misses a great deal of how contemporary social life is organized. By analyzing the institutional role of religion, additional insight can be gained with regard to religion's contribution to American civil society and democratic life. Such an institutional perspective suggests that religion's contribution to the maintenance of civic vitality needs to be considered just as much as its potential for revitalization or reform. By focusing only on religion's capacity for moral rejuvenation, scholars miss an important component of religion's contribution to civil society. Thus, to fully appreciate religion's contribution to civil society, religion's institutional role must also be emphasized—including its organized and routine relationships with other institutions.

Chapter 13 then concludes the volume with an assessment of religion's role in generating social capital and in promoting democratic life. The chapter assesses religion's contribution to social capital, the distinctiveness of religious social capital, and the limits of religious social capital. The chapter concludes with a discussion of religion's contribution to democratic life.

Chapter 2

Bowling Alone
But Serving Together
The Congregational Norm of
Community Involvement

Ram A. Cnaan, Stephanie C. Boddie, and
Gaynor I. Yancey

In contrast to European countries, people in the U.S. typically do not trust
their government nor do they expect it to assist them in performing tasks that
serve the needs of diverse groups (Inglehart et al. 1990). Government is typically expected to intervene only in those matters that affect a majority of citizens, and, as a result, Americans are often left with the choice of either attempting to influence governmental authorities to act or producing the desired goods
themselves. Because they frequently need to produce these desired goods themselves, the most common way Americans influence their environment and
become more empowered is through joining and forming voluntary, largely
nonprofit associations.

This chapter analyzes the voluntary associations of religious congregations
and their role in social and human capital formation. Overall, we argue (1) that
it is normative for most congregations that they be involved in social and community service provision; (2) that religious congregations are, in fact, highly
concerned with the quality of life of others in their neighborhood and beyond
in that they often form the basic social safety net that helps those who are
unable to provide for their own basic needs; and (3) that active participation in

The work of this chapter was supported by a generous grant from the Lilly Endowment to study
the role of local religious congregations in the provision of social and community services. We
also thank The Manhattan Institute and the Kellogg Foundation for supporting our work.

local religious congregations is a key element for acquiring human and social capital, the necessary tools for civic engagement.

NORMS OF SOCIAL INVOLVEMENT

The impressive, and often unrecognized, role that local religious congregations play in building human and social capital is more than a current social phenomenon; it is a long-held and enduring social norm. In essence, it is a norm that dictates the way in which people who come to worship together also become involved in community service. While one can be spiritually and religiously active without belonging to a congregation, seeking out a community of worshipers and joining a congregation necessarily involves accepting a set of norms—including the norms of contributing to the building of human and social capital and of being willing to participate in civic affairs.[1]

In individualistic societies, such as American society, members are not expected to be deeply concerned about the welfare of others. In fact, the freedom to do what one wants is a highly prized American possession, while self-interest and the struggle for individual success are key tenets of the American value system. Given these values, volunteerism and religious affiliation can easily be seen as being antithetical to them, as one accepts the subordination to a higher power in religion and conformity to the rules and guidelines of some other entity in volunteering.

Wuthnow (1991) sought to solve this tension between individual freedom/self-interest and religious affiliation/volunteerism by focusing on the rewards associated with volunteering and joining a religious congregation. According to Wuthnow, such rewards can range widely, but ultimately they all represent means by which to express one's control and individuality. In this respect both the individual and the corporate body benefit; the member chooses and the collective is strengthened. But, regardless of their motivational basis, the ideals of compassion and care still set the tone and form the foundation for a complex web of individual commitments and a rich civic life that is based on people's freedom to get involved and actively support whatever is dear to their hearts.

These norms of social capital-building and civic engagement held by local religious congregations have numerous positive externalities and very few negative ones.[2] They save the public sector money because they encourage the provision of numerous services to persons in need. Moreover, these norms form a nucleus of conformity, stability, and social order in communities that would otherwise be volatile.[3] And they help newly relocated people blend into the community and deal with culture shock. As such, the congregational norms of involvement are beneficial both to members of these congregations as well as to other members of society outside such congregations.

Millions of Americans, regardless of socioeconomic background, are members of religious congregations. In the United States, where church and state are legally and practically separate, religious congregations serve a broader function than in many other countries. Members of congregations form committees and task forces to carry out what is often called "social ministry." That is, members of religious congregations set out to influence their communities by performing a variety of activities that add to the quality of life in the community. Congregations play a critical role in community life by providing resources for the homeless, teaching religious classes, creating choirs, and engaging in many other important social activities. Such activities, performed by individuals who organize under the auspices of religious congregations, enable people to control and influence their immediate environment rather than remain helpless victims.

A recent cartoon by Gary Trudeau illustrates the extent to which congregational involvement in the community has penetrated our civic culture. The cartoon depicts a group of congregants planning a variety of social and community activities. As they schedule the activities, they realize they have to schedule some on Sunday. When one congregant asks what has happened to Sunday worship, the answer given is that it had to be canceled in order to allow time for all other social activities. As in all cartoons, the intended point is taken to the extreme in order to emphasize its meaning and make us laugh. Yet, the reality is that many people who are active in their congregations know just how busy their building is every day of the week, serving the community in numerous ways ranging from AA group meetings to day-care services.

Congregations are a major source of human and social capital in the American society.[4] By social capital we refer to the level of development of networks, both informal and formal, in a given community. In social capital, we start with face-to-face interactions and then progress to personal exchanges; these exchanges may grow into obligations, and ideally end up with trust. Trust in this respect refers to people's beliefs that others, such as one's neighbors or elected officials, will act on their behalf and not against them. When all these exist, groups can be formed and civic associations may emerge. By human capital we mean the skills, knowledge, experiences, and developed talents that individuals apply to solve problems and enhance their quality of life. Human capital can be increased by equipping people with skills and abilities or trusting them with leadership and organizational responsibilities so that they can function more productively.

Human and social capital are the foundation for creating civic culture (Potapchuk, Crocker, and Schechter 1997). Combined, they help local people organize and face collective problems. In civic cultures, community members work together to address problems when they arise, and they trust one another, so that different subgroups can collaborate in ways that are beneficial to all members of the community.

Putnam (1995a) contends that face-to-face contacts are declining in America today, a phenomenon that has resulted in declining civic engagement.

He does acknowledge that church-related groups are currently the most common type of organization that Americans join. But Putnam argues that religious sentiment in America seems to have become less tied to institutions and more self-defined. America may still be highly churched in terms of its number of local religious congregations, but Putnam contends that the number of people who report attending religious services is declining. According to him both participation in religious services and membership in church-related groups have declined by about one-sixth since the 1960s. However, this reported decline is not necessarily corroborated by other scholars (e.g., Finke & Stark 1992; Wuthnow 1988; Warner 1993), whose findings suggest stable or even increased religious participation over the past twenty years.

It is our thesis that religious congregations continue to provide social ties of exchange, obligations, and trust which produce social and human capital. Yet, Putnam largely dismisses religious congregations—contending that they are less relevant today than in the 1960s in that church members today participate less as members of a religious community and more as consumers of what they seek spiritually. His contention is that people who become church members for reasons of personal fulfillment are not likely to form strong associational ties of exchange. But in the following section we will demonstrate how religious communities continue to serve as major sources of human and social capital.

CONGREGATIONS AS SOURCES
OF HUMAN AND SOCIAL CAPITAL

Coleman (1990) noted that two elements are critical for social capital to be effective: a high level of trust among members of the system and the extent of obligations held. Let us view these elements as they pertain to local religious congregations. People who attend congregations do so as a manifestation of a religious commitment. They choose the congregation carefully and trust its clergy and members. Ample literature suggests that religious, denominational, and most importantly, congregational affiliation is a matter of personal choice and that this choice is carefully made (Warner 1993; Wuthnow 1988). But once this choice is made, one usually develops and demonstrates trust in the clergy and other congregants. Furthermore, through membership classes and interviews, after-service coffee, and informal discussions with other congregants, one becomes involved with others in the congregation and shares resources with them. Often, the new member is the beneficiary of the experiences of veteran members and their familiarity with both the congregation and the community. These tangible and intangible benefits are later reciprocated—whether directly to the veteran members or indirectly to newer members.

Consider the following. Almost every one of the more than 250 congregations that we visited over the past several years holds some form of regular Bible (or religious) classes for adults and/or children.[5] These classes are mostly conducted by congregational volunteers. This essential role of instruction is one that is familiar to all members of a religious congregation, and it sows the seeds of human and social capital. In these classes, knowledge is disseminated and new skills are acquired. Some learn to be teachers and group moderators, while others learn new ideas and information. Given that these volunteer teachers are caring for the education of others, those who are not teaching are in debt to those who do (particularly when it is one's own children who are being taught), and the infrastructure of exchange of favors is institutionalized. When someone voluntarily teaches my child what I consider to be important, I am happy to reciprocate— helping that person (and other members of the group) by using the skills and abilities that I uniquely possess, be it baking a cake or recommending a good mechanic. Now, multiply these reciprocations to include choir members, ushers, committee members, and other congregational volunteers and the level of social embeddedness, exchanges, and trust begins to be visible. It is in the very nature of congregations that members come together. Some may give more than others, but they will have accrued more social credit (obligations) for doing so, and they can anticipate being more fully supported in the future when they are in need.

But churches foster important human, as well as social, capital. Brady, Verba, and Schlozman (1995) found that one of the key places where people report acquiring these civic skills (e.g., concrete activities such as letter-writing, participation in decision-making meetings, planning and chairing meetings, and giving presentations or speeches in public forums) is within religious communities. While people can acquire these skills in other places (e.g., the workplace and nonpolitical organizations), these nonreligious contexts tend to attract and favor white middle/upper class members of society and, as such, perpetuate the power imbalance in society. Thus, it is in religious organizations that women, people of color, and the poor are provided opportunities to enhance their human capital and acquire skills of political participation (see also the Harris chapter in this volume). Accordingly, Verba, Schlozman, and Brady conclude that religion is the predominant institution working against the class bias of American civic engagement (because those who are already privileged economically also control a greater portion of the other resources needed for democratic participation).

Furthermore, membership in a religious congregation or a small religious group means belonging to a network of social relationships. Involvement in a congregation increases the likelihood an individual will be integrated into the community and will engage in activities shared by other members. Because many congregations are normatively involved in carrying out social services, there are many opportunities for an individual to become involved in volunteer work. People who join groups, especially religious congregations, are likely to internalize the norms and activities prevalent in these groups and to be able to use the skills gained therein outside the congregation in other groups and organizations. And, church-goers are more likely to volunteer than those who do not attend church (Wilson & Janoski 1995; see also Campbell & Yonish in this volume).

The Black Church, for example, has given birth to numerous social institutions that have strengthened the African-American community and helped its members (Lincoln & Mamiya 1990). Among these were mutual aid societies, fraternal lodges, benevolent societies, burial associations, and other mutual-help organizations. From 1950 to 1960, the Black Church discovered its political voice, mobilized its forces, and channeled its energy into the social justice movement. All these initiatives in combination contributed to empowering the African-American community. Indeed the hub of the civil rights movement was within local religious congregations in the South and many of the supporters who came from the North represented their own congregations (Morris 1984); in most rallies and protests, the front line consisted of clergy followed by thousands of congregants.

In times of natural disasters, endemic famine, and refugee crises, two organizations come to mind as organizing the provision of care: the Red Cross and the local religious congregation. This is evident in crisis after crisis when neighbors bring food, clothing, and other required goods to local congregations, trusting them to process the donations and forward them to the needy. Furthermore, at times of local crises, the community will often meet either in a local school or a local congregation as it seeks to cope with the problem. Both institutions, the school and the congregation, are viewed as trusted local pillars and spaces where the community can feel at "home."

Even today, congregations seek to address important community needs. Housing projects and social and economic development are two arenas within which increasing numbers of congregations are becoming involved. It is estimated that throughout the United States there are over 8,000 Community Development Corporations (CDCs) and about two-thirds of them are religiously based (Clemeston & Coates 1992; NCCED, 1999).[6]

In our study of congregations housed in historic properties across six different cities (Cnaan 1997), we found that the 111 congregations in the sample reported a total of 449 social programs, for an average of 4.04 programs per congregation. The beneficiaries of these services were mostly non-members, with a ratio of over 4 to 1 in favor of serving others rather than one's own members. The programs offered included: food pantries (60 percent); music performances (57 percent); clothing closets (53 percent); holiday celebrations (53 percent); community bazaars/fairs (51 percent); choral groups (51 percent); international relief (51 percent); recreational programs for teens (46 percent); alliance with neighborhood associations (45 percent); hospital visitation (44 percent); visitation of sick people including buddy programs (45 percent); recreational programs for children (42 percent); soup kitchens (41 percent); and tutoring (41 percent).

Most services were provided on the congregation's premises (approximately 80 percent). The vast majority of these programs (74 percent) reported the use of volunteers, with the mean number of volunteer hours provided monthly being 147.61 per program. Finally, the church's financial commitment allocated to social ministry was also significant—17.4 percent of the congregation's operating budget.

These findings that local religious congregations are highly active in social services provision and that they play a major role in the service delivery system for urban Americans is clearly in line with a host of other studies (e.g., Silverman 2000; Hill 1998; Grettenberger & Hovmand 1997; Hodgkinson & Weitzman 1993).[7] Thus, local congregations, whose primary goal is religious worship, frequently serve the larger community through their provisions of informal social safety nets.

CONGREGATIONS AS BUILDERS OF HUMAN AND SOCIAL CAPITAL

Five factors contribute to the high level of human and social capital-building in local religious congregations and their involvement in social and community social services provision. These factors are: (1) the group needs of congregants which can be met by actively joining other congregants in extra-worship activities; (2) the historical disestablishment of religion which necessitates the entrepreneurial spirit of congregations; (3) the homogeneity of congregations as a key factor in the willingness of congregants to donate money and volunteer alongside people like themselves; (4) the presence of religious teachings that emphasize social responsibility; and (5) the changing ecology of local associations, which left the religious congregation as the primary local institution.

The Group Needs of Congregants

Victor Frankl (1963) struggled with the question of why some survived the Holocaust and others did not, even when prisoners experienced identical circumstances. His conclusion was that people need to find meaning in their existence before they can be fueled with energy to cope with hardships. Relatedly, William Glasser (1965) has argued that all human beings struggle to experience love and attain self-worth. These three needs (meaning, love, and self-worth) are among the most powerful forces in our social life. While organized religion may not be the means by which all people find their meaning, it is the means for many. Moreover, "religion has a remarkable capacity to provide a sense of identity and rootedness for both the person and the group" (Joseph 1987, 17), and the religious congregation frequently provides an individual with friendship groups and a sense of purpose.

Thus, joining a religious congregation is not simply an act of finding spiritual meaning. Congregations are also social settings within which people of similar backgrounds and interests come together to form small groups. Even in the new mega-churches, people are prodded into forming small, home-study, prayer groups. Besides joining a congregation to find spiritual meaning, membership in a religious congregation or a small religious group means belonging to a network of social relations. Involvement in the social life of a congregation increases the likelihood that an individual will integrate into the religious community, internalize its norms, and engage in activities shared by other members (bonding social capital). Because they are involved in carrying out social services, many congregations multiply opportunities for the individual to come into contact with, and join in working with others who are outside their religious group (bridging social capital).

Wuthnow (1994c) has contended that Americans are transforming the way they contribute to community and the public good through a growing reliance on participation within small groups. He found that small groups are playing a vital role in institutional religious settings. According to his survey, 40 percent of the adult population in the U.S. claims involvement in "a small group that meets regularly and provides caring and support for those who participate in it" (Wuthnow 1994c, 45), with most attending regularly. From the participants' responses, Wuthnow concluded that "the members of small groups are quite often prompted to become more active in their communities, to help others who may be in need, and to think more deeply about pressing social and political issues" (Wuthnow 1994c, 346). In fact, most congregations are small groups in and of themselves, consisting of fewer than 200 people who often know each other quite well, while larger congregations frequently choose to form "small groups" as essential components of their ministry. In such small groups the problem of "free riding"[8] is minimal because the actions of each individual are quite noticeable, and prestige and social position within the group is dependent upon carrying one's load.

The Historical Disestablishment of Religion

In many European countries, including key welfare states such as Sweden, the state supports and protects the church. Salaries for clergy and maintenance of religious properties come from general taxes or from a publicly collected church-designated tax. In Greece, France, and Belgium clergy are state employees. In Germany and Sweden the state collects a church tax that is distributed among various religious groups (Monsma & Soper, 1997). In this practice of "establishment," one religion or denomination is designated as the state's religion and is publicly supported, while other recognized religious groups may receive less public support or may be wholly left on their own, if they are allowed to practice at all. When the American colonies came into being, most had an "established" religion: the Puritans in New England, the Dutch Reformed in New Amsterdam, the Anglicans in Virginia, and the Quakers in Pennsylvania. However, a movement to disestablish churches emerged along with the quest for independence, and this movement gathered momentum in the decades that followed.

Contrary to popular assumption, the colonial church of the seventeenth and eighteenth century played only a minor role in social service provision, although the church was an important social institution in each of the colonies. In colonial times, the church was not a benevolent institution per se. It focused on religious and moral matters and ignored other aspects of society. Most colonies had their own established religions, and the civil authority was empowered to punish those who persisted in false beliefs. This society of true believers, which tied civil order to common doctrine, only began to focus on the welfare of people in the community with the emergence of the separation of church and state.

The institutional or state churches in colonial America were supported by taxes imposed on believers and nonbelievers alike. Other forms of religions were strongly discouraged or even sanctioned. Membership in the established church was often a formal prerequisite for holding public office, serving on a jury, or sharing in the distribution of common and undivided lands. In addition, the formation of dissenting congregations was often forbidden or strongly discouraged and the advocacy of unorthodox views punished. As such, the American church of the period followed the European tradition and did not seek a new path.

Because their salaries were secure through state funding, clergy were not compelled to make special efforts to recruit new members, revive their preaching, and manifest a dynamic leadership style. Thus, clergy were not accountable to their congregants but were the representatives of the state and its church locally. Furthermore, religious leaders were discouraged from speaking or acting against the state. In such a system, clergy were also discouraged from developing social ministries, as these efforts were difficult to organize and unnecessary to establish the credibility and importance of the church in the community. In fact, in most European countries today, the level of congregational involvement in social welfare programs continues to be rather minimal.

After "disestablishment," however, congregants bore the cost of religious services and church leaders had to foster an environment in which members willingly provided the means to pay for the clergy and maintain the building (Warner 1993). Thus, in the U.S., the clergy are expected not only to bring the word of God but also to establish a community of members who voluntarily support the congregation. This expectation created a new brand of clergy. American clergy are much more accountable to their congregants, are frequently hired and fired by the congregation's executive committee, and are generally expected to attract sufficient numbers of members. The financial independence of congregations forces them to make sure that they are fiscally solvent and attractive. One method that has been shown to enhance group loyalty, to prevent members from leaving, and to improve the congregation's public image is to become collectively involved in caring for needy people in the community. Congregations with strong social ministries (services) are capable of attracting and retaining members who find their place of worship a source of "good works" (Ammerman 1997; Cnaan, Boddie, Handy, Yancey, & Schneider in press). American clergy are aware of the expectation to be engaged in social and community service provision as a mechanism for community building and member retention. Thus, the persons who spend the most time in the congregation (i.e., the clergy and lay leaders) know that social and community involvement is essential not only to practice the Word of the Lord but also for organizational survival and growth (Milofsky 1997).

The Homogeneity of Congregations

One element of American capitalist culture is the expectation of constant competition, i.e., economic individualism. Under this principle, each adult or family unit is expected to produce an income sufficient to meet one's needs without being dependent on others. Furthermore, inequality in income is culturally acceptable and even valued, as it is interpreted as an indication of one's success in life and valued contribution to society: "American culture contains a stable, widely held set of beliefs involving the availability of opportunity, individualistic explanations of achievement, and acceptance of unequal distribution of rewards" (Kluegel & Smith 1986, 11). Flowing from the principle of economic individualism is the belief that one is not responsible for another's welfare, unless the other person is a family member or is related in some other way—although a person may choose to be benevolent and help the other financially.

In America, a large segment of the poor are regarded as unworthy, and consequently, welfare is very limited; homelessness is an accepted social condition affecting some three million residents a year (Culhane, Dejowski, Ibanez, Needham, & Macchia 1994), and the welfare reform act demonstrates the norm of refusing to help the unworthy poor. This is especially so when the poor are not members of our ethnic, cultural, and social network.

Actually, America is a heterogeneous and divided society. It is composed of distinct ethnic groups that tend to see each other as competitors, and such pluralistic societies do not tend to support their citizens. There is no history of mutuality and shared destiny, but there is a strong sense of competition and suspicion. It is not surprising that welfare state services and trust of government are more frequent in homogeneous societies than in heterogeneous ones. In a homogeneous society one helps his or her fellows and feels the camaraderie in helping. In heterogeneous society, helping is too removed from the individual giver and the beneficiaries are people toward whom the helper feels no personal attachment. Furthermore, diverse groups tend to demand heterogeneous services, and the supply of such services by government is difficult because such services tend to cater to median voter preferences (Weisbrod 1988).

In the United States, the historic social and ethnic divisions, the cultural distrust of government, and the belief that inequality (given equal opportunity) is just have all combined to produce a weak public welfare system. Among industrialized nations, the United States has the least developed public social service system. This creates a vacuum: services are needed but are not publicly provided. The most common organization that steps into this vacuum is religious. It is precisely because congregations are a collective of homogeneous people who share common values and interests that they are able to motivate and enable members to get involved in welfare and advocacy for the poor.

The Religious Teaching

The desire to help others in need is not instinctive but a norm that one acquires through socialization and observation (Keith-Lucas 1972). All major religions have developed a theology, a corresponding set of rules, and mechanisms to help others in need (Queen 1996). All major religions emphasize collective responsibility for the welfare of others and for social justice.

Space is too limited here to discuss all theological teaching in this respect and such information can be found elsewhere (see for example, Cnaan, Wineburg, & Boddie 1999, chapter 6). But one example that can be discussed is Christianity's mandate to help others as illustrated in the parable of the "Good Samaritan."[9] Wuthnow (1991) has found that most Christians who are engaged in helping others know this parable. The New Testament, like the Old Testament, has many references to helping the less fortunate. This passage about the Good Samaritan taken from the gospel of Matthew (25:31-46) is often cited as a direct command to feed the hungry, clothe the needy, help the stranger, and save the prisoner. When we asked people in our interviews why they were involved in caring for others and acting as representatives of their community, we were often told in response that this is their religious calling, with several passages from religious texts used as reference for their motivation.

There are three important points to be noted regarding theological teachings on helping the needy and preserving social justice. First, teachings of all major religions emphasize mutual responsibility, the need to assist strangers in need, and most importantly, the legitimate claim of the weak and needy upon the community. Second, the major religions have advocated for social care and compassion for the needy regardless of location and economic conditions. Third, religious teachings, even when they are not put into practice, are still part of the socialization process of younger generations into adult roles in society and serve as instructions for desired behaviors of compassion and social care. If we assume that religion has a powerful and lasting effect on people's attitudes and behaviors, then religious teaching may contribute to a more civil and caring society.

We are not claiming that such teaching directly influences behavior. However, as a result of such teaching, social care, concern, and social activity have become crucial to our social discourse (see also Chapter 11 in this volume). Such is the moral foundation that makes congregational social action a legitimate cause and allows congregants to organize around any common cause they deem relevant. Religious teaching fosters the ideal of just relationships among people. Consequently, congregants are implicitly (through the internalization of its teaching) and explicitly (through clergy sermons) encouraged to practice such theological instruction and apply these principles to everyday life.

The Changing Ecology of Local Associations

Local institutions can serve as mediating organizations between local residents and broader, more powerful institutions such as the state or big corporations, and the ecology of local institutions is changing. Local religious congregations are the most visible, stable, and trusted community institutions in the U.S. Any one who travels through the United States cannot help but notice its many places of worship. Be it a minaret at the top of a mosque, a steeple on top of a church, Hebrew words or the Star of David on a synagogue wall, they all reflect the massive presence of local congregations. There are approximately 350,000 local religious congregations ranging from small store-front churches to mega-churches in the United States. And religious-based organizations have become central to the operation of local human service networks; it is estimated that they command 34 percent of all volunteer labor and 10 percent of all wages and salaries in the nonprofit sector (Hall 1990, 38). Although these numbers are not based solely on congregations, they impressively reveal the extent to which U.S. citizens support religious causes and campaigns.

The presence of such local congregations is particularly important in declining or depressed neighborhoods. While other institutions and services tend to leave such neighborhoods, religious congregations frequently remain. For example, Peter Dobkin Hall (1996) found that in New Haven, Connecticut, the number of local voluntary associations remained stable from 1850 to 1990. However, this stability masked two contrary trends. What is interesting is that, during this period of time, the number of fraternal/sororal organizations dramatically decreased, almost to the point of extinction, while the number of religious congregations increased dramatically. Such findings provide further evidence that the one community institution that remains alive and active in most U.S. communities is the local religious congregation.

This massive presence of local congregations is further evident in a study of four Los Angeles neighborhoods, where it is reported that "there is an average of 35 religious congregations and 12.5 religiously-affiliated nonprofit corporations per square mile, far more than the number of gasoline stations, liquor stores, and supermarkets combined" (Orr 1998, 3). Likewise, in our study of West Philadelphia, we found 321 places of worship in a territory estimated to comprise between six and nine square miles, a number quite similar to that found in Los Angeles.

In our study we also asked congregations if they plan to relocate in the near future. Almost all reported negatively and most continued to stress their commitment to the neighborhood where they are located—even if many members are now residing away from the congregation. In fact, with the exception of Jewish orthodox synagogues (whose members must not drive on the Sabbath), most congregants live some distance from their congregations. Yet, almost all congregational members reported commitment to the community and their desire to be known as the "compassionate big building on the corner."

CONCLUSIONS

The public and the media are in agreement that religious congregations are expected to serve their neighborhoods and are the most capable community institutions to cope with our social ills. When an expectation is so publicly explicit, the norm is not only internalized among the actors expected to carry it out, but also by the public at large. Effective norms may constitute a powerful form of social capital. A norm of meeting and discussing shared problems can facilitate the mobilization of local response to a communal threat. Similarly, the congregational norm of social and community involvement facilitates social capital-building. This process is an ongoing cycle in which members are meeting regularly, exchanging favors, developing trust, and joining together to practice their faith in a manner that is essential for civic engagement and civil society.

Congregations in America form a basis for social and human capital development. Over the course of time, social and cultural norms have developed that dictate that congregations are to be involved in enhancing the standard of living in and around their community. These norms have developed and continue to be sustained for several reasons: the group processes of congregational life, the disestablishment of religion in America, the homogeneity of congregations, the power of religious moral teaching, and the ecology of local voluntary organizations that has left the religious congregation as the primary local institution. In a society that celebrates individualism and inequality, local religious congregations are at the forefront of meeting people's basic needs and serving as our national social safety net, a function that in other advanced democracies is reserved for governments.

Chapter 3

Religious Social Capital
Its Nature, Social Location, and Limits

John A. Coleman, S.J.

It has become now almost a cliché that religion in the United States generates more "social capital" than any other American institution. The sociological evidence linking religion to social capital seems overwhelming. For example, two-thirds of all small groups in America are directly connected with churches and synagogues (Wuthnow 1994b, 56-57). Likewise, two-thirds of those active in social movements in America claim that they draw on religious motivation for their involvement (Cunningham 1995, 97). As Wuthnow states in his national study of student volunteers in America, "churches and synagogues remain the primary place where instruction is given about the spiritual dimension of caring" (Wuthnow 1996b, 9).

While there is considerable evidence that indicates that religion is a major generator of social capital, there still remain a variety of questions with regard to the manner and extent to which it does so. This chapter analyzes the social capital generated through religion—its nature, location, and limits. First, it briefly presents some of the empirical evidence that suggests religion disproportionately generates social capital and holds considerable democratic potential. In this first section of the essay, we ask why this might be the case. Is there really some genuine special nexus between religion and social capital?

Secondly, the chapter examines the sites for religious social capital—are they principally or exclusively local congregations? For example, beyond the social capital forged in congregations, do religious schools and other religious organizations also generate social capital? In recent years there has been a huge upsurge of para-church special interest groups engaged in community organizing or lobbying (Wuthnow 1988, 100–31). Do such groups also play a crucial role in aggregating religious social capital?

Finally, the chapter probes whether religious social capital has distinctive elements that serve to differentiate it from the kind of social capital produced by other civic associations or organizations. In trying to answer this question, the chapter identifies certain limits in the very metaphor of "social capital" and its difficulty in dealing with important qualitative variations between different kinds of groups. The chapter ends with a cautionary discussion of the limits that any expansionary investment of religious social capital may hold.

THE DEMOCRATIC POTENTIAL OF RELIGION

Churches regularly and straightforwardly act as communication networks that foster civic volunteerism. Princeton sociologist Robert Wuthnow puts it this way: "Religious organizations tell people of opportunities to serve, both within and beyond the congregation itself, and provide personal contacts, committees, phone numbers, meeting space, transportation or whatever it may take to help turn good intention into action" (Wuthnow 1994a, 242).

Religiously motivated volunteers are more likely than the non-religious to employ a communitarian language to describe their involvement and to appeal to some sense of the common good rather than simply some individualistic language to explain their behavior (Wuthnow 1991, 325). People are more likely to give money and time, even to secular efforts, if they are church members (Wuthnow 1996, 87; see also Campbell & Yonish, Chapter 6 of this volume), and they are also significantly more likely to vote if they are church members (Wald, Kellstedt, & Leege 1993, 49).

Even having neighbors who attend church can be a critical factor in predicting whether the youth in a neighborhood will have jobs, use drugs, or engage in criminal activity (Case & Katze 1991, 58); the social capital of churches, it seems, spills over beyond their members into whole neighborhoods. Glenn Loury has noted that "the reports of successful efforts at reconstruction of ghetto communities invariably reveal a religious institution or a set of devout believers at the center of the effort" (Schambra 1994, 32). This ability of church-based community organizing efforts to turn around low-income neighborhoods is further documented by the discussions of Warren (Chapter 4) and Wood (Chapter 5) in this volume.

In fact, many Americans believe that churches and synagogues are better able than other institutions to deal with "the problems facing our city or local community." In one Gallup survey, 57 percent of the respondents deemed churches to be more apt to deal with such problems than other social institutions, while less than a third thought local business, government, or political parties were apt vehicles for "compassionate and just solutions to the problems of our local communities" (*Emerging Trends* 1990, 3–4).

When American Christians think about matters of economic justice, both individualist and communitarian Christians can be found (Hart 1992). Such differences are not surprising given that both individualistic and communal motifs are found in the very normative foundations of Christianity. As a result, not only may some Christians draw from different ethical frameworks when making decisions about economic justice in our society, but other Christians may simply compartmentalize their faith and their attitudes about economic justice. Accordingly, some Christians may distrust any government action, while other Christians may hold strongly to social democratic views of the obligations of government to care for the needy. Still, as Steven Hart sums up his evidence about Christians and attitudes toward economic and social justice, he notes:

> In the uses of the Christian faith we have been examining, individualistic and communal strands seem in some balance, with perhaps a slight edge for the communal side. In secular culture, the balance is more weighted to the individualistic side. As a result, when people put on their Christian hat, they have more chance to bring communal values to bear on economic life than they do without that hat. (Hart 1992, 125)

Religion's contribution to democracy is not limited simply to its more communitarian vision; it also provides civic skills among those who participate in its structures. In their massive study of political and civic volunteerism in America, Sidney Verba, Kay Schlozman, and Henry Brady (1995) argue that religion significantly increases the democratic potential of the United States. Churches are superior to their two main competitors (i.e., the workplace setting and non-political civic organizations, such as the Rotary Club) in bringing transferable civic skills to the more disenfranchised. The workplace and non-political civic organizations tend to reward those who already have human capital and are middle-class; those who already have get even more opportunities. Verba and his colleagues contend:

> Only the religious institutions provide a counter-balance in this cumulative resource process. They play an unusual role in the American participatory system by providing opportunities for the development of civic skills to those who would be otherwise resource poor. (Verba et al. 1995, 18–19)

Indeed, a blue-collar worker in America is more apt to gain opportunities to develop and practice civic skills in church than in a union. This is "not because American unions are particularly deficient as skill builders but because so few American blue-collar workers are union members and so many are church members" (Verba et al. 1995, 520). Thus, a working-class deacon in a black church receives organizing and communication skills beyond what his job would provide. Verba, Schlozman, and Brady's study exhibits the distinctive strength of the black churches in generating and investing social capital, and this role is further discussed by Harris in Chapter 8 of this volume. These authors see churches as providing our society with a more participatory, more egalitarian, and a more communitarian ethos than would be evident in our society without them.

We should not be surprised therefore that churches, especially local congregations, are major sites for the generation of social capital. Few other organizations think of themselves so explicitly as communities. Few so insistently raise up norms of reciprocity—"neighbor love and care." It is almost part of the expected ethos of a church that it will exhibit some wider form of outreach to the needy. Indeed, the American public tends to identify "care for the needy" and "care" more generally as religious values (Ammerman 1997, 367).

THREE CAVEATS

Despite the evidence discussed above, there are three important caveats that need to be raised with regard to this initial generalization that religion in the United States generates more social capital than any other institution. First, the phrase "in the United States" signals a need to distinguish national settings and varying structures of religious authority (see also Chapter 10 of this volume). Robert Putnam, in his study of civic tradition in modern Italy, found consistently negative correlations between Catholic religiosity and civic engagement, though he did not probe other forms of religiosity among members of minority religious faiths—e.g., among Italian Protestants or among Italian Jews (Putnam 1993a, 107). And, in their study of religious volunteerism, Verba, Schlozman, and Brady found that American Catholics exhibit less civic participation than Protestants, although Catholicism still remains more strongly predictive of civic engagement than secularity (Verba et al. 1995, 245–46).

A crucial distinction to explain variance in religiosity and the generation of social capital lies in a differentiation between *horizontal* and *vertical* relations of religious authority. For example, some forms of religiosity, such as traditional Catholicism in Italy, remain intensely hierarchical in structure. They foster vertical relations (between bishops and priests and priests and people) of passivity and subordination. Other forms (e.g., congregational forms of Protestantism and Judaism and variant forms of congregational Catholicism, such as those found in post-Vatican II American Catholic parishes) nurture horizontal relations of interaction between congregants in parish councils, finance and worship committees, lay leadership and faith groups (Sweetser 1983). Recent studies among American Catholics reveal a growth in support, with a clear majority of respondents supporting, horizontal authority relations within the church (D'Antonio, Davidson, Hoge, & Wallace 1996, 25–42). As historian Jay Dolan has noted, Catholicism in America tends to become de facto congregational in style (Dolan 1985, 158–94). And where Catholics adopt a congregational style—as in African-American parishes—they look much like black Protestants in their propensity toward volunteering. Consequently, it is likely that denominational affiliation is "less significant than the particular congregation's own internal structure" (Cavendish 2000, 338). Only horizontal authority structures, generally, seem to generate social capital.

The size of congregation is also an important variable to monitor in studying religion and social capital—Catholic parishes tend, typically, to be two to three times the size of modal Protestant congregations. Large congregations may become much more like audiences than communities. Those large congregations or megachurches that generate social capital tend to do so because they sponsor or facilitate small sub-group formations (e.g., prayer cells, social action groups, fellowship groups) within the larger parish. Membership in these small groups within congregations has positive consequences for civic engagement (Wuthnow 1994b, 325–38). Those forms of religiosity that are mainly individualistic in nature and unrelated to, or anchored by, real ongoing groups do not seem to generate much social capital. Even intense, purely personal spirituality that is cut off from churches or some ongoing groups has almost no predictive value for civic engagement or social activism (Wuthnow 1994b, 329). Perhaps it should be obvious that, absent any embeddedness in the social, the likelihood of any social capital investment of individual spirituality is small (Coleman 1997).

A second caveat has to do with the very notion of social capital. It is important to remember that Robert Putnam, in his classic "Bowling Alone" essay, contends that social capital is clearly "not a unidimensional concept" (Putnam 1995a, 76). In economic terms, capital refers to a stock of accumulated wealth: an aggregation of (economic) goods or services *capable* of being used to promote the production of other goods and services, instead of being valuable for immediate enjoyment. The word "capable" is emphasized to stress that someone could simply "sit on" their capital and be unable or unwilling to invest it and reap its potential rewards. The derivative notions of "human" and "social" capital carry similar connotations of investment possibility, a pool of skills and resources or social networks capable of multiplying and expanding into a larger pool. Social capital, in particular, focuses primarily on norms and networks of organized reciprocity, trust and civic solidarity that are capable of spinning off—for education, urban poverty, unemployment, control of crime and drugs, health—new solidarities and potentialities. As Putnam has argued, even the economic health of communities may depend on underlying social networks of friends, cooperators, and neighbors who espouse and embody reciprocity, trust, solidarity, and engagement (Putnam 1993a,152–62).

But like capital in wealth, human and social capital can lie dormant. James Coleman has pointed to the way parents mediate social capital to their children (Coleman 1988, 115). But research psychologists have argued that it is not just the potentiality of social capital that is important but the energy, commitment, and actual "investment" with which it is communicated (McClanahan & Sandefur 1994, 38). It is important to remember that some religious units either pay scant attention to the social capital they generate or do not know how to turn it into politically or civically relevant social movements, service, and volunteerism. As a result, much of the social capital of some congregations remains frozen within the local unit, or it becomes isolated in separate pockets of friendship cliques within the congregation, failing to spill out into the larger society. Daniel Olson has suggested, for example, that friendship networks within congregations can implode, thus impeding any outward reach either in evangelism or civic service (Olson 1989, 442, 447). Similarly, John Wilson and Thomas Janoski (1995) have noted that conservative Protestants who are active in their churches are actually less likely to get involved in secular volunteerism because they turn their energies into their own congregations rather than outward to the community at large. More recent studies, however, demonstrate the need to differentiate between "evangelicals" and "fundamentalists" among such conservative Protestants: only the latter are much more prone to community insularity (Park & Smith 2000, 283; see also Campbell & Yonish, Chapter 6 of this volume).

Some congregations define themselves essentially as sanctuary havens from a heartless world. Not every congregation sees itself as having a civic, public mission (Roozen, McKinney, & Carroll 1984, 177–216). In particular, as Robert Wuthnow claims, the local congregation may find that public debates about economics and civic matters inside the very heart of the church "can easily become polarized, taking on an aura of antagonism that runs against the grain of religious teachings about fellowship and reconciliation" (Wuthnow 1994a, 263). There exists, as Gallup data repeatedly show, a widespread and strong public dislike in America of religious leaders playing too direct a role in politics. Finally, there is some empirical evidence that congregations are reluctant to become involved in civic outreach endeavors that they do not sponsor. They want to keep outreach programs "close to home," with very close ties to their own congregation (Wuthnow 1997, 192). Obviously, such factors limit the expansionary potential of any social capital they might generate.

A final caveat is related to this second one. Almost all of the studies on religion and social capital focus on the congregation as the only relevant unit of analysis (Ammerman 1997). Much of the research on religious social capital correlates it with formal church membership and measures of church attendance. Yet congregations frequently find themselves too small and limited to address even local and neighborhood problems such as homelessness, ecological deterioration of a neighborhood, or police protection. At best their civic outreach tends toward immediate "pay-offs." Churches do not provide *massive* monetary relief, health care, or housing to the poor. But churches meet short-term emergency needs among their own members, contribute to the needs of other people who may be working to keep their churches alive, and provide volunteer assistance that may be lacking from other agencies (Wuthnow 1997, 192–93).

CONGREGATIONS AND PARA-CHURCH ORGANIZATIONS

Any adequate account of the social capital generated by churches, however, must reach beyond the mere study of congregations and their own programs of outreach.[1] To be sure, the overwhelming majority of congregations do have some outreach program (Ammerman 1997, 360–62). But, even at local levels, many food banks, soup kitchens, homeless shelter programs, and low-cost housing initiatives derive not directly from congregations but from special-purpose para-church organizations, independently incorporated and autonomous from congregations and denominations. These para-church special purpose groups turn to the local congregations to obtain volunteers.

Few studies of para-church groups, their constituencies, and their relationship to local congregations currently exist at the national and even the regional and local levels (Willmer, Schmidt, & Smith 1999). As a result, we analyzed, over a three-year period, six national para-church organizations engaged in citizen activism or education. The research involved 300 formal interviews and participant observation at forty different sites across the country (Coleman 1996, 1998). The six groups that formed the basis for the study were: (1) Habitat for Humanity,[2] (2) Bread for the World,[3] (3) Focus on the Family,[4] (4) Pax Christi USA,[5] (5) PICO,[6] and (6) five congregations within the African-American Episcopal Church (three of them megachurches) that spun off nonprofit organizations for housing, education, and health clinics to renew whole African-American neighborhoods (Lincoln & Mamiya 1990; Mimaya 1994). This research has revealed that congregations and para-church organizations exist in a symbiotic relationship—in both creating and investing social capital.

The Symbiosis of Congregations and Para-Church Organizations

Congregations and para-church organizations may need each other to generate an effective public church in America. Many local congregations do not really know how to use the social capital they generate in more public settings. They lack, at times, the practical or organizational skills to turn it effectively toward broader civic engagement and public policy. Ron Snyder, from the PICO sample, puts it succinctly: "I don't think local congregations know how to make their values real. I think they want to but they don't know how." Sally Klein, from the Habitat for Humanity sample, echoes this point: "The relationship between the church and groups like Habitat is not a competition." Habitat's Harry Mijnstra puts it this way: "Our main emphasis has to be the churches. We are the servants of the churches."

Again and again, in our research, the para-church organizations brought new vitality to local congregations. Community organizers told how such community organizing was the only way in which Hispanic and Anglo congregants in Catholic parishes socialized or their two disparate social networks of the parish intersected. To build their own networks, para-church organizations both depend on and add to the social capital they find in congregational set-tings. These para-church groups rely on pre-existing strands of community they find in and through congregations. But, in many congregations, these strands of social networking exist largely in isolation from one another—as friendship cliques, service societies, lifestyle enclaves, or as other "clumps" of individuals. When groups such as Habitat for Humanity or PICO speak of renewing the fabric of society, they can point to the ways in which they establish new link-ages among the many isolated strands of relationships they pick up from with-in congregations.

Para-church organizations are also essential to forge linkages between and across congregations. As Mary Cole-Burns, a west-coast affiliate director of Habitat for Humanity puts it: "I always tell people the housing is merely the vehicle. The real work of Habitat is our notion of community and what it means to be together. It expands my notion of who my neighbors are." Without the social capital and sense of community found in congregations, Habitat for Humanity would lack the essential initial social capital it needs to build upon. Yet, it also expands the social capital it receives from congregations through its bridging processes. At Habitat building sites, the typical congregational volun-teer will rub shoulders with the sweat-equity, lower-income homeowner and other volunteers of different religions and race. In their own home congrega-tion, church members are unlikely to meet such a social mix.

Congregations and para-church organizations relate in a symbiotic fashion. By and large, para-church groups are not good initial discipling units, because they are so specifically focused and involve limited liability commitments. Few of the unchurched participants in our research (a minority in the sample) were moved to join congregations simply because of their experiences with these para-church organizations (for example, with PICO or Habitat for Humanity). Nor did those who were members of congregations expect primary discipling from the para-church groups: "I don't look to Habitat to fulfill basic religious needs. That's what the church is for" and "I always expect that we should bring our religious sentiments and beliefs to Habitat rather than vice-versa" were typ-ical comments. Discipling, i.e., taking seriously the Christian message or norms and joining churches, either takes place in families or congregations or not at all.

The Contribution of Para-Church Groups to Congregations

It seems clear what congregations do for para-church groups: they provide the initial network of social friendships and reciprocity on which to build. What do para-church groups give to congregations in return? The same people who say that their sense of discipleship inculcated in local congregations primarily moved them to civic action, wax enthusiastic about how it was the para-church group, rather than the parish, that taught them how to put their faith into con-crete action and have larger civic consequences. A Bread for the World member from Albuquerque, New Mexico, puts it this way: "I find more encouragement to exemplify my Christianity in Bread than in my local congregation." A San Francisco Habitat for Humanity executive catches the symbiosis between congregations and para-church groups in the process of expanding and investing the local congregation's initial social capital in his statement that "Habitat is not a church but an 'outward sign' of what we do and believe in the church."

Precisely because of the widespread taboo against introducing controversial political issues into the local congregation, even when they have some clear religious or moral overtones, para-church groups serve local congregations by providing outlets for a social and public faith without dividing the congregation as such. One Bread informant puts it this way: "I see in my own church where talking about Nicaragua and the arms race raises a lot of hackles and divides people." But many of her fellow congregants could work together on hunger issues around the world through Bread for the World. Those interviewed almost universally expressed gratitude to their para-church groups for providing them with a sense of "efficacy," for helping them "lean our weight on the side of an answer" or "give legs to Christianity."

Does Religious Social Capital Have a Special Character?

We have already seen that religion's social capital is more open to the disadvantaged in our society than are other forms of social capital. Allan Hertzke's study of religious lobbies with offices in Washington, D.C., reinforces this conclusion. Interest groups and lobbies are, generally speaking, decidedly unrepresentative of the American public at large. Voting may, in principle, tilt toward equality of voice (one person, one vote), but even voting in America clearly mirrors the class structure because educated, middle-class Americans are more likely to vote. But while lobbying generally does not promote equality, "religious lobbies," Hertzke contends, "play a unique representational role in the pressure system, articulating the values of many non-elite citizens and modestly correcting the skewed nature of the lobbying system" (Hertzke 1988, xiii).

The main conclusion of Hertzke's study is that church lobbies actually increase the range of voices represented in Washington. To be sure, they lobby for and represent their own church institutions and interests (focused primarily on tax code and religious freedom questions). But they also represent theological and biblical values, especially the Bible's concern for social justice. Religious lobbies speak out on legislation about welfare, the arms race, and foreign policy. Almost uniquely among lobby groups, they view themselves as representing not only the American churches but constituents outside the United States.

Hertzke argues that religious lobbies bring in the voices of the poor, or at least the under-represented, that are not heard elsewhere. They mobilize people who otherwise never have had a voice in Washington or learned how to lobby. One notes, for example, the careful way Bread for the World orchestrates letters from ordinary constituents on hunger issues and leads them, almost by the hand, on their annual lobby-days to the corridors of the House and Senate. Kay Carlson from Albuquerque, a retired woman in her sixties, expresses her gratitude for the way Bread provides her with opportunities for quiet, yet effective, political voice:

> I like the set up of Bread. The newsletter that comes out. I like those ties with the local people from elsewhere. The telephone tree that we have. The lady calls me from El Paso and I call this lady in Los Cruces and I like that a lot because we have ties with others and Bread encourages that kind of participation. That's the kind of thing that anybody can do. Anybody can write a letter to their congress member. Anybody can get on the phone and it doesn't jeopardize our busy time of day. Anybody can do it.

In the light of the generally sober picture of a fragmented congressional politics dominated by elite-based organizations working for often narrow interests, Hertzke contends that "religious lobbies are significant because they potentially represent non-elite constituencies and attempt to articulate broad (albeit competing) visions of the public good" (Hertzke 1988, 94). In short, Hertzke contends, our democracy is more representative because of the presence of religious lobbies.

Nancy Ammerman in her important book, *Congregation and Community*, has broached this question explicitly. She suggests that the social capital generated by congregations gives them a leg up for three reasons. First, they are presumptively legitimate. "Groups recognized as congregations receive, by definition, a measure of acceptance and the social identities of those congregations are therefore recognized" (Ammerman 1997, 363). Second, congregations (and presumably, by inference, at least some para-church groups) are presumed in American society to be driven by a moral imperative. Given the pervasive American cynicism about the "putatively moral" rhetoric of politicians, corporations, and other secular public agencies, congregations retain a weight of cultural expectation that their behavior will involve not just narrow self-interest but some altruism and concern for the public good (p. 368). Finally, congregations "have the most pervasive infrastructure for meeting community need, along with the expectations that their provision of services will be trusted" (p. 367).

Our study reaches conclusions that resonate with Ammerman's (Coleman 1996, 1998). But, in addition to the points mentioned by Ammerman, our study reveals three other elements about the social capital of religious groups.

The "Stick-To-It," Long-Range Social Commitments

Most of the informants in our research project claimed that they "were in it for the long haul." Joel Underwood, the Director of Development for Bread for the World, makes this point explicitly: "Art Simon [the founder of Bread] made it a major point not to appeal to people's self-interest. What is done is done for obedience to God, regardless of results. This gives the Christian a 'leg up' on the general population. We are in it for the long haul." A Focus on the Family brochure echoes this point: "The Family Policy Councils offer no quick-fix solutions. Rather, they are digging in for the long haul, laboring for both morality and justice in public policies." This larger sense of being in it for the long haul may explain—from an individual motivational stand-point—the organizational reality that McCarthy and Zald have found in their study of social mobilization phases of social movements. As more secular groups may ebb away when interest in the issues becomes less salient, religious groups can continue to hold out—as survival units—against this more general decline (Zald & McCarthy 1987, 73). This characterization of religious groups, for example, is dramatically true for the ebbs and surges in peace mobilization during this century (Marullo & Lofland 1990, 116).

A Tension Between Efficacy and Witness

The long-haul mentality that is behind the social capital that religion generates is related to a tension between efficacy and witness found in all of the groups in our study. Bread for the World prides itself on being able to show to its constituency some concrete pieces of legislation enacted each year that make a difference on hunger. PICO purposely looks to "winnable" local actions to give its members in community-organizing units a sense of empowerment. The successful megachurches of the African Methodist Episcopal Church thrive and grow, in number of congregants, partially because of the demonstrated effects their spin-off corporations (e.g., medical clinics, job bureaus, low-cost housing) have in their neighborhoods. Focus on the Family tries to effect legislation on same-sex tolerance, taxes on families, no-fault divorce laws. Habitat for Humanity has its quota of houses built to show off as signs of its can-do efficacy. Even Pax Christi can boast of its impact in removing, in places, ROTC programs from the schools.[7]

But no religious group could survive for long just on efficacy or issue-oriented civic action alone. Each group in our study appeals to witness and fidelity to some religious truth. "We are in it for the long haul," Bread's Underwood states. One of the PICO respondents says that she continues to remain hopeful, even when community organizing strategies are not going well, "because I think there is a God."

In general, the tension between efficacy and witness takes on different balance points across the six groups in our study. PICO, Focus, and Habitat may lay greater stress on efficacy than the other groups, but even that emphasis finds a counter-balance in its appeals to religious witness, truth, and more transcendent goals. Pax may lean much more strongly toward the witness pole, but it too wants to show results. This witness motif gives to religious special-interest groups a kind of staying power. Whether or not they win day-by-day on the issues, they look to another source for staying power.

Local and Global Notions of Citizenship Prevail

The typical conceptualization of citizenship found in our interviews shows a strong localist, anti-federalist sympathy. The bias toward localism, of course, should not be entirely unexpected. After all, in national surveys, Americans consistently report that they are more likely to trust government the closer it lies to home. Yet so many of the problems and issues that contribute to the erosion of an active citizenship cannot be addressed adequately only at the local level.

Clearly, our respondents across the various para-church organizations differed in their sense of the legitimate range and limits of governmental activity. Some, most predominantly found in the Focus on the Family sample, would restrict the government to the barest minimum, night-watchman state. And Habitat for Humanity members were, by and large, strangely reticent about how much of their ministry might be explicitly aided by government actions through the waiving of tax or zoning laws. Bread and PICO respondents were most open to a strong governmental presence in welfare, while the main focus of the PICO activists focused on issues of their neighborhoods or, at best, cities.

Countering this local bias, however, was a vital sense of a more global citizenship and solidarity. In the words of a Detroit Bread member: "We are citizens of the world and not just the United States." The theme of global citizenship (and hence, a sense of solidarity and mutuality beyond national boundaries) was most dominant in the Bread, Habitat, and Pax Christi samples, less evident (although not absent) among PICO respondents. It was almost entirely absent among the Focus on the Family informants. David Snell, Director of Educational Ministries at the national headquarters of Habitat for Humanity in Americus, Georgia, touched on this theme of international citizenship when he was asked "Is Habitat a good citizen organization?":

> Yes it is and I'll tell you why. We are an international organization so we are citizens of the world. The greatest by-product of any Habitat project-affiliate, special event, you name it—is the bridging between rich and poor, black and white, Catholic and Baptist and Christian and Jew. You take, for example, 1000 white, middle-class or rich suburbanites and dump them in Ward 7 of Southeast Washington D.C. (as was done during the Jimmy Carter Work Project) something happens!

Part of the difficulty in answering the question of whether religious social capital differs from other forms of social capital relates to the inherent limits associated with the social capital metaphor.[8] In a sense, the economic, rational-choice, and market models implicit in the metaphor make it exceedingly difficult to make qualitative distinctions or to address, more directly, what constitutes a community. Clearly, some of the social norms (reciprocity, trust) carried by what James Coleman calls "social capital" cannot really be justified by appeals to economic or rational-choice models. As Don Browning has recently remarked:

It is dangerous to think of churches in terms of social capital. Churches are carriers of religious stories that reveal God's will and grace. Salvation, not the increase of social capital, is the primary purpose of churches and their narratives. Christianity tells the story of how God's creation and grace empower us not only to live an ethic of equal regard but to risk moments of self-sacrifice with a sense that God's grace will sustain us. Salvation is having the trust to risk sacrificial love and self-giving, even though the mutuality of equal regard is its ultimate goal. Christians do not live the Christian life to produce social capital but it appears that increased social capital is a long-term, secondary consequence of Christian life. (Browning et al. 1997, 268)

What Browning's remarks force us to consider is that we may have to employ other metaphors besides "social capital" to deal with differences in the quality of communities in order to answer the question about whether religious social capital may differ from its secular variants. The economic leveling metaphor of social capital systematically erodes all possibility of direct qualitative comparison.

The Limits of Religious Social Capital

Finally, we need to remain realistic about the limitations of congregations and para-church groups for the renewal of American social capital. To be effective in reaching a primarily religious constituency, religious entities will continue to need to balance (and this involves time, attention, and staffing) both efficacy and witness. This puts such groups, at least in the short run, in some competitive disadvantage when they are compared to purely secular interest groups that can focus entirely on efficacy. Again, because of American fears and taboos about any close ties between religious groups and political parties, religious special-purpose groups will generally stand at the margins of a major vehicle for determining public policy—the political party.

Para-church groups frequently tend to equate the sacred with large, but specific, causes, but that taps into only a portion of religious America. For many Americans, the sacred is more rooted in private concerns and spirituality. Clearly, the majority of congregations do not seem willing to join para-church groups. Moreover, most congregations show a certain bias toward their own "hands-on" programs (and, therefore, more personal and less structural approaches) to address those in need in society. Given new and growing constraints on congregational (and para-church) budgets, the niche for growth and investment of their social capital is neither universal nor ever expanding.

A significant minority in the Habitat sample want to secularize the organization and drop its particularist Christian inspiration. PICO, with all its successes, has not been especially resourceful in building effective coalitions with more secular groups (e.g., labor unions) in metropolitan and regional settings. While members of congregations who belong to para-church groups express great gratitude for the resources of the para-church group, they resist turning the local congregation itself too fully into a special-purpose group. Most parishes try to avoid controversial issues, and few sermons get preached in local parishes on social justice.

In the end, those who would hope to renew American social capital only, or even primarily, based on religious social capital will find that their hope rests on too thin a reed. At best, religious social capital remains a potent source that other civic organizations' social efforts can enlist for the renewal of an American sense of mutual trust, community, and solidarity. Even in the religious community, many remain, as Steven Hart has shown, primarily religious individualists (Hart 1992, 74-78). Many religious people would circumscribe the social scope and role of congregations simply to being sanctuary havens against a larger social world, and many non-religious people remain wary of a coalition of interests whose largest umbrella is religious in nature. Of course, we have not, as a society, fully tested the limits of the exportability of religious social capital. Nevertheless, there seem to be only finite niches into which it can be invested, exported, or magnified. Robert Wuthnow's sober words from his study of churches and stewardship in a time of diminishing revenues reminds us of these limits to expanding religious social capital:

> In the final analysis, churches are now at the point where even those that have been most active in helping the needy are beginning to wonder if they can continue at existing levels. Clergy recognize that it is easy to operate social programs when times are good. None of the tough choices have to be faced. The new wing can still be built. The choir can still purchase new music. Belt-tightening makes the choice to help others harder. "We haven't had to make a choice between heating the place and feeding people," admitted the pastor of one of the most affluent churches we studied. "I don't know what would happen," he said. "Probably, we'd act like most churches. We'd heat the place." (Wuthnow 1997, 196)

CONCLUSION

We have seen pervasive evidence that church or group-based religion generates more social capital in the United States than any other institution. Moreover, purely individual religiosity does not generate these same social effects. Organized church groups are an especially potent source for norms of reciprocity and trust, and they carry, almost intrinsically, strong communitarian overtones. Studies of religion and social capital have focused too narrowly on congregational membership and practice. Often congregations do not know how to invest or multiply their social capital into the larger society. Para-church groups, in symbiosis with congregations, can be very effective multipliers of religious social capital.

The limits in the economic model ingredient in the social capital metaphor make it difficult to compare the kinds of social capital generated by religious groups with more secular forms of social capital. Much evidence, however, suggests that they are not simply the same. A congregation is not a soccer club. There seem to be distinctive niches in which religious social capital can be multiplied as well as limits to its totally free exportability into secular spheres.

Chapter 4

Faith and Leadership in the Inner City

How Social Capital Contributes to Democratic Renewal

Mark R. Warren

"Them bones, them bones," Father Al Jost began his prayer.[1] The thirty community leaders present were nervous. These women—school secretaries, homemakers, and nurses—came from poor Mexican-American neighborhoods of San Antonio, Texas. They were nervous because they were about to take the stage to lead the twentieth anniversary convention of their organization, Communities Organized for Public Service (COPS). Thirty-five hundred supporters waited for them behind placards announcing "Saint Leo's" and "Saint Gabriel," the Catholic parishes of the west and south sides of San Antonio. The leaders were going to face the governor of Texas, the mayor, a majority of San Antonio's city councilors, and the CEOs of the largest local banks. They intended to demand support for COPS's programs in the areas of affordable housing, job training, and school reform.

The leaders formed a circle, gathered hands, and Father Al prayed: "them bones, them bones." He told the story of Ezekiel's prophecy of the valley of the dry bones, a symbol of a community in ruins physically and spiritually, a community without hope and in despair. Father Al spoke of the bones beginning to rattle, to come together, of sinews forming, and flesh and blood growing. He told of a great army emerging as a symbol of the community coming together to rebuild itself. When Father Al finished, the COPS leaders said "Amen" and marched out to the stage. To the sounds of a mariachi band, they climbed the steps to the podium, exuding an attitude of confidence and collective determi-

49

nation. Over the next two hours, Texas Governor Ann Richards pledged $500,000 to COPS's job training program, and bank executives promised $110 million in housing loans for COPS neighborhoods.

COPS is one of sixty or so local affiliates of the Industrial Areas Foundation (IAF), a national network of faith-based community organizations. With over one hundred professional organizers on staff, the network claims to reach one thousand congregations, schools, and other community institutions, that, in turn, include more than 1 million member families. The IAF is rapidly growing, with more than twenty new organizing projects underway. This makes the IAF the largest network in an emerging set of faith-based community organizing efforts. The faith-based field incorporates three other networks, including the PICO network discussed by Richard Wood (Chapter 10 of this volume), as well as a large number of independent, non-affiliated local church-based community initiatives.[2] Faith-based organizations are an important variety of the para-church organizations discussed by Coleman (Chapter 3 of this volume).

Drawing upon its deep roots in religious institutions, the IAF network has proved able to draw large numbers of participants, particularly from low-income communities of color, into sustained political action for community betterment in a way that has become quite unusual in American society. While many advocacy groups remain staff-dominated with few roots in local communities, IAF affiliates consistently engage community residents in political action at a variety of levels. For example, the Texas state network drew ten thousand participants to its founding convention in 1990. Affiliates across the country regularly draw two to three thousand participants to yearly conventions and engage hundreds in campaigns for affordable housing, job training, school reform, public safety, and neighborhood improvements.[3]

The faith-based network's success in engaging many Americans often excluded from political participation suggests the gains that can be made by linking religiously based social capital to democratic action. This chapter analyzes how the IAF makes that link, drawing upon research on the IAF in Texas reported more fully elsewhere (Warren 2001).[4] The IAF has built its largest state network in Texas. It began its organizing in Texas when Southwest IAF director Ernesto Cortes, Jr., founded COPS in his native San Antonio in 1973. It now has eleven local affiliates across the state, and it has become a powerful state-wide political influence. Since the IAF makes a conscious effort to engage religious communities in political action, it offers an opportunity to deepen our understanding of how social capital can contribute to democratic renewal.

SOCIAL CAPITAL AND DEMOCRATIC PARTICIPATION

Recent research suggests the connections between social capital and democracy. In his study of Italy, Robert Putnam (1993a) shows that regions with greater stocks of social capital have more effective democratic institutions and higher levels of social and economic development. In the United States, according to Putnam (1993b, 1995a, 2000), social capital has been seriously eroded, as can be seen in the decline in associational membership and levels of social trust. Social capital underpins democracy because it provides the relationships of trust and habits of cooperation essential for citizens to work together to solve common problems.

This decline in social capital can help explain present low levels of political participation, particularly if we recognize that many social organizations in the past sought to engage people in politics. Political participation in the U.S. has declined as political parties have lost their ties to community-based organizations and have become candidate-centered vehicles for election (Wattenberg 1990). Despite the rise of many advocacy groups since the 1960s, few encourage active participation in cooperative efforts, and most exclude low-income and minority communities (Judis 1992; Walker 1991).

Putnam's approach points us towards an understanding of how to rebuild political participation by thinking about how to connect Americans to politics through their social organizations. He has emphasized the resources of trust and habits of cooperation that can be gained through participation in all kinds of social institutions, from bowling leagues to civic associations. But, thus far, he has paid less attention to the structures and unifying beliefs of the specific social institutions that engage Americans (see Smidt, Chapter 1 of this volume).

The advantage of Putnam's approach is that social capital can be measured as a universal cultural resource. What remains less explored is how the specific institutional settings in which social capital is embedded affect its ability to be translated into the political arena. In his early work on Italy, Putnam (1993a) equated social capital with purely equal, horizontal relationships within associations and institutions. But most concrete social institutions exhibit complicated patterns of authority and equality, of hierarchy and participation—patterns that may be important for developing democratic leadership and accountability.

Some important steps have been made to specify the kinds of social institutions that are important to democratic participation and the mechanisms through which social capital resources can be translated into politics (Verba et al. 1995). Religious institutions can play a particularly important role in equalizing political participation because they are sites where people of color and low-income people have the opportunity to learn skills that can be translated to politics, skills like letter writing, speech making, and how to plan and make decisions in meetings (see also Harris, Chapter 8 of this volume). The other venues for skill acquisition reside in workplaces and non-political organizations where people of lower socioeconomic status are less likely to attain them. Churches are places where many low income and minority people participate and have a relatively equal opportunity for skill acquisition (Verba et al. 1995, chapter 11).[5]

The study by Verba, Schlozman, and Brady is important because the authors point us to religious institutions as key social capital sites for increasing political participation and because they are able to quantify the impact of social capital through the mechanism of skill acquisition. Accepting the current institutional arrangements of the American polity, they show how religious communities can offset class and racial bias. But, despite the equalizing role of churches, many Americans remain marginalized because current institutional arrangements limit participation considerably. Our political institutions fail especially to engage many residents of low-income communities of color.

Nevertheless, the approach used by Verba, Scholozman, and Brady follows an individualist bias in understanding political participation, as it sees social capital as a set of assets (skills) that inhere in an individual, instead of more properly viewing social capital as a structural feature of communities (see Chapter 1 of this volume).[6] The real strength of the social capital concept is that it directs our attention to the resources that inhere in the relationships between people. It suggests an approach to engage people in democratic politics not as disconnected individuals, but as persons embedded in communities. To significantly expand political participation requires thinking about how to engage communities in political action.

Those institutions, like churches, that mediate these communities, however, have specific traditions and structures through which trust and cooperation are developed. The theological beliefs and traditions as well as the institutional structures of these churches provide an important potential basis for the expansion of democracy. Shared religious convictions can motivate people to cooperate and act together (see Chapter 9), while churches can provide networks of trusted leaders and followers (see Chapters 3 and 5). But denominations vary in their theological traditions and in their institutional structures in ways that might affect the potential of religious communities to become engaged in politics.

The IAF pursues a strategy that has had significant success in expanding democratic participation, especially within low-income communities of color. It creates a different type of political institution—local organizations like COPS that have engaged people broadly in political action through their religious communities. The IAF's experience with different churches offers an excellent opportunity to explore the contributions that religiously based social capital can make to democratic renewal, and to understand the way that different institutional structures and unifying beliefs affect that contribution.

RELIGIOUS COMMUNITIES IN THE TEXAS IAF NETWORK

The IAF seeks to engage religious communities in political action for community development broadly conceived. To do so, the IAF employs what it calls a "relational organizing" strategy (Warren 1998). Rather than first identifying an issue around which to mobilize people, it brings together community residents drawn from its various churches for purposes of discussion of community needs and capabilities. Out of these discussions, a commitment emerges to act to achieve winnable goals that can improve the community. Professional IAF organizers train these indigenous community leaders, mostly women, in all facets of political organizing—including research, policy development, lobbying, negotiation, and community mobilization. The community residents who become leaders of local IAF affiliates are drawn primarily from these churches, and to a lesser extent from other institutions such as schools. These churches constitute the formal, dues-paying members of the affiliates. The IAF follows a nonpartisan strategy. Local affiliates derive their ultimate power from their community base, organizing large actions to pressure public officials and to win their commitment to support IAF campaigns. At the same time, the IAF involves community leaders in developing their own policy proposals, which they negotiate with public officials.[7]

Faith communities offer an important set of social capital resources that help explain the success of IAF organizing. Faith communities contain pre-existing networks of clergy and lay leaders who, in turn, are further connected to broader networks of friends and neighbors. These networks contain a degree of trust and legitimate authority that can help initiate cooperative action. The pastor's endorsement of the IAF effort opens the door to church members who may be initially suspicious of "outsiders." The IAF can then work to strengthen these networks and direct them towards political action. Churches provide a pool of lay leaders from which IAF organizers can draw recruits to its affiliates. The IAF trains these community residents to be political leaders who will act to improve their communities. Churches also provide these networks with leaders who are better positioned to mobilize others to vote and to engage in public actions, activities that give IAF affiliates their political power. A religious motivation for community care plays an important role in encouraging participation. Religious traditions can motivate ministers and lay leaders to engage in political action, and to sustain their participation through victories as well as defeats, because they provide a moral foundation that can deepen and sustain interest-based political action.

I use the term "engagement" because the IAF does not mobilize—or draw from—the capacities of religious institutions in a one-sided or utilitarian fashion. Wood (Chapter 5 of this volume) has used the term "symbiosis" to describe this sort of relationship, as demonstrated by the PICO community organizing network and its religious community affiliates (see also Coleman, Chapter 3). Religious institutions do have much to gain from political action through the IAF. Many people of faith find an opportunity to implement their social ministry commitments and to make real improvements in their communities though the IAF. In addition, church institutions can become strengthened through the development of its lay leadership. Finally, successful IAF campaigns work directly to improve the neighborhoods of these churches and thereby make the faith community more viable in the long run. Thus, religious institutions enter a collaboration with the IAF that offers important gains to, but also certain transformations of, both parties. The IAF has to reshape and focus religious traditions in order to direct them towards IAF-style political action. But these traditions, in turn, have contributed to the IAF's "theology of organizing." The IAF does not simply mobilize existing networks around a predetermined agenda, but works to develop their leaders and strengthen the social fabric of communities. These lay leaders, in turn, become leaders of IAF affiliates, and these leaders shape issue campaigns.

The Texas IAF has been able to engage many types of religious communities in its local affiliates. Some denominations are more likely to be involved than are others, and not all important denominations have been engaged. About half of the churches active in the Texas IAF are Hispanic Catholic parishes. The other half is made up in roughly equal proportions of African-American and Anglo churches, both of which are largely Protestant. Although white and black Catholics, and several Jewish synagogues, have played important roles from time to time, these three groups (Hispanic Catholics, African-American Protestants and Anglo Protestants) represent the large majority of IAF member institutions in Texas. Anglo faith communities, however, are largely middle class, while the bulk of the network's organizing activity lies in low-income communities of color where political participation is often low.

This chapter will contrast the involvement in the Texas IAF of Hispanic Catholic and African-American Protestant communities, whose institutional structure and religious traditions turn out to vary in significant ways (for a fuller treatment, see Warren 2001). Examining these differences will help reveal why some churches are more likely than others to join the IAF and why some are better able to mobilize a larger base of support for its effort.

The preponderance of Hispanic Catholic parishes can be attributed, in part, to the fact that the rapidly growing Hispanic population makes up almost 25 percent of the state's total. And, Hispanics are heavily concentrated in low-income communities. African Americans, meanwhile, constitute about 13 percent of the state's population. Moreover, the origins of the IAF in the Mexican-American communities of San Antonio gave the network an initial grounding and reputation among the state's Hispanics. In addition to COPS, the Texas IAF has three local affiliates in areas where low-income Mexican Americans make up the large majority of the entire population: Valley Interfaith in the lower Rio Grande Valley, EPISO in El Paso, and the Border Organization in the Del Rio/Eagle Pass area. IAF organizers have worked hard to involve African-American Protestants in their efforts in Texas, and they have met with growing success (Warren, 2001). Part of the difficulty in engaging African Americans lies in the different institutional structure and religious traditions of black Protestants, as will be discussed below.

In addition to their availability for recruitment as members of IAF affiliates, denominations vary in their ability to provide a broader base of supporters. In absolute numbers, Catholic churches can mobilize for IAF actions, on average, almost twice as many followers as Protestant churches.[8] Per capita figures, however, show a less marked difference, with Catholic parishes mobilizing roughly 25 percent more followers. The overall greater capacity of Catholic over Protestants churches for IAF mobilization, therefore, rests both upon their larger average size and upon their ability to mobilize a greater proportion of parishioners and neighborhood residents.

Exploring more deeply the theological traditions and institutional structures of Mexican-American Catholic and African-American Protestant churches can help clarify the contributions that religiously based social capital can make to expanding democratic participation. Comparing the two types of churches will make clear why differences in beliefs and structures matter for efforts, like the IAF's, to engage people in political action through their religious communities.

Mexican-American Catholic Communities

Theological Tradition: Catholic Social Thought

Hispanic Catholics and their priests bring a rich faith tradition to their participation in the IAF. That tradition finds its roots in the social teaching of the Catholic Church that began with Pope Leo XIII's encyclical Rerum Novarum in 1891. In that papal encyclical, Pope Leo defended the rights of workers in the face of powerful economic and political institutions. The Second Vatican Council (Vatican II) reactivated this tradition for the modern era. Held between 1962 and 1965, the Vatican II council meetings served to strengthen the church's commitment to social and economic justice and to inspire action by Catholics throughout the world. In 1982, the American Bishops published their letter on the economy, which called for the church to take action for economic justice. Although Pope John Paul II has taken conservative stands on certain social issues, he has continued to articulate a strong role for the church in defending the rights of the poor.[9]

The IAF's organizing efforts among Hispanics also drew energy from the theological and social ferment stimulated by liberation theology developed in Latin America. In 1968 the bishops of Latin America issued a manifesto from Medellin, Colombia, that called for the participation of the poor in their own liberation and salvation. In many Latin American countries, Catholic priests and lay activists began to oppose ruling elites and military dictatorships. They organized small Christian "base communities" that took political action for social and economic justice. Although Catholics in the IAF took some inspiration from liberation theology, they never followed the base community strategy, which seemed, to many of them, more appropriate to Latin American conditions. Instead, IAF Catholics sought to participate within mainstream church structures, seeking to engage parishes in political action for community needs.[10]

More important to the IAF's effort to counter the individualism and atomization of contemporary American social and political life is the fact that

Catholic social thought articulates a strong communitarian conception of human beings. In *Gaudium et Specs,* the church asserts that it is only "through [man's] dealings with others, through reciprocal duties, and through fraternal dialogue he develops all his gifts and is able to rise to his destiny."[11] According to IAF director Cortes (1991, 160), "this conception imagines human beings as 'persons,' not as 'individuals.' They are mothers, father, brothers, daughters, workers, employers, pastors, governors, and so on, not isolated, self-directed singularities."

In interviews conducted for this study, the large majority of IAF-affiliated priests and lay leaders explain their involvement in the IAF in terms of a Catholic concern for community and a responsibility to take action for social and economic justice. Participation in the IAF offers the opportunity to make the social commitments of their faith real. Moreover, since many Hispanic parishioners live in low-income communities themselves, there is a tight connection between the demands of their religious faith and the immediate interests and needs of their communities. Father Mike Haney of St. Leonard's parish explains why he joined COPS:

> COPS is a way of implementing the Gospel's call to justice that it impos-
> es on us. This happens in a couple of ways: dealing with issues themselves;
> and COPS calls us to work as a collective, to find strength in community
> and that's a gospel call itself.[12]

While IAF does have to convince socially committed priests that political action is a legitimate way to pursue community building, the non-partisan character of IAF organizations makes these affiliates an attractive venue for priests with a variety of political affiliations, except the most conservative.

Institutional Structure: Authority and Participation in the Parish

The institutional structure of the Catholic Church has proven quite beneficial to IAF organizing. The Catholic Church has historically placed a stress on authority, and continues to be more hierarchically organized than most Protestant denominations. Since Vatican II, though, the church has worked to increase lay participation in its parishes and in the broader life of the church.[13] Exactly how to balance authority with participation is a matter of contention within the church, with Pope John Paul struggling to assert papal authority over many doctrinal matters at the same time as he reiterates the church's commitment to the poor. Catholic women, meanwhile, have worked to assert their leadership in the church in the face of the Pope's defense of the traditional monopoly of men in positions of power. Nevertheless, Catholic dioceses have been encouraging the development of lay leaders, including women, and have been giving them much more responsibility for pastoral duties, especially as the shortage of priests has become increasingly more pronounced. Consequently, IAF organizers today have a much more significant pool of lay leaders from which to draw than they would have had prior to the 1970s.

The combination of authority with participation benefits political partici-pation in the IAF in several important ways. The hierarchical structure of the Catholic Church encourages many priests to join the IAF because Texas bish-ops have fairly consistently supported the Texas IAF organizations. San Antonio's Archbishop Patricio Flores, the nation's first Hispanic bishop, played a key role in supporting COPS early on, and regularly encourages priests to involve their parishes in the effort. Flores has also used his influence to encour-age other Texas bishops to support local IAF affiliates. They have seldom been hesitant to do so. Consequently, priests who do get involved in local IAF affil-iates can expect recognition from their bishops. In San Antonio, several priests active in COPS have been appointed to important posts in the church, includ-ing David Garcia as secretary to the Archbishop and Rosendo Urrabazo as director of the Mexican American Cultural Center. While there appears to be no evidence of retribution against priests who decline to support IAF initiatives, diocesan support makes many priests more likely to get involved.[14]

Within individual parishes the Catholic priest commands authority as well. So his support of IAF efforts carries great weight in encouraging participation by the parish's lay leaders. According to former COPS co-chair Reverend Urrabazo, "participation can be charted according to the pastors. When the clergy is on-board, the parish takes off. When the clergy is not with COPS, par-ticipation falls off."[15]

For its part, the Catholic Church in Texas has much to gain from partici-pating in the IAF. Hispanics constitute, by far, the most rapidly growing Catholic community. The allegiance of Hispanics to the church is vital to its survival. The Texas church would like to avoid the growth of Pentecostal churches that has occurred in Hispanic communities elsewhere in the country (see also Skerry 1993: 190–91). Moreover, because the Catholic Church has a parish structure, the vitality of parish churches depends on the health of the neighborhoods in which they are located. The IAF works directly to help these communities survive and grow, so its work is vital to the long-term health of the Catholic Church itself.

Finally, the IAF can offer direct assistance in developing lay leadership for the church. As the number of priests and nuns has dropped precipitously, the church has become dependent on lay ministries. Because of a long tradition in which priests monopolized these responsibilities, the church must train lay parishioners to become ministerial leaders. Many dioceses have set up parish development offices for precisely this purpose. But IAF organizers are experts in leadership development. In the late 1970s, IAF director Cortes and his staff established their own parish development program to offer to priests and min-isters. In San Antonio, the IAF and the Catholic Church work so closely on these matters that the diocese actually hired former COPS President Carmen Badillo to head up its parish development office.

Parish development and IAF involvement, however, is not necessarily with-out conflict. Once lay leaders take on more responsibility, they have the opportunity to challenge parish priests on at least some of the issues facing the church. In some cases, it has been lay leaders who get the priest to join the IAF effort, not the other way around. In the early days of COPS, Ernesto Cortes recruited Beatrice Cortez and some fellow parishioners at St. Patrick's in San Antonio to get involved in a campaign to stop the closing of a neighborhood school. It was Beatrice Cortez and other parishioners who then got the pastor to commit St. Patrick's to join COPS.[16] In many cases, when an originally supportive pastor moves on only to be replaced by a less supportive one, it is the lay leadership of the church that continues its IAF involvement. Over time, parishes go through cycles of involvement in this way. If a priest is hostile to the IAF, though, participation normally ends.

In a surprising way, the authority of the parish priest often makes lay leadership in IAF efforts more likely. Catholic priests derive their authority from the church, i.e., they are appointed by bishops and not elected by parishioners. Since their position in the parish is relatively secure, and their authority does not come from their talent as a community leader, they often let lay parishioners become the IAF leaders in their parish. In COPS, Metro Alliance, and ACT, only several pastors out of the forty or so member parishes are highly active.[17] Catholic pastors often find it relatively easy to commit their parish to join the IAF, because membership does not necessarily mean extra work for them. As we will see below, African-American Protestant ministers face a sharply different institutional structure, and consequently such pastors find that they must play a direct leadership role in their church's IAF work.[18]

Institutional Structure: The Neighborhood-based Parish

The geographically based parish structure of the Catholic Church contributes to the ability of the IAF to build an extensive base of support within low-income Hispanic neighborhoods. Catholic churches tend to be large in membership, and they incorporate all Catholics in the parish neighborhood. Since the residents of COPS neighborhoods are almost entirely Mexican American and at least nominally Catholic, each member church provides the IAF with access to a large proportion of neighborhood residents. The 27 parishes in COPS represent 70 percent of the Catholic parishes in the south, west, and central sections of San Antonio. Thus, by recruiting only 27 churches, COPS has direct access to 70 percent of church-going Hispanics, a total of about 50,000 families. Moreover, lay leaders and church members can reach beyond church-goers to their families, friends, and neighbors, most of whom are concentrated in a local community surrounding the parish.

Because they normally live in the neighborhoods of their parish, Hispanic Catholic IAF leaders are tied particularly closely to neighborhood networks. Although working- and middle-class Hispanics appear to be more likely than the very poor to serve as church and neighborhood leaders, they share an Hispanic identity and live with the poor in one neighborhood. Consequently, there is a tight connection between their own self-interest, the needs of the broader community, and a religious commitment to social ministry. In other words, fixing the street in front of their house meets the personal self-interest of an IAF leader, helps the larger neighborhood, and fulfills a commitment to social ministry as well.

Metro Alliance leader Pauline Cabello discusses why she seized the leadership opportunities offered by IAF participation. Cabello lives in San Antonio's near north side, a working class community becoming predominantly Hispanic, and is a member of St. Mary Magdalene's parish.

> My grandmother lives in the deep west side. When it rained, her street was a river of mud. My grandmother always said it was the will of God. A young priest at St. Timothy's changed their lives—Father Benavides [an early COPS leader]. . . . When Father Benavides came to St. Mary Magdalene's, he set up ministries and leaders developed [including me]. It gave me a sense of ownership. That I'm important and I don't have to be a tamale or taco-maker. I can have a voice and a vision for me and my family. . . .
>
> What we do comes from our gut—being mothers, we have a sense of community. In the last two to three years we [Linda Froebane and myself] got more involved in Metro because they hit on our area of interest, education. That hit us: it's our kids, the children of the community. We buried two or three; we don't want to do that anymore.[19]

Other Hispanic IAF leaders stress the connection between the effective power offered by IAF participation and their religious beliefs. Veteran COPS leader Patricia Ozuna takes pleasure from tough meetings with public officials where she advocates for the community in which she lives. "I like banging heads, or using my skills to accomplish something—knowing you moved an issue forward. . . . With COPS you see the changes—streets, sidewalks. We have the power to do things for the community." But Ozuna's desire for personal power is tempered by her religious vocation. Although Ozuna likes "banging heads," she says that two things keep her going, "anger at injustice and that I'm doing the Lord's work. It's my ministry for social justice."[20] In fact, many Hispanic IAF leaders report that involvement in the IAF has strengthened their religious commitment. For Beatrice Cortez, COPS's fourth president, IAF involvement gave meaning to her faith. "I could now relate scripture to my life. . . . Faith is a matter of developing, creating the right situation for people. If you don't make a choice, your faith won't mean anything."[21]

The extensive access to neighborhood networks offered by the parish structure combined with the direct interest of the residents of low-income Hispanic communities in the work of the IAF help explain why Catholic parishes stand out in their consistent ability to engage large numbers of neighborhood residents in supporting IAF campaigns. The authority of a supportive priest who encourages participation from the pulpit provides an important incentive for support as well. Meanwhile, the parish and neighborhood stand to gain from their IAF participation. The IAF works to strengthen the community's social fabric and to bring the necessary resources for community revitalization. Moreover, through participation in the IAF, the parish can draw the neighborhood more closely around the parish, enhancing the allegiance of Hispanic Catholics and attracting new parishioners as well.

Hispanic Catholic communities, therefore, contain a nexus of characteristics that have a close elective affinity to IAF organizing. The tradition of Catholic social thought directs clergy and parishioners towards action for the benefit of their own community. The church's institutional structure combines authority and lay participation in a way that encourages priests to join and lay leaders to emerge. Finally, its parish base provides the IAF with broad and dense access to neighborhood-based social networks, which can be more easily drawn into action with the support of a priest that carries the authority of the church behind him. At the same time, the church itself benefits from IAF participation. Clergy and lay leaders find a way to activate their faith and to pursue their social ministry through the IAF. Meanwhile, IAF organizers help develop the lay leadership on which the future of the church depends. Finally, IAF organizing strengthens the economic and social health of the communities on which Catholic parishes both serve and depend. Through this process of mutual interaction and benefit, the IAF and Hispanic Catholic communities have developed a very close collaboration.

African American Protestant Congregations

Theological Tradition: Racial Justice and Liberation

Theologically, the themes of deliverance and freedom lie at the heart of black Christian spirituality (Cone 1969; West 1982). Freedom suggests deliverance both into God's kingdom as well as from slavery and racial oppression in the real world. The African-American worldview relies deeply upon its religious theology, and its practice draws heavily from the church's cultural styles of worship, such as call and response (Lincoln & Mamiya 1990; Pattillo-McCoy 1998). The theological tradition of the black church, then, offers a rich resource for efforts to sustain the African-American community and work for its liberation.

African-American churches have a long tradition of engagement with social and political issues in the black community (see Harris 1999, and Chapter 8 in this volume). During the era of legal segregation, as Aldon Morris (1984) has shown, black churches became *the* center of black community life in the urban South. Excluded from mainstream civic and political institutions, African Americans concentrated their community and political leadership in their independent churches. In the 1950s and 1960s, these churches provided a crucial foundation for the civil rights movement through its pre-existing networks of leaders and followers under the influence of their pastors. In order to engage black churches and their pastors, religious leaders like Martin Luther King, Jr., refocused religious beliefs to direct them towards active engagement in the struggle for racial justice and equality. Some ministers declined to participate because they thought the church should concentrate on personal salvation, not political action. But a large number of ministers did play central roles in local civil rights movement organizations.

After the decline of the civil rights movement, many ministers continued to participate in African-American social and political efforts. Although King had tried to broaden the movement's perspective to deal with poverty and economic problems facing Americans across racial lines, the primary direction of these efforts remained racially based. Black ministers played key roles in organizations like the NAACP and in efforts to empower African Americans through the election of black candidates to office (Tate 1991).

This rich African-American religious tradition has not been as readily available for IAF organizing as the tradition of Catholic social thought in the Hispanic community because the black tradition has focused primarily on racial justice. The IAF has a different emphasis, avoiding race-based organizing in favor of community organizing in a multiracial context. While participation in the IAF does not require a rejection of theological concern for liberation or for the needs of the black community, it does require a shift and re-emphasis in social and political theology.

For its part, the IAF had long seen its purpose as providing a vehicle for the inclusion of marginalized and oppressed communities. Once African Americans started participating in the Texas IAF and in local IAF organizations in other parts of the country, the network proved open to their theological influence. One of the central themes in the IAF's "theology of organizing" became the inclusion of the stranger. Cortes and other IAF organizers began to stress the origins of that theme in Exodus, a central symbol in black religious traditions. According to Cortes, "the black tradition is important because it cannot escape Exodus. At Exodus the narrative is about the formation of peoplehood. So that's real rich [for our organizing]."[22] But, rather than emphasize the theme of liberation of a people in Exodus, the IAF has stressed the themes of inclusion and community-building that are also present there.

This shift away from racial justice and towards a broader multiracial and community-building approach in the IAF proved difficult for some black ministers to make, because they were personally involved in advocacy groups with a specifically racial mission (like the NAACP) or in current electoral arrangements. Many important black ministers held elective office, particularly at the local level, or they had relationships with elected officials that committed them to support those officials in exchange for favors or resources to their neighborhoods. And many ministers, seeing the continued effect of racism on their communities, felt committed to independent black organizations.[23] Participation in the IAF not only required a theological shift, it required the breaking of relationships and the development of a nonpartisan style of political activity. That was a risk—particularly given the importance of the benefits, no matter how few, that came from connections to political parties and public officials that held power and controlled resources.

The IAF challenged Hispanic priests who were mostly uninvolved politically to take their faith commitments into the political arena. Many African-American ministers, however, already did that. The IAF challenged them, instead, to direct those political commitments in a different way, namely towards fostering democratic practice rather than towards direct involvement in party and governmental institutions.

While this shift proved unappealing to some African-American ministers, others were looking precisely for such an opportunity. Seeing their communities crumble while black candidates ran for office and while the NAACP pursued legal strategies, many black ministers saw the IAF as an opportunity to create effective power and real improvement for their communities. Reverend Barry Jackson, an African-American leader of Dallas Area Interfaith, recognized the importance of black power, but did not want to be limited to it. When he accepted the pastorship of Munger Avenue Baptist Church, he inherited a church with a rich tradition in efforts to address racial justice, but one located in a rapidly deteriorating inner-city neighborhood. According to Jackson, "there was a time for black theology as race-based. I don't reject that. Integration hurt us more than helped us. Our businesses were destroyed. We forfeited who we are. It's okay to claim your history and culture. But it's not okay to limit yourself to that. It doesn't understand that our welfare is tied up together. . . . I talked to black ministers. I said we can't continue to engage on racial issues. We need to address issues of families, neighborhoods, and if we build multiracial alliances, we can win."[24]

Some black congregations still emphasize personal salvation so exclusively that they reject political participation of any kind, and that is why the more mainstream black denominations constitute the majority of black church participation in the Texas IAF. Nevertheless, the IAF has drawn some significant amount of participation from congregations in denominations that have been fairly apolitical generally. In particular, a number of churches belonging to the Church of God in Christ (COGIC), a fast-growing Pentecostal denomination, participate in local IAF affiliates. Often counting among their congregants the poorest African Americans, these COGIC ministers tend to emphasize social ministry as much as evangelism.[25]

Institutional Structure: The Independent Congregation

The Protestant congregational structure contrasts sharply with the Catholic ecclesiastic hierarchy and parish base. In Baptist denominations, congregations are fiercely independent. There is no equivalent to an Archbishop Flores to encourage black ministers to join IAF efforts. At the same time, Baptists do form associations, and black ministers often form ministerial alliances in their cities. Pastor networks have proven crucial to IAF organizing. Many pastors joined the Fort Worth IAF affiliate ACT when encouraged to do so by

Reverend Nehemiah Davis and others in the Baptist Ministerial Alliance in Fort Worth. The support of Baptist minister Barry Jackson, who had been involved with the IAF in Austin before his move to Dallas, proved crucial to the IAF's success in recruiting a core group of black Baptist churches to its more recent effort in Dallas.[26]

The congregation is typically understood as a more horizontal structure than the parish because the independence of congregations places power in the hands of lay leaders. Black Baptist congregations hire their pastors. Their leadership boards, not the priest or his bishop, hold ultimate authority. Verba and his associates (1995, chapter 11) argue that this structure holds out an advantage to political participation. According to these authors, lay leaders in Protestant churches have more of an opportunity than those in the Catholic Church to learn civic skills because they participate more fully and directly in church life.

But this understanding misses a crucial aspect of black congregational dynamics. First, it turns out that, despite the fact that ultimate authority rests with the congregation's governing board, many black ministers have developed a reputation for authoritarian leadership styles. Authoritarianism has deep roots in theocratic and patriarchal traditions in the black church (Harris, 1999). But another reason for this apparent paradox lies in the way that black pastors must operate in order to keep their jobs. Because in many black congregations the job security of the black Baptist minister does not rest with some bishop, the African-American pastor must constantly work to maintain the allegiance of one's congregants. The pastor acquires this support through demonstrating leadership as well as through charismatic speaking. Given the particular history of black churches as centers for community life, pastors are expected to be community and political leaders as part of their ministerial responsibilities. The tremendous demands placed on black pastors for broad leadership, coupled with the need to maintain constant support, has contributed to an authoritarian style among many within their ranks.

The responsibility of the African-American pastor to be the political leader of his or her congregation presents, perhaps paradoxically, an obstacle to the recruitment of black churches into the IAF. Since the Catholic hierarchy assigns priests to parishes, the priest does not have to be the parish's political leader, although some may desire that role. A Catholic priest can sign his parish up with the IAF and then step back to let lay parishioners do the actual work required for participation. Black ministers are not as able to do so. Apparently, if a black minister wants to maintain his or her leadership position in the congregation, the pastor must take an active role personally in the IAF when the church joins. An examination of clergy participation in Texas IAF organizations supports this conclusion. Only a few priests of the forty or so Catholic parishes in COPS, Metro Alliance, and ACT are engaged in the organizations on a regular basis. Some associate pastors and nuns also play prominent roles. On the other hand, all pastors of the ten African-American Protestant churches in ACT and the Metro Alliance are actively engaged in the affiliates.[27]

The participation of black ministers, of course, often contributes important leadership to IAF organizations. The problem lies in recruitment. For a black pastor to commit his or her church to the IAF, the pastor must be willing to put in the time and effort required of IAF leaders. Many pastors may be supportive of the IAF, but unwilling to commit their own time. Consequently, they will not join the IAF effort, whereas similar passive support by a Catholic priest will often be sufficient for the church to join.[28]

If the black minister is committed enough to join, the IAF can usually count on his active participation. In turn, that minister can gain from IAF's assistance in "parish development." Many black congregations are institutionally weak. They suffer from inadequate income and old buildings in need of repair. Many cannot pay a salary sufficient to support a minister full-time. Although black congregations do provide the opportunity for greater lay involvement, often their lay leaders are inexperienced and untrained. The IAF helps interested ministers build a leadership team to strengthen the church's finances and programs. But the minister has to be open to a new style of leadership—one of collaboration with lay members. According to African-American minister and Dallas Area Interfaith co-chair Gerald Britt, the black ministers who come to embrace the IAF are those who can see the compatibility of the work with their religious mission and can see the advantages of shared leadership. "It's a different day and time. . . . The idea of shared leadership within the congregation and within the [IAF] organization—that's a new model of leadership. But when you've been raised in a hierarchy, where you're the final authority. . . ."[29] IAF leader and black minister Barry Jackson argues that the IAF's approach meets the needs of a new era for black churches, declaring "it's time out for the 'big daddy'!"[30]

Institutional Structure: Pan-neighborhood Congregations

The congregational structure of the black church exhibits strengths and weaknesses as well in the way it provides access for IAF organizing to neighborhood social networks. African-American congregations typically provide access to a comparatively smaller number of neighborhood-based social networks than Catholic parishes. First, black churches tend to be smaller in size than Catholic parishes. In San Antonio and Fort Worth, the average Catholic parish in the IAF includes about two thousand families. By contrast, the average black Protestant church includes about five hundred families, and several are quite small.[31] IAF organizers, therefore, would have to recruit four black pastors to have access to the same number of people and neighborhood networks provided by one Catholic parish.

Moreover, being congregationally based, black churches draw their membership from across the city, not just in their neighborhood. In fact, many inner-city black congregations have more members from outside, than inside, the neighborhood in which the church stands. A large number of these members are commuters who grew up in the neighborhood of the church. As the more affluent left for the suburbs, many continue to return to their old church on Sunday morning. Many of these more middle-class congregants dominate in church leadership, and often in IAF participation as well. On the one hand, this is a great strength and contribution of black churches: they often help overcome the isolation of poor communities by bringing the more affluent together with the poor within one congregation. On the other hand, the IAF's ability to tap the networks of the church's neighborhood is weakened. The smaller size and less dense access to neighborhood networks helps explain why black churches mobilize, on average, fewer supporters than Hispanic Catholic parishes to the large public actions that provide the foundation for the political power of IAF affiliates.

Although IAF campaigns speak to the immediate interests of inner-city black neighborhoods, for housing, education, public safety, etc., many of the leaders that emerge from African-American churches in the IAF do not live in those neighborhoods. Mexican-American Catholic leaders have a strong material self-interest in IAF participation that combines with their religious commitments. The involvement of African-American leaders from outside the church's neighborhood has to rely more strongly upon a religiously derived concern for the broader black community. Maurice Simpson, an African-American leader in ACT, got involved "because I believe in the Great Communion— Matthew 19 and 20. You reach out and teach. If you teach a person to read and write, then they can be a good Christian. It's part of my ministry. Being from the black community, you learn to share resources and help your neighbor. It took those things to survive."[32]

For their part, African-American ministers see some important gains from their participation in the IAF for their own institutions. Taking action for community improvement through the IAF helps root the church in its neighborhood. IAF organizing engages neighborhood residents, draws them around the church, and connects them to suburban members within the congregation. Unlike parishes, congregations can move. But many black ministers are committed to their neighborhoods and their residents. Many IAF ministers pastor historic black churches in the inner city, churches with a rich heritage. But, in many cases, these inner-city communities suffer from extreme distress. Participation in the IAF can directly improve these communities, and therefore sustain the church as a community institution. According to Reverend Barry Jackson, he participates in the IAF because "the church's very survival is at stake."[33]

SOME LIMITATIONS TO THE IAF APPROACH

Since the IAF has succeeded, where many have failed, in engaging indigenous leaders of low-income communities in political participation as well as sustaining high levels of participation, it is important to consider some of the limitations to the IAF's approach.[34] While IAF organizing draws in people from a variety of class backgrounds, the poorest and most marginalized members of these communities appear less likely than low-income workers or middle-class congregants to become leaders of IAF organizations. The majority of IAF leaders in Texas are poor or low-income, especially in the largely Hispanic organizations. To its credit, the IAF encourages these leaders to develop relationships with fellow congregants and residents from all walks of life. But few people on public assistance or members of the long-term unemployed participate directly in IAF leadership, although some do.[35] Other studies of faith-based community organizing efforts have also found that the most marginalized members of poor communities participate less in direct leadership (Appleman 1996; Delgado n.d.). Nevertheless, they may be represented by the leadership of other community members to which they are tied in various ways.

Institutional factors explain part of this failure. Since the poor are less likely to attend church and become lay church leaders, they are less present in the pool out of which IAF leaders are recruited.[36] In recognition of the fact that the poorest Americans are among the most socially isolated, the IAF has made special efforts to organize them in a variety of venues beyond churches. For example, the network has built immigrant associations, and it works in colonias (the American equivalent of shantytowns along the border with Mexico), and organizes them as parents where their children attend school.

Another limitation to the IAF's contribution to democratic renewal can be found in the fact that the many residents of communities of color who do become IAF leaders appear to keep their political participation within the scope of IAF campaigns. Few seem to increase their participation in politics outside that sphere by, for example, running for office or taking positions on the boards of public institutions unrelated to IAF efforts. On the one hand, such concentration of activity within the IAF can be seen as a strength, certainly in regards to the capacities of IAF affiliates. The tendency to stay within the IAF may also mitigate against the kind of co-optation of leaders so often experienced by low-income communities. But it also means that the broader effects of IAF activity on American democracy remain constrained. The study conducted by Berry, Portney, and Thomson (1993), which found that San Antonio ranked low in measures of political activity despite IAF organizing, is consistent with this evaluation. At the same time, their study is ultimately inconclusive because it failed to measure and compare levels of political activity before and after IAF organizing efforts. In other words, IAF organizing may have increased political participation in a significant way in San Antonio, yet that level of activity remains low compared to other cities.

CONCLUSION

Despite the weaknesses just discussed, the IAF's faith-based organizing strategy does significantly expand the basis of political participation in America. It does so by providing a sharp contrast to mainstream forms of political mobilization. Rather than mobilize disconnected individuals, the IAF engages people through their institutionally based social networks. Rather than tap an individual's commitment to an issue, the IAF engages a religious commitment to community well-being and social justice. The significance of the IAF's efforts lies not just in the numbers of people it can mobilize. Rather, it lies in the connection between these leaders and their communities—a connection that comes from membership in a local congregation or parish and from the common faith shared in this institution. Although this study is limited by locality and by its attention to one specific organizing network, it does strongly suggest the importance of considering institutional structure and culture in our understanding of the contribution that social capital can make to democratic renewal.

While many types of churches have proven conducive to IAF organizing, some do appear to have a greater elective affinity than others. In particular, Catholic parishes in Hispanic communities provide lay leaders to IAF organizations that are well-rooted in parish neighborhoods and that mobilize the largest number of supporters to public actions. Parishes provide dense access to neighborhood-based social networks. The combination of authority and participation within the parish seems to be most conducive to IAF organizing.

This finding runs counter to the exclusive emphasis on horizontal relations found in Robert Putnam's (1993a) treatment of social capital in Italy and in Sidney Verba's (1995) conclusions about the greater opportunities for skill development in black Protestant congregations (see also Coleman, Chapter 3 of this volume). Putnam argued that it was the horizontal relations of voluntary associations in north-central Italy that made democracy work in that region, while Italy's South remained mired in vertical forms of clientelism embedded in the Catholic Church and personalistic politics. If a church, or any other institution, is organized entirely along vertical lines, with no opportunity for participation at all, then it probably will not contribute much to democratic politics. Putnam's Catholic Church in southern Italy may well exhibit such a vertical monopoly. But in Texas, and most everywhere in the United States, the Catholic Church combines authority and participation in a way quite powerful for expanding democratic participation, at least through the IAF. The authority of pastors and bishops provides legitimacy and encouragement for lay participation and support. Meanwhile, the lay leaders who play an increasingly important role in the church provide a pool of potential recruits well-rooted in parish neighborhoods. Indeed, the structure of most social institutions exhibits some combination of authority and participation. A bias against any form of authority can blind us to the necessary requirement of leadership in politics— a leadership, of course, that must be accountable if it is to be democratic.

Verba, Schlozman, and Brady (1995) made their argument for the greater democratic potential of black congregations vis-a-vis Hispanic parishes by examining skill development in individuals. They did not, however, look at processes of political engagement and mobilization within church communities. Yet if we are concerned about expanding democratic participation beyond its current level, we need to look precisely at these community dynamics. And here we see that opportunities for authoritative leadership, as well as for participation, remain important. The advantages of the "participatory hierarchy" of the Catholic Church suggest that we must pay attention to the structure of social capital, as it is mediated by concrete social institutions, rather than bias our approach to favor horizontalness. The real question for democratic renewal, at least in low-income communities, may be how to develop forms of accountable, authoritative leadership that encourages broad participation and collective responsibility.

The IAF experience also suggests that faith beliefs, which are of course authoritative traditions, are important to expanding political participation. IAF participants are motivated to become involved in politics in large part by their religious beliefs. The IAF works to unlock the commitment to action for community well-being that exists within various faith traditions. Beliefs matter both to motivate participation and to influence the kind of participation people of faith will undertake. Beliefs do not necessarily determine, a priori, a political agenda—and they are often malleable. So, for example, African-American religious commitments to racial justice can be turned towards multi-racial community-building efforts. Nevertheless, beliefs do shape commitments and influence the direction of political action.

Moreover, religious beliefs can temper the self-interested basis for political action with a broader dedication to the common good grounded in deep moral commitments (Smidt, Chapter 1 of this volume). Many Americans fear the intervention of religious groups in politics because some have pursued a political agenda that is derived narrowly from theology. The IAF, by contrast, attempts to engage religious traditions in the broad questions of American public life and community well-being. Although the institutional members of IAF affiliates are religious groups, the organizations themselves are political, not religious. Although they attempt to speak with a religious voice, they are speaking about public issues that are subject to rational debate and compromise (see the discussion by Williams, Chapter 11 of this volume, on religious language as a cultural resource for political discourse).

IAF organizations are concerned both about "all God's children" and about the specific needs of their constituent communities. That tension between "faith and works" proves particularly powerful in low-income communities of color, where theology and self-interest are immediately connected and palpably felt. The national polity may never experience that connection so strongly. But the faith traditions of religious communities can play an important role in broadening American democracy through the participation of communities long neglected, communities that bring to political action a deeply rooted interpretation of the common good.

Chapter 5

Does Religion Matter?
Projecting Democratic Power into the
Public Arena

Richard L. Wood

This chapter seeks to contribute to the current conversation regarding religion, social capital, and democratic life in two ways. The bulk of the chapter utilizes the concept of social capital to analyze two leading forms of democratic civic engagement among low-income Americans today. This analysis shows first how religion can, and does, contribute to democratic public life (democratic both in the sense of wider participation in political life and in the sense of outcomes that benefit the less well-off in society).[1] Second, it argues, contrary to much recent criticism, that the social capital concept provides an analytic framework useful for both social science and political praxis.

Why concern ourselves with democratic engagement among low-income Americans? American democracy is built on the ideal of relatively equal access to influence over the political decision-making process by all citizens, regardless of economic status. Of course, our democratic institutions were designed part-

Please send correspondence to the author at Department of Sociology, 1915 Roma NE, SSCI #1103, University of New Mexico, Albuquerque, NM 87131-1166 or rlwood@unm.edu. The initial research was funded primarily by the Lilly Foundation through a grant to John Coleman, S.J. at the Center for Ethics and Social Policy in Berkeley, California. The author thanks these institutions for their support, as well as the Pew Charitable Trusts and the Center for the Study of Religion and American Culture for subsequent support. In addition, Ann Swidler, Bob Bellah, Bert Useem, Gary LaFree, Felipe Gonzales, Nancy Ammerman, Jim Keddy, Dan Hosang, Tim McClosky, Stephen Hart, Dana Bell, and Paul Lichterman provided valuable feedback. Finally thanks to the staff of the Pacific Institute for Contemporary Organizations and the Center for Third World Organizing for access and inspiration.

ly to blunt any radical excesses of democratic initiative—but the ideal has remained equal democratic rights for all. As our political system has come to depend more heavily upon donated money, the ability of the poor to influence the decisions that shape their future has been increasingly compromised (Verba et al. 1995). Thus, analyzing democratic participation among the poor matters for both the process and the *outcomes* of our political life—e.g., the degree of economic polarization in American society, the extent of alienation between classes, the level of crime present in society, all depend partly on whether the less privileged among us are able to participate effectively in politics at all levels. This chapter analyzes that participation by comparing two approaches to democratic organizing built on different sources of social capital: one religious, the other racial.

This analysis contributes to two salient debates centered around Robert Putnam's work on social capital in Italy and the United States.[2] First, various critics have noted that—whatever the merits of Putnam and his colleagues' careful empirical work on Italy (1993a)—his initial application of the social capital framework to the United States (1995a) was much weaker.[3] His conclusions were taken by elite leaders in political institutions and foundations as suggesting that "building social capital" would be a panacea for society and would allow them to avoid the hard political work of building more democratic political coalitions and policies (see especially Foley & Edwards 1996, 1997; Edwards & Foley 1998). By using social capital as the key theoretical lens for examining precisely this kind of hard political work, this chapter suggests that the social-capital-as-panacea perspective is rooted not in the concept itself, but rather in the proclivities of elite leaders.

Second, scholars have debated whether religiously generated social capital has different political value from social capital arising within other kinds of social institutions, and whether it can make up for the "democratic deficit" caused by the relative weakness of labor institutions, political parties of the left, and the like (Greeley 1997a, 1997b; Verba, Schlozman, & Brady 1995, 1997; see also Coleman, Chapter 3). By examining the difference made by religiously generated vs. racially generated social capital, this analysis begins to lay the groundwork for answering these questions.

This analysis conceptualizes social capital in terms that stay true to the work of James Coleman and Pierre Bourdieu (see Foley & Edwards 1997; Edwards & Foley 1998), by conceiving of it as neither a social-psychological nor a purely social-structural phenomenon. Rather, it considers social capital as inhering between these two levels of analysis, in the networks of relationships that connect individuals and institutions in society (see Chapter 1 to this volume for a discussion of this distinction). More precisely, social capital has to do with the number and quality of those relationships; analyzing it requires a *cultural analysis* of those networks. Thus, as discussed below, this study relies on the interpretation of qualitative data gathered to assess how organizations draw on social ties to mobilize people for political action, and to assess the *nature* of those ties.

For example, in analyzing the "trust" dimension of social capital, the degree to which residents trust one another and therefore collaborate is here much more relevant than is the extent to which they "trust government" in the abstract. Likewise, the focus here on social action means that trust is important because it allows collective action, not because it is somehow "more civic" to trust government. More generally, defining social capital in these terms leads to a focus on the microdynamics of political organizing, and how those dynamics lead to differing outcomes. This chapter thus directly addresses the question asked in the Introduction regarding "which kinds of associations [foster social capital], under what circumstances, and with what effects for the polity?" (Foley & Edwards 1998, 15).

TWO MODELS OF CIVIC ENGAGEMENT IN URBAN AMERICA

Two models of grassroots political participation, typically described by participants as "community organizing," provide the focus of this analysis. The most widespread community organizing model in use today roots itself institutionally in urban religious congregations and culturally in the diverse religious cultures of participants; it is known as "church-based," "faith-based," or "congregation-based" community organizing. Church-based community organizing efforts exist in some 130 metropolitan areas around the country, through efforts linked to religious congregations but sponsored by autonomous organizations.[4] Four main national or regional networks promote these efforts and train leaders from low- to moderate-income neighborhoods. Each network joins together federations of affiliated churches in various metropolitan areas. The Industrial Areas Foundation (IAF), with some 48 federations, is the largest and most studied. PICO (the Pacific Institute for Community Organization, founded on the West coast but now nationwide) and the Gamaliel Network are next largest, each with nearly 30 federations in some 40 cities. The remaining network, DART, has some 20 federations. In turn, each federation is linked to sponsoring religious congregations—from a half dozen to 60 or more in a given metropolitan area. As documented in a study by Interfaith Funders (Warren & Wood 2001), church-based organizing arguably represents the most widespread movement for social justice among poor and working-class Americans today. Some two million people are members of the approximately 2,600 participating congregations.[5]

A second community-organizing model roots itself culturally in the racial identities of participants and is known as "race-based" or "multiracial" organizing. Race-based organizing operates on a much smaller scale, though such efforts can also be found in metropolitan areas throughout the country. Like church-based organizing, it represents an influential movement for social justice in America. It has gained particular influence in urban settings with populations of high racial diversity.[6] Multiracial organizing is important here, due both to its local influence and for the light it sheds on how social capital shapes democratic engagement.

These two models of community organizing represent contrasting cultural strategies for promoting democracy among low-income urban Americans.[7] This analysis focuses on successful examples of each model: PICO in the case of church-based organizing, and the Center for Third World Organizing (CTWO) in the case of multiracial organizing. Rather than comparing CTWO and PICO in the abstract or on the level of their overall efforts, this study looks more concretely and empirically at their respective projects in one city: Oakland, California. This approach holds constant the wider social environment (including demographics and political opportunity structure) faced by the two organizations, and thus it can assess the role of social capital in their organizing efforts.

Three years of participant-observation and interviewing in PICO's local project and two years in CTWO's local project provide the primary data for this comparative account. Supplementary data come from 30 extensive interviews with participants in their respective organizing projects in Oakland and in Denver, Colorado (the only other city where organizing projects associated with CTWO and PICO existed at the time of this study), and from 30 additional interviews in PICO federations in five cities nationwide.[8]

As important as their location in the same city is the fact that PICO and CTWO organize within essentially identical neighborhoods in East and West Oakland; CTWO appears to target particular sections of those neighborhoods, notably the poorer sections and those sections where incidents (such as police abuse) may have generated discontent around issues related to their organizing. PICO's church-affiliated organizing committees typically include members from within these areas, but also incorporate broad swaths of low- and moderate-income inner city neighborhoods, and a few somewhat more affluent settings. In Oakland, both organizations are highly multiracial.

Likewise, the two organizations draw on very similar resources. Annual budgets during the course of this study were approximately $180,000 for PICO and $150,000 for CTWO with regard to their organizing efforts in Oakland. Their in-kind resources were basically the same—primarily meeting space in churches and social service agencies. Finally, both had access to the consulting services of their respective national networks, in both cases recognized as experts in these organizing models.

Thus, other than their divergent cultural strategies, PICO and CTWO display significant similarities: they use similar organizing techniques to organize in essentially identical neighborhoods of Oakland; they work primarily within the same "political opportunity structure"; they address similar, but not identical, issues; they have access to comparable financial, in-kind, and consulting resources; and they display overlapping demographic profiles whose limited differences are rooted in their contrasting cultural strategies. Thus, the key contrast being analyzed lies in their divergent cultural strategies—precisely the factor that leads to differing resources of social capital.

THE PUBLIC REALM

Both PICO and CTWO express one of their primary goals as promoting the "accountability" of government leaders and institutions to citizens. "Accountability" represents these organizations' way of talking about their role in what democratic theorists call the public realm (Habermas 1984, 1989; Cohen & Arato 1992). My analysis of the role of social capital in these organizing efforts draws heavily on this concept; later, it will also help us see more clearly what makes these efforts important as well as understand their dilemmas.

For present purposes, we may think of the public realm as made up of all those arenas of social life in which members of a community reflect upon, argue about, and make decisions regarding the problems they face and the rules under which they live. This clearly includes all levels of the state, from local to national government, particularly those settings in which elected representatives deliberate the rules by which the wider society lives. These include: the legislative process in city councils, schools boards, state legislatures, and Congress; judicial review at all levels; and executive policy formulation by mayors, governors, and presidents and their aides, especially as this occurs in dialogue with their constituencies.

But the public realm also includes far more than this. It includes all those arenas connected to, but outside, the state in which citizen demands are aggregated and possible responses are formulated—that is, "political society." Most notably, it includes political parties, lobbyists and political action committees, labor unions and business associations, and similar organizations with political goals.

And, the public realm includes civil society: all those settings in which members of a society, as individuals and in associations of all kinds, reflect upon and form values and attitudes regarding their life together, social problems, and the future of their society. These politically relevant conversations occur in myriad settings throughout society—civic groups, political discussion groups, issue study groups, ethnic associations, and churches, to name only a few. (See Wood [1995] for a full discussion of civil society, political society, and the state in community organizing, drawing on Stepan [1988] and Casanova [1994]; see also Warren, Chapter 4 in this volume for a parallel discussion.)

So the public realm can be understood analytically as constituted at three levels of societal life: the state, political society, and civil society. The linking of these three levels and their reciprocal influence on each other are central to a thriving democratic public life; it is this linking and reciprocal influence that gives democratic direction to society and legitimacy to government. The anemia of American democracy can be seen in the breakdown of this ideal: the three levels of the public realm have become severed from one another, as state-based political elites have used the power of the media and money-raising technologies to become autonomous from political society, which itself has lost much substantial grounding in civil society. Thus, the process of democratic deliberation through the three levels of the public realm has broken down. As a result, political decision-making has become less democratically controlled, with the unsurprising result that elites have harnessed the political process to serve their own interests rather than serving democratic ends.

BUILDING DEMOCRACY BY PROJECTING POWER IN THE PUBLIC REALM

Both organizations in this study strive to build stronger democracy by drawing together low-income residents around issues of concern to them and "building power" within their organizations; they then use that organizational power to influence public policy concerning those issues. Organizational power is brought to bear on public policy in two ways. First, they do so through public events called "actions" or "accountability sessions," at which political leaders appear before the community organization and are asked to commit to a specific policy defined by the organization. Second, they do so through negotiations prior to and following such public events. Much of the actual shaping of policy comes through the negotiations—but the organizations' power to engage in those negotiations from a position of strength depends crucially on the public political actions, and on the number of participants who attend them.

Analytically, we can understand this process as first parlaying existing social capital embedded in low-income communities into organizational power, then projecting this power into the public realm in pursuit of more democratic public policies. Each organization's ability to project power into the public realm will be assessed in two ways: by examining its ability to succeed on issues that help promote democratic outcomes, and by examining the organization's position in the public realm, what I label its *structural position in the public arena.* This latter consideration provides the basis for assessing what each organization's position allows it to contribute to addressing the contemporary anemia of American democracy.

The key questions then become how the two cultural strategies of these organizations differ with regard to the stores of social capital that they open up, how this shapes their respective structural positions and abilities to project power into the public realm, and the implications this holds for extending democracy more deeply in American life.

CENTER FOR THIRD WORLD ORGANIZING (CTWO)

Cultural Strategy, Social Capital, and Democratic Power

CTWO's cultural strategy of appealing to racial identity means that participants explicitly target "communities of color" and highlight racial and ethnic identity in their organizing campaigns. Clearly, racial identity has provided a powerful basis for social movements in the history of the United States—examples include the Black Power, Chicano, and American Indian movements, and, in a different way, the Ku Klux Klan and other white power movements. But CTWO's commitment to democratic multiculturalism excludes the kind of cultural strategy of ethnic or racial nationalism used by these movements to mobilize along exclusive racial lines. Such a strategy might give an organization access to the intra-racial trust and social networks that still exist in minority communities. But CTWO staff have learned the lessons of the experience of divided ethnic power groups of the 1960s and 1970s: minority communities working in isolation from one another are easily balkanized and defeated. To successfully reform society demands a broader movement (see Williams's insightful discussion, Chapter 11 of this volume, regarding the difficulty of making authoritative claims via identity politics).

So CTWO seeks to build a "multiracial organization." In doing so, however, it faces a dilemma: the trust and social networks to which it gains access through appeal to racial identity are largely intra-racial resources. Trust within ethnic-identity-based social networks primarily exists as trust of others in one's own ethnic group. Drawing on Putnam's differentiation (Putnam 2000) between bonding and bridging social capital that is noted in Chapter 1 of this volume, "bonding social capital" is strong within these distinct ethnic groups. In contrast, inter-ethnic trust is thin and inter-ethnic social networks weak. As a result, cross-cultural organizing is an uphill struggle, because "bridging social capital" must be constructed.

Certainly, many members of CTWO were remarkable for the extent of their cross-cultural friendships (this was true of PICO as well). The rich racial diversity present in gatherings of both organizations remains sadly rare in today's America. But CTWO must either *develop* leaders capable of and interested in multicultural organizing, or do extensive outreach work to find individuals *already* holding this kind of capability and already embedded in extensive cross-cultural networks. Because the latter individuals are rare, the former approach predominates; bonds are initially thin within the organization, and staff must expend a considerable part of its effort on building and maintaining a multiracial identity within the membership.

The difficulty of doing so becomes clearer when one considers the paucity of shared history or culture existing between urban African Americans, with their historical experience of slavery, and recent immigrants to this country, e.g., Asian Americans and Mexican Americans. Certainly, the subaltern status of many of these groups, and their experience of racism in various forms and various degrees of virulence, give them shared experiences within American society and thus shared interests. But constructing a self-conscious reform movement out of those shared interests demands constructing what Fantasia calls a "culture of solidarity" (Fantasia 1988). The task is more difficult still, since the elements of culture most widely shared among these diverse groups come, unsurprisingly, from American popular culture with its indelible marks of the dominant culture. Since CTWO's cultural system rejects that culture, it is of little use in constructing a culture of solidarity.

So CTWO puts considerable effort into building its own multiracial culture within the organization, setting up social events in which participants are exposed to the food, music, or political experience of the various ethnic cultures represented among its constituents. Such events might be termed "cultural action," as distinct from more directly strategic "political action." The prevalence of cultural action within the CTWO organizing process partly stems from the need to build—essentially from the ground up—an organizational culture to unite its diverse members: these actions serve to build a reservoir of shared symbols and ritualized experiences to mark group identity. The organization must do a great deal of work to generate this shared culture and sustain the cross-cultural trust and social networks needed for democratic mobilization. As a result, it invests significant time and effort into cultural action and informal visiting among members.

This work represents a kind of preliminary effort to the organization's ultimate goal of being politically effective in the public realm. Unless the organizing work can project sufficient power into the public realm to make an impact there, it cannot contribute to effective political reform. CTWO has done so successfully, around such issues as testing children for lead contamination, translation services at local hospitals, asset forfeiture, etc. To project that power it must mobilize people by drawing on the trust embedded in their social networks. So the organization must focus on both the political organizing tasks associated with mobilizing its membership and the cultural tasks of generating trust and sustaining social networks through a shared multiracial culture.

Organizational Dilemma

The constant need to engage in both sets of tasks produces an organizational dilemma: at any given time, should it concentrate its energies primarily on political action or cultural action? Of course, these are not *inherently* in conflict; indeed, CTWO successfully combines them in an "action/reflection" model. But the constant shifting of organizational focus from one to the other leads to two results. First, CTWO mobilizes fewer people than PICO does, both internally during the organizing process and publicly during political actions. So it projects less power into the public realm and carries less influence there. In Oakland, CTWO turned out 100-120 people for its public actions, whereas PICO turned out anywhere from 500 to 2,000 for citywide actions. Second, CTWO's less stable internal culture forces the organization to find other ways of producing internal cohesion. External conflict and a hostile view of mainstream institutions are classic organizational responses to the need to produce internal cohesion in sectarian communities (Kanter 1972). CTWO's organizing efforts engage in both to a significant degree, through such tactics as "direct action" takeovers of public offices and a generalized suspicion of those working in "dominant institutions" within the "dominant culture."

The organization appears to recognize the dilemmas arising from its relatively weaker access to social capital for mobilizing: it has periodically attempted to draw on staff allies in social service agencies to involve their clientele in CTWO-sponsored political actions. But these patron-client networks are functionally similar to the vertical networks Putnam observed in southern Italy. In both CTWO and southern Italy, patron-client networks fail badly at effective democratic participation. This stands in contrast to the "participative hierarchies" that Warren, in the previous chapter of this volume, found underpinning Catholic participation in church-based organizing.

As a result, CTWO must largely organize its turnout at political actions through door-to-door campaigns and extended family networks. The organization can turn out over a hundred people at a time through these efforts, which is no small feat. Such efforts have allowed them to gain sufficient political leverage to extract concessions from local government regarding public services and funding. But such mobilization efforts have not been sufficient to win the larger issues to which they aspire.

CTWO's Structural Position

Several characteristics of CTWO's structural position are noteworthy and suggest that CTWO is essentially a civic institution (in contrast to PICO's status as a "bridging institution," see below). First, several factors point to this direction: the salience of "cultural action" within CTWO's work; the fact that these produced the organization's largest attendance during the course of this study; and the importance of relationships within the organization in offering participants a sense of primary community.

Second, CTWO's most common form of cultural action was "political education," sessions that attempted to refashion individual perceptions and attitudes rather than to affect political institutions directly. This focus on political education also suggests that CTWO strives to change American culture on the level of civil society.

Third, to the extent that this political education does ultimately aim to influence public policy, it seeks to do so primarily through direct action aimed at government institutions. Little effort is made to address the intermediate level of political society, to appeal to the ideals or self-interest of individual decision-makers in political institutions. As players within the institutions of the dominant culture, these individuals are distrusted and most such political institutions are bypassed in favor of disruptive direct engagement with governing institutions, aimed at disclosing the power relations at work there. In a sense, this disclosure becomes an end in itself—political education partially displaces political influence as the primary goal being pursued.

As a result of these factors, CTWO's structural position in the public realm looks essentially like a classic institution of civil society, much like any of a myriad of cultural associations that have been present throughout American history. But it is a civic institution with a twist: one with a highly systematized political ideology that attempts to project itself rather directly into the workings of the state. Thus, in terms of structural position in public life, CTWO might best be characterized as a *politicized civic association:* essentially located and focused in civil society, with a highly politicized internal culture, and limited (though not negligible) political leverage on the wider society.

The preceding interpretation of how CTWO's cultural strategy has shaped the political experience of its Oakland project is depicted in Figure 5.1:

As we will discuss shortly, PICO's different cultural strategy and its resulting greater access to social capital place it in a different and, in a significant sense, more powerful structural position. Nevertheless, CTWO's structural position does bring some significant strengths with it. First, the organization can focus on cultural tasks crucial to transforming America's racial history. Second, its efforts at shaping political perceptions in civil society have real political implications: part of changing American society's political orientation surely entails changing its grassroots political culture, the values and racial assumptions shap-

Fig. 5.1 Multiracial Organizing: Cultural Strategy, Social Capital and Public Power

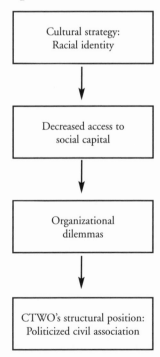

ing our politics. And, finally, the struggle to enrich and strengthen American democracy surely benefits from a plurality of differing organizational approaches working in complementary ways. All that being said, CTWO's structural position, arising from its thin access to social capital, does constrain the organization's immediate prospects for influencing social reform. As a result, it looks much like the urban social movements analyzed by Castells (1983), which led him to pessimism—albeit sympathetic pessimism—regarding their prospects for advancing democracy.

PACIFIC INSTITUTE FOR COMMUNITY ORGANIZATION

Cultural Strategy, Social Capital, and Democratic Power

In analyzing how PICO's religious cultural strategy provided it with access to social capital and resulted in a different structural position in public life, two comparisons are illuminating: between PICO's work before and after adopting the church-based model, and between the results of PICO's religious cultural strategy and CTWO's racial cultural strategy.

From its founding in 1972 until 1984, PICO did not use its current model, but rather operated under an organizing model less grounded in religious institutions and less focused on a religious cultural strategy. During this time, PICO did use churches for meeting space and as a source of legitimacy for gaining entree to neighborhoods, and thus was in a sense church-tied. But it was so only in a very restricted sense. Current PICO staff who were involved in the organization twenty years ago think of their work at that time as "neighborhood based." The shift to a more fully church-based model occurred for reasons I have analyzed elsewhere (Wood 1995); here, the key question to be addressed is how this shift in cultural strategy may have affected PICO's organizing efforts.

To abbreviate a complex story: the shift revolutionized PICO's organizing effort. From 1972 to 1984, under the neighborhood-based model, PICO grew to sponsor a total of four federations. By the end of this period, all were quite weak. From 1985, when the shift in cultural strategy began to take shape, to 1995, PICO grew to 25 federations in cities throughout California, the deep South, and the Midwest. As of 1998, 29 federations in 40 cities make up the PICO network, with growth primarily limited by the difficulty of finding talented organizers to carry the church-based organizing model to new sites.

The organizing capacity brought by the church-based model is also reflected in the numbers of people attending PICO actions in recent years and by the kinds of issues the federations address. At least ten PICO federations have brought 1,500 or more participants together in a single political action, and the New Orleans federation has repeatedly brought 4,000 or more people together in meetings with the governor, mayor, or other local politicians. Whereas previously PICO was only able to influence fairly low-level resource allocation issues, today PICO federations address issues of public education reform, police reform, economic development policy, and minimum wage laws. Previously, PICO federations targeted local politicians exclusively; today, they deal with politicians from mayors to state-level cabinet members to governors.[9]

In Oakland, PICO's success occurred over the same time period as CTWO's success—but at a higher level. On at least two occasions the Oakland federation brought 2,000 participants to political actions, and it has, at least once a year, brought local political leaders before 600 to 1,500 constituents. It has spearheaded efforts to focus Oakland city government on local economic development so as to revive neighborhoods shattered by economic restructuring; it has pushed police reform forward; and, it has collaborated with the local teachers' union to increase public school funding. The Oakland federation is also a key participant in the PICO California Project, a statewide initiative that has drawn increased state funding for public education from a state government then controlled by conservatives opposed to increased government spending.[10]

How can we best interpret this heightened success, both locally in Oakland and nationally? PICO's cultural strategy appears to have allowed the organization to draw on the heightened trust existing among members of some congregations by virtue of their shared membership in a moral community (see also the discussion by Curry in Chapter 9). This has afforded PICO greater access to the social networks embedded in congregations—including, in some of the most supportive congregations, full access to phone lists, computer databases, church social and ministerial groups, announcement times at services, bulletin space, etc. This heightened access to the moral resources and social capital of church life appears to be the key factor in explaining the success of the church-based organizing model. These patterns bear witness to effective mobilization of religious believers for civic purposes through sophisticated use of religiously rooted social capital.

Structural Symbiosis

Note that PICO's access to religiously rooted social capital depends upon a constructive relationship with churches, and thus ultimately on its cultural strategy of appeal to religious belief as the basis of organizing. That strategy makes PICO dependent on and indebted to religious institutions; PICO needs these religious institutions to be effective communities that inspire individual religious commitment through worship, help participants see the social implications of their faith, and build networks of trust. These things do not just occur naturally; they take shape through socialization in communities. To a great extent, PICO relies on churches to carry this burden—in contrast to CTWO's need to carry out much of this function itself. If religious institutions did not gain something from the bargain, such a reliance could be seen as parasitic exploitation of them. But, in fact, a relatively symbiotic relationship between

PICO and member churches is more typical, especially in the stronger local federations. This symbiosis is crucial to the long-term democratic promise of church-based organizing.

The image of symbiosis comes from the plant world, in which two species mutually benefit from their interaction. The benefits that PICO gains from its relationship to churches are by now clear: above all, unhindered access to the networks and trust embedded in church congregations—i.e., the congregation's social capital. Also significant in those congregations where the pastor fully endorses and participates in the organizing process is the pastor's role in "calling out the troops," as one organizer put it—that is, using "participative hierarchy" to encourage members to attend actions and other meetings. In addition, as Coleman notes in Chapter 3 of this volume, congregations bear a presumption of legitimacy in American culture; PICO thus gains some level of legitimacy both among local residents who are non-church members and in the wider social world of the city.[11] Finally, PICO gains great motivational benefit from being able to speak of its work in the language that many Americans hold as fundamental to their sense of self (see Williams' discussion of this point in Chapter 11). The moral language and symbolism of religion moves from being a "second language" that remains in the background for people to draw on privately, to being a "first language" of shared commitment, solidarity, and calling (Bellah, Madsen, Sullivan, Swidler, & Tipton 1985).

But what do religious congregations gain from their collaboration with PICO? Pastors generally identified two primary benefits. First, most pastors consistently identified "leadership development," the formation of individual leaders, as a benefit to their congregations. Most saw their members' leadership experience in PICO translating effectively into leadership roles in church affairs; for example, Fr. Joseph Justice watched his PICO-trained leaders organize on their own initiative to successfully pay off the parish debt.

Second, pastors spoke of deriving great satisfaction from seeing their members active in transforming society in keeping with the social ethical teachings of their traditions. They expressed this in various ways, such as "implementing the gospel vision in the world," "building the Kingdom of God," "making the world the place God wants it to be," or, more ambiguously, as "taking the city for our Lord Jesus Christ." Many noted the frustration of trying to transform the world from the pulpit, and saw such efforts at transformation as a calling specific to lay people so as to "carry the message from the church community into the political world."

There may also be significant benefits to churches that pastors rarely recognize, yet receive nonetheless. First, since they are part of and dependent on the wider social fabric of American society, churches stand to benefit from whatever success a federation has in improving life in their communities. Second, if it is not abused, the church-constituted social capital on which PICO draws is not used up in the process of organizing; indeed, the whole notion of social capital conceives of trust and networks as "moral resources" whose utilization does not deplete them but rather deepens the reservoir of trust and relationship (Olson 1964). Indeed, bringing religiously rooted trust and networks to bear on this-worldly concerns may well strengthen these moral resources. Third, extensive involvement in community affairs can give congregational life a solid, "rooted" feel by anchoring the worship-based experience of transcendence in the every-day lives and struggles of church-goers (see Wood 1999). And, finally, commu-nity organizing sponsored by religious institutions may bring heightened pub-lic authority to religious leaders. In fact, the therapy-based model of the role of pastors popularized in American seminaries in the last two decades appears to have contributed to the declining social prestige of pastors in American society. But engagement with successful organizing projects may be quite satisfying to pastors uncomfortable with this therapy-based understanding of the pastorate, and may offer them a more public role.

The primary benefit that lay leaders derive from the collaboration between PICO and their churches appears to be a sense of integration between their "spiritual lives" and their "civic lives." That is, as religious discourse has moved from being a private second language to a public first language of PICO's polit-ical culture, the religious believers who lead the organizing effort have come to experience civic engagement as an integral dimension of their religious com-mitment rather than as extraneous to or, at best, vaguely related to that com-mitment. Some speak of a spirituality of engagement that has brought deep meaning to their lives.

For all these reasons, the church-PICO collaboration represents not the uti-lization or exploitation of the former by the latter, but rather, at its best, a *struc-tural symbiosis* between the two institutions: both gain important benefits from the relationship. Churches provide an anchor in civil society that allows PICO to venture far out into political society without losing its mooring in the moral worlds of individuals' everyday lives. At the same time, church-based commu-nity organizing offers the churches a way to channel their ethical teachings more effectively into the public realm and create stronger bonds among their members. Essentially, this represents a division of labor: congregations as moral communities become privileged sites for generating "bonding social capital," while the church-based organizing networks specialize in drawing on this as a resource, linking it to other congregations and other institutions—i.e., gener-ating "bridging social capital" (see Warren, Chapter 4).

PICO's Structural Position

PICO's symbiotic relationship with religious institutions, in turn, has allowed it to assume a new structural position in public life. Clarifying this structural position will help reveal what makes this kind of organizing successful and why it holds promise for democratic renewal.

In one sense, the structural position of local church-based organizing federations is clearly within civil society. These federations are rigorously non-partisan in relationship to political parties, withhold endorsement of specific political candidates, and actively strive to avoid close identification with political office-holders.[12] Yet they exist precisely to pursue power to address public issues, albeit not as contenders for political office. The most successful of them—in cities like New Orleans, Oakland, and San Diego—have clearly attained sufficient influence within city politics to have become important players at the level of political society. This was made evident in interviews with political officials in these cities, who cited the local PICO federations as key players in the city arena. Thus, in dozens of local jurisdictions and through powerful statewide initiatives like the PICO California Project and the Texas Industrial Areas Foundation, church-based organizing federations function partially as institutions of political society, oriented toward power and focused on shaping the decisions of elite decision-makers.

Together, these facets of PICO's work constitute the organization's structural position in the public sphere, which can best be understood by seeing church-based organizing federations as "bridging institutions" straddling the divide between civil society and political society. Analogous to the classic role of political parties, they aggregate the interests and value-commitments of individuals and collectivities in civil society and channel them into the decision-making processes of governing elites, "holding them accountable to the community." Yet in their focus on subjecting the dynamics of political power to the ethical traditions and moral-political vision of moral communities, they hold political society and the state at arm's length and remain rooted in civil society. With a foot in both worlds, church-based organizing like that of PICO provides precisely the kind of democratically controlled links from society to the state that are so scarce in contemporary American society.

Despite similar terminology, this emphasis on church-based organizing's role in establishing "bridging institutions" between civil society, political society, and the state differs profoundly from conceiving of their role only as fostering "bridging social capital." Both are important, but the latter concept draws attention to building links between individuals who are members of different communities *within* civil society. As Robert Wuthnow argues in Chapter 12 of this volume, the social capital metaphor only partially captures the dynamics crucial to diagnosing and addressing our contemporary situation; we need to pay at least equal attention to our *institutions*. Church-based organizing not only helps build "bridging social capital," it also addresses a crucial institutional shortcoming of contemporary democracy, the divide between communities and the institutions of political society, the state, and the corporate world. As a bridging institution, church-based organizing helps sustain, renew, and re-direct those institutions.

Figure 5.2 depicts how PICO's cultural strategy and religious social capital make this possible:

Fig. 5.2 Church-based Organizing: Cultural Strategy, Social Capital and Public Power

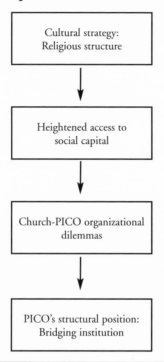

By drawing on religious social capital to project political power, PICO and the other church-based organizing networks are re-linking state, political society, and civil society and opening them up to greater reciprocal influence. In this way, they may be forerunners of the kinds of bridging institutions needed if we are to overcome the democratic anemia of American life.

CONCLUSION

This comparison between political organizing based on religiously-rooted and racially-rooted social capital reveals that both can contribute in important ways to greater political efficacy among less-advantaged members of American society, and thus to more egalitarian political and economic outcomes. Both approaches may therefore play important roles in renewing American democracy in the years ahead.

However, this analysis also reveals how the vigor of American religious institutions and religious culture brings comparative advantages for projecting political power into public life. The strength of horizontal social networks and the stores of trust between relative peers within religious institutions allows faith-based community organizing to unburden itself of significant organizational demands, project greater power into the political arena, and bridge the gulf that has come to separate civil society from political society and the state. Because this status as a "bridging institution" addresses one of the key structural weaknesses of modern democratic life, faith-based organizing offers important resources for forging a more democratic future for American society.

But delivering on this democratic future depends precisely upon the hard democratic work of community organizing with an explicit (non-partisan) political agenda: empowerment of the poor and middle class for greater democratic participation and more egalitarian political policies. Simply building social capital with no effort to make it politically effective promises no such democratic pay-off. Thus, the critics of "social capital-as-panacea" have it right: democratic social capital indeed helps foster democratic action, but to be effective it must be mobilized politically. This is precisely what CTWO and PICO are all about: multiplying the social capital of low-income Americans and making it more politically effective. Thus, social capital is important, but it can never replace the hard, much-belittled, and sometimes conflictive work of politics. When "generating social capital" is seen as a universal cure for what ails American democracy, as promoted by some American foundations with an emphasis on community-building for its own sake, social capital obscures at least as much as it illuminates. Greater clarity comes from seeing community-building as one element within a broader agenda for reinvigorating American democratic life: promoting local community organizing in its various forms and linking these efforts into statewide networks, strengthening religious institutions and minority communities, re-invigorating labor unions, reforming and refinancing public education, strengthening campaign finance laws, and creating democratic controls on international capital flows are all important elements within such an agenda (Bellah, Madsen, Sullivan, Swidler, & Tipton 1991). So religion matters for democratic thriving—but so do a host of other institutions. Church-based organizing represents an important movement partly because it offers religious congregations an appropriate way to exert ethical pressure on other institutions by standing in a constructive-yet-critical relationship to them, and also because it offers a way to draw on social capital "to help people accomplish tasks that require change in institutions" (Wuthnow, Chapter 12 of this volume).

Finally, is religious social capital any different than social capital rooted in other spheres of life? *In principle,* it is not. Like other forms of social capital, religious social capital holds important democratic potential—but it can also contribute to strongly anti-democratic efforts. This truth, however, must not blind those engaged in political analysis or practice from seeing another crucial fact. In practice, religious social capital in the contemporary American setting matters in crucial ways: because the vitality of religious institutions in America makes them veritable engines of social capital production; because religious social capital—rightly or wrongly—carries a presumption of social legitimacy; and, because religious social capital comes bundled with religious ethical traditions that help hold American institutions to democratic ideals. This is especially important in low-income settings, where other institutions are often under siege and non-religious forms of social capital are often comparatively weak. So any effort at democratic reform that marginalizes religious faith is destined to fail.

Given their tendency toward secularism or highly intellectualized forms of religious faith, some scholars may feel uncomfortable with the role played by religious institutions in low-income settings. But this should not blind them or us to the importance of religious institutions *as institutions* with a presence in poorer urban areas. They generate social capital, giving poor folks the resources they need to work together. They feed and clothe multitudes of the most desperate victims of rising economic inequality. They help many others emerge from the ravages of addiction or destructive behavior. They organize politically, sometimes calling the powerful to new accountability. They sustain hope, when much of what the poor see around them is cause for despair. And when all else falters, they offer consolation and comfort. In all these ways, religion matters—both politically and in ways that transcend politics.

Chapter 6

Religion and Volunteering in America

David E. Campbell and Steven J. Yonish

Religion should hold pride of place in any discussion of the state of social capital in America. Churches are by far the most prevalent form of voluntary association, and previous research has shown that religious involvement is linked with other forms of civic engagement (Hodgkinson, Gorski, Noga, & Knauft 1995; Greeley 1997b). Churches enhance civic engagement by teaching civic skills (Verba et al. 1995), serving as the focal point of a shared social network (Huckfeldt & Sprague 1995), and by providing the psychological motivation for participation (Harris 1999). Indeed, two seminal works employing the concept of social capital—Coleman and Hoffer's (1987) *Public and Private High Schools* and Putnam's (1993) *Making Democracy Work*[1]—discuss religion at some length.

But while religion has been integral to the development of social capital as a theory, until this volume there have been few systematic studies specifying how churches facilitate the creation, sustenance, and growth of social capital. This chapter focuses on one important aspect of religiously based social capital—the link between religion and volunteering. It carefully examines the religious roots of volunteering in the United States, across levels of religiosity, different religious traditions, and different types of voluntary activity. Our study is in the spirit of Putnam's call for "social capital botany field work," in an attempt to assist in developing "a *Peterson's Field Guide* to the forms of social capital" (1998, vii). In particular, we hope to shed some light on a central theme of this volume, how religion shapes civic values. To foreshadow our findings, we find that religion both pushes people into the public sphere and, in some cases, pulls them out of generalized participation and into particularized religious activity. However, religious activity is not alone in this regard; participation in secular organizations has a similar effect, directing people away from religious activity.

Like many concepts in social science, "social capital," as we operationalize it, cannot be observed directly. In this sense, it is no different from other concepts regularly studied by social scientists like rationality, partisanship, or power. Social capital has the added complication, however, of having both an individual and a collective component. Drawing on the insights of Coleman, Putnam defines it as "features of social organization, such as trust, norms, and networks, that can improve the efficiency of society by facilitating coordinated actions" (1993a, 167). By definition, such features are collective in nature. This is not to say, though, that individuals cannot be said to have more or less social capital. They can. But, when employing data at the individual level, any social-capital-building interaction with others must be inferred, a point discussed at greater length by Nemeth and Luidens in the next chapter of this volume. Consequently, scholars measuring social capital often use participation in group settings, whether formal as in a fraternal club or informal as in a dinner party, as measures of connectedness to others, and thus proxies for social capital. One important proxy measure of social capital is involvement in one's church, because it facilitates the creation of social networks, which in turn "foster sturdy norms of generalized reciprocity and encourage the emergence of social trust" (Putnam 1995a, 67). Thus, while there are many venues in which social capital is fostered—like informal personal relationships and voluntary associations, to name just two—this chapter will narrow its focus to that formed within places of worship. We are interested in how "general" the reciprocity facilitated within a religious community is—does it extend beyond a believer's specific congregation?

Social capital has been shown to have many effects, but this chapter will narrow its focus further to examine how the social capital formed during religious activity relates to volunteering—activities for which one does not receive financial remuneration. Many observers, from Tocqueville (1969) to Almond and Verba (1963) to Putnam (1995, 2000), have drawn a connection between the voluntarism of Americans and the health of American democracy. More specific to the theme of this volume, volunteering is, according to Putnam, "by some interpretations a central measure of social capital" (2000, 116). Similarly, one of the most-cited books in this volume is Verba, Schlozman, and Brady's book *Voice and Equality,* subtitled *Civic Voluntarism in American Politics.*

We must note that there are differences in perspectives over voluntarism's proper place in democratic society. Most notably, political conservatives and liberals disagree on the appropriate role for voluntarism—liberals generally holding that it should buttress action by the state, conservatives that it should substitute for government programs. Both camps do agree, however, that voluntarism is something to be valued. Among Republicans, both President George Bush W. Bush and his father have advocated an enhanced role for private charities in welfare programs. Among Democrats, Bill Clinton made the creation of AmeriCorps an early priority of his administration. And, during the 2000 presidential campaign, both George W. Bush and Al Gore endorsed "charitable choice," whereby religious organizations—staffed largely by volunteers—are granted public funds to provide social services to the poor.

The bulk of this chapter compares people across religious traditions and frequency of church attendance. However, it will also examine whether the form of social capital fostered by churches is *sui generis*, or rather can be compared to that found within secular voluntary associations. In other words, to extend Putnam's analogy of the *Peterson's Field Guide,* this chapter asks whether, when it comes to facilitating voluntarism, secular social capital is better characterized as being of the same species or merely the same genus as social capital formed in sacred spaces.   In asking this question, we follow the lead of Coleman in Chapter 3, although as the reader will see, we arrive at some different (although not necessarily contradictory) conclusions.

DATA

The data for this analysis are drawn from a series of surveys conducted by the Gallup Organization for Independent Sector, a nonprofit organization that promotes voluntarism and philanthropy. These Giving and Volunteering Surveys were conducted every two years from 1989 to 1995. They are a remarkably rich source of data, with many questions asked about the respondents' participation in every imaginable voluntary group, including their religious identification and involvement. This richness in the questions is enhanced by the large sample size (N = 9626) which results when all four of the separate surveys are combined. Thus, not only are there a wide array of data for each individual, but there are enough individuals representing different religious traditions that we can have confidence in the differences and similarities observed across those groups. The reader should note that these are the same data employed by Nemeth and Luidens in Chapter 7 in their discussion of financial contributions. While some of our analytical methods differ from theirs, the findings of the two chapters complement one another.

DESCRIPTIVE STATISTICS
ON RELIGION AND VOLUNTEERING

The Giving and Volunteering surveys are such a rich source of data that they allow for a thorough description of voluntarism in America. These data confirm what observers since at least Tocqueville have consistently noted: Americans are both a philanthropic and a religious people. Table 6.1 presents the percentage of Americans who report volunteering in an extensive range of activities in the previous year and month, as well as how long they spent doing each type of activity in the previous month. It also reports the percentage who participate in each type of activity when looking only at those who volunteer. Fifty-one percent of Americans report having volunteered in the last year; 40 percent in the previous month. Twenty-seven percent—more than for any other type—have volunteered for a religious organization in the last year; 20 percent in the last month.[2] And, if we assume that having volunteered in the previous month is a reflection of one's dedication to that cause, then religious volunteers appear to be most dedicated.[3] When looking only at that portion of the population that volunteered "last year," 52 percent spent time working on behalf of a religious organization. By comparison, only 16 percent of Americans report volunteering for an organization relating to education in the last year, while just 10 percent of all respondents volunteered for such a group in the last month. Of those who volunteered in the last year, 32 percent did so for education. Even informal volunteering, which is defined so broadly as to include "helping a neighbor, friend, or organization on an ad hoc basis, spending time caring for an elderly person or babysitting children of a friend," is not as common as religious volunteering.

Turning to the column that lists how much time respondents spend volunteering, one can see that the average American devotes 8 hours per month to voluntary activity, and almost 2 of those hours volunteering for a religious organization. This is more time than is spent on any other single form of volunteering. Again restricting our attention to that subset of the population that reports volunteering in the previous thirty days, we find that during that month they spent an average of 20 hours volunteering. Religiously oriented volunteer work occupies 4.5 hours of their time. The intention here is not to overwhelm the reader with an avalanche of descriptive statistics, but instead to reinforce the point that *no matter how the measure is taken, Americans volunteer more for religious organizations than any other type of group.* This mirrors the finding of Nemeth and Luidens in the next chapter that Americans give more money to religious causes than any other type of charity.

The Giving and Volunteering data also allow for an examination of people according to religious tradition. The analysis here is restricted to Mainline Protestants, Evangelical Protestants, Black Protestants, and Catholics,[4] and where appropriate, a group that encompasses all who report adhering to no religious tradition. Table 6.2 displays the percentages[5] of those who volunteer[6] for any type of activity in each of these religious traditions, compared to those who claim no religious affiliation. Looking down the column labeled "Any Voluntary Activity," which is the percentage of respondents who report volunteering of any type, we can see that fully 59 percent of Mainline Protestants reported volunteering in the last month, more than for any other group.[7]

In an analysis that employed a single year of the Giving and Volunteering series, Robert Wuthnow (1999) has argued that there is an important distinc-

Table 6.1 Frequency of and Time Devoted to Volunteering

	All Respondents			Volunteers Only	
	Volunteered in last year[a]	Volunteered in previous month[a]	Avg. hours spent in previous month[b]	Volunteered in last year[a]	Avg. hours spent in previous month[b]
All types of volunteering	50.9%	40.2%	8.0	--	19.9
Religion	26.6	19.7	1.67	52.4%	4.29
Informal	22.2	14.4	1.66	43.7	4.22
Education	16.3	10.3	0.96	32.0	2.41
Youth	14.7	8.7	0.85	29.0	2.13
Service	12.5	6.9	0.66	24.5	1.66
Health	12.3	7.6	0.63	24.3	1.58
Work	7.7	3.8	0.27	15.2	0.68
Recreation	7.2	3.3	0.27	14.2	0.67
Environmental	7.1	2.6	0.12	14.0	0.31
Public Interest	6.7	3.5	0.23	13.1	0.57
Art	6.3	3.2	0.31	12.3	0.76
Political	4.3	2.3	0.15	8.5	0.39
Foundation	2.4	1.3	0.07	4.7	0.18
International	1.8	0.1	0.04	3.4	0.11
Other	2.5	1.7	0.17	4.9	0.42

Source: *Giving and Volunteering 1989–95*
[a] Cell entries are percentages.
[b] Cell entries are hours.

tion to be made between volunteering for the internal maintenance of one's church and volunteering for activities and organizations that stretch beyond the church. Mainline Protestants and Catholics are more likely to volunteer in activities designed explicitly to benefit the broader community; conversely, the energies of Evangelical Protestants are more likely to be expended on within-church voluntarism, benefiting only members of their denomination. To account for the different types of voluntarism, four specific types of volunteer acts are included in the analysis: religious, nonreligious, informal, and political. Religious volunteering was specifically addressed in the Giving and Volunteering questionnaire, as respondents were asked whether they participat-

Table 6.2 Church Attendance and Volunteering

	Frequency of Church Attendance (%)	Type of Volunteering				Any Voluntary Activity
		Religious	Non-religious	Informal	Advocacy	
Evangelical Protestants (N = 1545)		**29.4**[a]	**36.3**	**24.5**	**14.2**	**51.3**
Roughly every week	38.8	57.9	46.9	33.5	21.4	72.3
Once/twice a month	14.8	32.8	43.0	25.8	13.1	54.1
Few times a year	27.2	6.2	28.6	16.4	10.5	35.9
Not at all	19.2	2.0	20.7	16.9	5.8	28.4
Mainline Protestants (N = 2509)		**33.1**	**43.7**	**27.9**	**17.6**	**59.2**
Rouchly every week	39.9	62.8	50.9	35.4	21.6	75.0
Once/twice a month	14.2	34.3	52.2	28.1	17.7	61.0
Few times a year	26.8	11.1	38.3	24.2	15.3	50.2
Not at all	19.1	0.8	29.9	17.3	12.5	37.4

Table 6.2 Church Attendance and Volunteering (cont.)

	Frequency of Church Attendance (%)	Type of Volunteering				
		Religious	Non-religious	Informal	Advocacy	Any Voluntary Activity
Black Protestants (N = 843)		**24.3**	**23.8**	**9.7**	**7.2**	**36.1**
Roughly every week	45.9	42.0	31.3	13.2	12.6	50.4
Once/twice a month	24.8	14.4	24.4	8.6	3.8	22.7
Few times a year	22.7	5.8	14.7	3.1	1.6	11.8
Not at all	6.6	1.8	1.8	3.6	1.8	1.3
Roman Catholics (N = 2582)		**24.9**	**38.7**	**21.0**	**13.1**	**48.8**
Roughly every week	43.8	43.1	46.3	25.1	14.6	60.0
Once/twice a month	18.3	18.9	37.7	17.8	14.2	44.2
Few times a year	25.1	8.3	32.6	17.9	11.3	39.8
Not at all	12.7	3.6	26.2	17.9	9.7	34.3
None (N = 959)		3.7	28.8	14.2	13.5	38.3

Source: *Giving and Volunteering 1989–95.*

[a] Bold-faced entries are column averages for each religious tradition.

ed in "religion-related or spiritual development" groups. Nonreligious volunteering consists of all the other categories of volunteering asked about in the questionnaire, with two exceptions.[8] First, informal volunteering is a separate category. As mentioned above, informal volunteering consists of volunteer work that is not sponsored by an institution. It represents the presumably spontaneous helping acts that, in turn, foster individualized networks of reciprocity. Second, a separate category labeled "advocacy organizations" was created by combining three types of groups included in the Giving and Volunteering Surveys: political organizations, environmental groups, and public benefit groups.[9] Our interest in this type of volunteering relates to the fact that churches have historically played an important role in mobilizing Americans to political action, and perhaps even an enhanced role over the last twenty or so years.[10]

Table 6.2 presents the proportion of each religious tradition participating in these four types of volunteering. It also displays these proportions across different levels of church attendance.[11] Note that the general pattern observed for voluntary activity in general holds for each individual type of volunteering. Mainline Protestants are the most likely to volunteer, with Black Protestants the least. Evangelical Protestants and Catholics fall in between, often close enough to be statistically indistinguishable. The reader should be reminded that this table displays only the raw, descriptive statistics for each religious tradition, without accounting for any other factors known to facilitate volunteering, such as education or income. Thus, while it is descriptively true that Mainline Protestants are more likely to volunteer than people of the comparison groups, we cannot be sure that this is due to their "Mainline Protestant-ness" or to other characteristics, such as advanced education which may be shared by many within this group. The argument that religion acts as a catalyst for voluntarism requires more rigorous evidence.

Church as a Catalyst for Voluntarism

It is also clear from Table 6.2 that the proportion of people volunteering increases as church attendance increases. In particular, note the increase in the percentage of Black Protestants who report volunteering as church attendance increases—from 6.6 percent of those who never attend church, to 45.9 percent of those who attend roughly every week. The results for the four specific types of volunteering share a remarkably consistent pattern: for all four religious traditions and all types of volunteering, more frequent church attendance corresponds with a greater proportion of volunteers. And it is not the case that church attendance varies widely across denominations.

The first column of Table 6.2 displays the rates of church attendance across denominational groups, and it reveals that the differences are slight. In particular, note that the percentage of each religious tradition that report attending church "every week or nearly every week" holds steady at about 40 percent (although it should be noted that Black Protestants and Catholics report slightly higher rates of attendance, 45.9 percent and 43.8 percent, respectively[12]). What these data reveal is that, when one speaks of religion serving as the impetus to voluntarism, there does not appear to be a compositional effect leading to a voluntary sector that is disproportionately of one faith rather than another.

As further evidence for church attendance serving as a catalyst for voluntarism, the Giving and Volunteering data also allow us to examine how people are recruited into volunteering. Table 6.3 compares a number of different "pathways" into volunteering and does so for each of the four types of volunteering under examination.[13] Respondents were asked where they received an invitation to volunteer, and the results are quite striking. Looking across each row one can see that church is always one of the most common pathways to volunteering. Not surprisingly, a majority of people who volunteer for religious organizations were recruited through their church. But church is a common path of recruitment for other types of volunteering as well—for advocacy volunteering, for example, church (32.5 percent) ranks with both family (34.6 percent) and friends (36.3 percent). Indeed, of the four basic institutions of contemporary American society—family, church, work, and membership organizations—church follows only family as a vehicle to recruit volunteers, and stands well ahead of work and membership organizations.

Not only does church facilitate the voluntarism of individuals, it does so for entire families. Contrary to the image of harried parents serving the community or their church at the expense of their family, the Giving and Volunteering data paint a picture of church-going families volunteering together. The proportion of respondents reporting that they perform volunteer work as a family increases markedly as church attendance increases (results not shown).

Summarizing our data thus far, there is considerable evidence for the claim that churches serve to facilitate volunteering in America. Those who attend church more, volunteer more; churches are the most common pathway into the voluntary sector; and, increased churchgoing is associated with increased volunteering with one's family.

Table 6.3 Recruitment into Volunteering

Type of volunteering	Church	Membership organization	Work	Friend	Family member	Sought it out oneself
All types	34.8%	12.6%	13.2%	25.8%	29.8%	22.8%
Religious	60.0	13.2	11.5	24.6	29.6	22.0
Nonreligious	30.4	15.6	16.6	27.9	33.8	24.9
Inofrmal	35.2	17.2	16.5	33.7	37.7	28.1
Advocacy	32.5	21.7	18.3	34.6	36.3	30.8

Source: *Giving and Volunteering 1989–95.*

FROM DESCRIPTION TO EXPLANATION

The real test of the relationship between religious involvement and volunteering is to include a number of other potential, rival causes in a model designed to predict whether someone volunteers. Because this model predicts the outcome of a dichotomous dependent variable—whether or not someone volunteers—logistic regression is employed. This statistical technique is used to estimate the effect of each explanatory variable when the observed outcome has only two possibilities. An intuitive interpretation of the model's results is presented using predicted probabilities calculated from its coefficient estimates. In other words, our statistical models result in a probability that someone with the specified characteristics has engaged in volunteer activity. By varying the value of a single independent variable while holding the others constant at sensible values, we can observe its "effect" on the probability of volunteering for someone with that given set of attributes (King 1989).

This is a rigorous test of religion's influence on volunteering, since the model controls for a wide range of factors identified in previous research as determinants of civic engagement and the likelihood of volunteering. These controls include age (as well as age squared, to account for physical infirmity among the elderly),[14] income, sex, marital status, region, job status (full-time, part-time, etc.), size of community (suburban, rural, etc.), length of residence in current location, whether one has children under eighteen, the respondent's degree of financial worry, and the year in which the survey was conducted. We include this extensive set of rival causes of voluntarism in the model in order to be sure that the relationship that we observe between church attendance and voluntary activity is not merely spurious. Terms for eight religious traditions (including "none" as a tradition) are included, even though results for only five are discussed here. The other traditions are different enough in a number of ways to be disaggregated for a properly specified model, but not large enough numerically to warrant inclusion in the results, as the small number of cases in each group limits our confidence in any conclusions drawn about them.[15] Most importantly, a control has been introduced for level of education, consistently the single greatest predictor of civic engagement (Nie, Junn, and Stehlik-Berry 1996). Given the causal primacy of education in explanations of a wide array of civic and social activities, the impact of religious involvement on volunteering can perhaps best be underscored with a comparison to that of education.

No better evidence exists for the role of churches as facilitators of voluntarism than the fact that, *ceteris paribus,* church attendance rivals education as a predictor of volunteering. This is comparable to the finding reported by Smidt, Green, Guth, and Kellstedt in Chapter 10 that church attendance has a slightly larger effect than education on their index of social engagement. Figure 6.1 presents a graphical display comparing the impact of education and church attendance on the decision to volunteer in the last year for "typical" Evangelical Protestants. In interpreting these graphs, note that education and church attendance are both measured on four-point scales. While varying education and church attendance across these four categories, the other variables have been held constant. In effect, a "hypothetical respondent" with the following characteristics has been created: a 35-year-old, white, male Southerner with a household income of $40,000 to $74,999. He is married, has a full-time job, children under eighteen, "a lot" of worry about his financial future, and has resided in his suburban community for five years. Unless otherwise specified, this hypothetical respondent is a high school graduate, and an Evangelical Protestant who attends church "a few times per year."

*Figure 6.1 Predicted Probabilities of Volunteering
for Typical Evangelical Protestant*

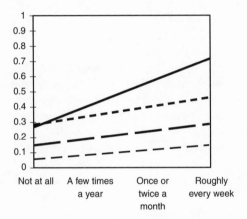

Frequency of church attendance

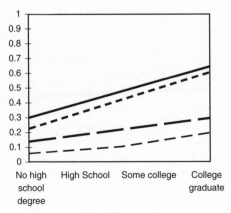

Education level

Figure 1 displays that an increase in the frequency of church attendance from "not at all" to "roughly every week" increases the probability of our respondent engaging in any type of volunteer work from .26 to .71, an increase of .45. Similarly, an increase in education from "not a high school graduate" to "college graduate" corresponds to an increase in the probability of volunteering from .29 to .64, an increase of .35. That religion even approaches, let alone surpasses, education as a predictor of voluntary activity speaks to its role as a catalyst for voluntarism in America.

Figure 6.1 not only compares the impact of religion versus that of education on volunteering in general, it also presents the changing probabilities for each specific type of volunteering. Not surprisingly, religious volunteering increases most dramatically as church attendance increases. More interesting is the observation that education's impact does not differ across types of volunteering, while that of church attendance does. The probability of engaging in other forms of volunteering does not increase nearly as much as the frequency of church attendance rises. The probability of engaging in informal volunteering, for example, only increases from .14 to .28 as church attendance increases across its entire range. Figure 6.1 only includes results for an Evangelical Protestant respondent, but they do not change substantively for the other religious traditions. Indeed, once a variable for church attendance is included in the model, none of the three religious traditions continues to have any predictive power. In other words, how often you go to church is far more important in predicting whether you volunteer than which church you attend. Again, this parallels Smidt et al.'s (Chapter 10) finding that church attendance has a stronger impact on social engagement than does religious tradition.

Beyond this general point, there are a few specific findings to note. First, increasing education predicts a dramatic rise in the probability of religious volunteering only for Evangelical Protestants. Somewhat consistent with the image of Christian Right mobilization in Evangelical Protestant congregations, it is this group that also shows the greatest rise in the probability of advocacy volunteering, from .06 to .14—or over 100 percent—as church attendance increases from its lowest to highest value (data not shown). Contrary to the conventional wisdom that evangelical churches are hotbeds of political activism, though, we must note that, while the increase in the probability is substantial, the probability itself is quite low.

Second, note also that informal volunteering is comparable to the other types of voluntary activity (data not shown). One might hypothesize that given its non-institutional character, informal volunteering would differ from the other types of voluntary activity. That is not the case. Informal volunteering increases as both education and church attendance increase. Whatever it is that schools and churches do to facilitate volunteering, it is not restricted to voluntary activity coordinated by institutions. This is not totally surprising: social capital theory rests on the premise that the social networks, which are both a cause and an effect of informal volunteering, are themselves fostered by institutions. No doubt the causal arrow goes both ways here: people who volunteer informally are more likely to be recruited into institutionally based volunteering (you watch a family's kids and they invite you to help at their church's soup kitchen), and people who participate in institutionally based volunteering are more likely to volunteer informally (someone you volunteer with at your church's soup kitchen asks you to watch his kids).

VOLUNTARY ACTIVITIES LINKED ACROSS TIME

Thus far church attendance has been presented as a predictor of volunteering cross-sectionally. A more stringent test of church's impact, however, would be to test whether it has any effect *over time*. Because these data do not consist of a panel of respondents interviewed repeatedly across time, the Giving and Volunteering data do not allow us to perform the most stringent form of longitudinal analysis. But in 1995, the survey did ask respondents to report whether they had any of a number of experiences when they were "young": e.g., being active in a religious organization; doing some kind of volunteer work; having a parent who volunteered in the community[16]; belonging to a youth group or something similar; or being active in student government. These youthful experiences turn out to be potent predictors of volunteering as an adult. If we take two people with identical sociodemographic characteristics *and frequency of church attendance,* the one who belonged to a religious group while a youth is more likely to participate in religious volunteering as an adult. Table 6.4 again presents changing predicted probabilities calculated from a logit model. The independent variables are the same "usual suspects" as in the models above, while the dependent variable is whether our hypothetical respondent has engaged in any of our four voluntary activities in the last year. Note also the first column of the table, which displays the percentage of respondents who report having each experience while young. The fact that 54 percent were members of religious organizations while young just underscores the wide-ranging impact religion has on the American voluntary sector.

The first row records the probability that the typical respondent volunteers if he had none of these experiences while young, the last row if he had all of the experiences. In between are the probabilities of volunteering if he reports only each individual experience. Looking at the column for religious volunteering, therefore, we observe that having had none of these experiences as a youth, our respondent has a probability of volunteering for a religious organization of only .28. However, that probability increases 50 percent, to .42, if he was active in a religious organization while young. In contrast, being active in a religious organization while young does not make a dent in the predicted probabilities of participating in the other types of voluntary activity.[17] That is, religious involvement as a youth predicts religious, *but not nonreligious,* volunteering as an adult.

In addition to our specific point about religious volunteering, Table 6.4 also

Table 6.4 Impact of Youth Experiences on Volunteering

Volunteer experience when young	Percent of adults	All types	Religious	Nonreligious	Informal	Advocacy
None	16.1%	.48	.28	.21	.11	.06
Volunteered	53.2	.65	.40	.34	.19	.12
Active in religious group	54.1	.50	.42	.20	.11	.06
Belonger to a youth group	63.2	.61	.35	.31	.17	.07
Active in student government	22.5	.53	.25	.28	.12	.10
Parents volunteered	52.6	.58	.36	.28	.13	.09
All	9.0	8.7	.67	.65	.35	.31

Source: *Giving and Volunteering 1995*. Cells contain predicted probabilities calculated from a logistic regression model which includes the following control variables: education, religious tradition, age, age squared, income, sex, marital status, region, job status (full-time, part-time, etc.), size of community, length of residence in current location, children under 18, and financial worry.

makes the general point that experiences while young have a measurable correlation with activities as an adult. For example, the probability that our hypothetical respondent will volunteer is .87 if while a youth he was active in a religious group and student government, participated in volunteer work, belonged to a youth group, and at least one of his parents volunteered. The evidence that religious involvement's impact on voluntarism extends across time dovetails with the observation that church attendance facilitates volunteering in the here and now. In both cases, churches serve to spur voluntary activity.

The unequivocal message from these findings is that church involvement provides a powerful impetus for individuals to engage in voluntary activity. But, if we look at volunteering from a slightly different angle, it also serves to channel volunteers into internal church-maintenance activity at the expense of more general-purpose volunteering. The findings regarding experiences as a youth have already hinted at this phenomenon, in that religious involvement while young only has a measurable impact on religious volunteering as an adult.

THE ROLE OF THE CHURCH IN CHANNELING VOLUNTARY ACTIVITY

To this point, church attendance has been shown to be a catalyst for voluntarism. But it not only "gets the ball rolling," it also serves to channel the direction in which the ball rolls. Among people who volunteer, increased church attendance leads to less general-purpose volunteering, instead directing their energies to religious volunteering. This may seem common-sensical, but previous research suggests that it is not so obvious that this would be the case. Verba, Schlozman, and Brady (1995, 291) provide evidence for the apparently accurate cliché that if "you want something done, ask a busy person." Even though time spent volunteering has an unavoidable ceiling—there are only twenty-four hours in a day—the general relationship is nonetheless striking: those who spend a lot of time volunteering for one thing are likely to spend a lot of time volunteering for another.[18]

The point, however, is that this relationship does not hold when the analysis is limited only to those respondents who volunteer. Within this group, more frequent church attendance leads to a lower probability of engaging in secular, informal, or advocacy voluntary activities. Some descriptive insight into this dynamic is presented in Table 6.5. Here we see the contrast between all respondents and only those who volunteer. For both groups, the average number of hours spent on each type of voluntary activity is reported by frequency of church attendance. Looking at the first column under each type of volunteering, it is once again clear that churchgoers spend more time volunteering than those who do not attend church, and as church attendance increases, time spent in each type of volunteering increases. The second column, which is restricted to volunteers only, shows the inverse relationship between church attendance and volunteering outside of the religious sector. The pattern is clearest for informal and advocacy volunteering: more frequent church attendance, less time spent volunteering. Admittedly, there is a slight increase for nonreligious volunteering, but this seems to be more accurately interpreted as no change, at least when church attendance moves from "a few times per year" to "every or almost every week."

As with the claim that church attendance fosters volunteer work, the real test that church inhibits nonreligious volunteering comes with the introduction of rival factors that affect voluntarism. Table 6.6 again displays changing predicted probabilities based on a logit model containing the full gamut of sociodemographic control variables, set to the same values as our earlier hypothetical respondent. To simplify the presentation, we show results based on levels of education and church attendance for only one type of volunteering: nonreligious. While more education corresponds to a greater likelihood of all types of volunteering, as it did when the full sample was analyzed, this is not the case for increasing church attendance. Among those who volunteer for any type of activity, going to church more frequently predicts a lower probability of nonreligious volunteering. Thus, if our hypothetical volunteer has a college degree and never attends church, the probability that he engages in nonreligious voluntary activity is .92. That drops considerably to .55 if he has no high school diploma and attends church every or almost every week.[19]

Whether or not this observed decline in nonreligious volunteering is meaningful rests on whether there is a clear distinction to be made between religious and nonreligious activities. Wuthnow (1999) assumes so, and thus contrasts the voluntary activities of Evangelical Protestants, which are more likely to be directed inward toward the maintenance of the church community, and those of Mainline Protestants and Catholics, which are more likely to be directed toward the wider community.[20] While using survey data to determine just what people do when they volunteer is quite difficult, the Giving and Volunteering data fortunately provide some purchase on the question of what people actually do when they volunteer for a religious organization. In 1995, 82 percent of religious volunteers indicated that the work they did for their religious organization was what has been classified as internal church maintenance activities.[21] Such a high percentage suggests that there *is* a distinction to be made between nonreligious and religious volunteering.

Interpreting churches' channeling effect in promoting voluntarism yields two alternative viewpoints. As Wuthnow reads results like these, the glass is half-empty: more church attendance, particularly for Evangelical Protestant volunteers, corresponds with less volunteering outside of one's church. But while that observation is technically correct, recall that church attendance increases the likelihood of participation in all forms of voluntary activity. Perhaps the glass is really half-full. Volunteers do, after all, face an unavoidable ceiling in the amount of time they have to give.

The Giving and Volunteering data suggest that it is because of time constraints that churchgoers volunteer for their churches at the expense of nonreligious organizations.[22] When asked why they did not volunteer more in the last year, 38 percent of those who attend church every or almost every week replied that their "personal schedule is too full." This percentage decreases as the frequency of church attendance decreases. Only 18 percent of those who never attend church offered the same reason. Similarly, 19 percent of the most frequent churchgoers report that they do not volunteer more because they "already volunteer as much as they can." Again, this percentage drops as church atten-

Table 6.5   Church Attendance and Hours Spent Volunteering (Monthly)

	Type of volunteering						
	Religious		Nonreligious		Informal		Advocacy	
Church attendance	All	Volunteers	All	Volunteers	All	Volunteers	All	Volunteers
---	---	---	---	---	---	---	---	---
Not at all	0.12	0.34	2.56	7.65	1.31	3.80	0.49	1.43
A few times a year	0.20	0.49	3.19	8.05	1.44	3.54	0.43	1.06
Once/twice a month	0.99	2.03	3.84	8.01	1.69	3.44	0.51	1.03
Roughly every week	3.98	6.00	5.33	8.09	2.02	3.03	0.57	0.85

Source: *Giving and Volunteering 1989–95.*

dance drops. Only 8 percent of respondents who are not churchgoers chose this reason for not volunteering more.

While some evidence has been offered that this displacement is because of time constraints, there is at least one other possible explanation. It could be that the constraint is not temporal, but rather psychological. It could be, in other words, that people who engage in religious volunteering may identify with their religion first and with other organizations second. Church may psychologically "crowd out" other forms of volunteering, as the churchgoer sees the church as the primary vehicle through which to deliver service. Going to church more may mean that one does not *feel* a need to go to Kiwanis, Sierra Club, or League of Women Voters meetings.

We must note that our observation of this channeling effect would be enhanced with data collected at levels other than the atomized individual, as many other authors in this volume have done. To what extent do particular religious collectivities—whether congregations (Cnaan et al., Chapter 2), parachurch groups (Coleman, Chapter 3), or communities (Curry, Chapter 9)—encourage voluntary activity beyond the walls of one's group? And how is this accomplished—through direct encouragement or more subtle behavioral norms, or some combination of both?

COMPARING RELIGIOUS AND SECULAR ORGANIZATIONS

This study focuses primarily on the positive link between church attendance and voluntarism. We hypothesized that this relationship is attributable to the social capital—networks of reciprocity—found within church communities.

Table 6.6 Probability of "Typical" Evangelical Protestant Volunteering for a Nonreligious Activity

Church attendance	No high school diploma	High school diploma	Some college	College degree
		Education level		
Not at all	0.78	0.84	0.89	0.92
A few times a year	0.72	0.79	0.85	0.89
Once/twice a month	0.63	0.72	0.79	0.85
Roughly every week	0.55	0.64	0.72	0.79

Source: *Giving and Volunteering 1989–95.* Cells contain predicted probabilities calculated from a logistic regression model which includes the following control variables: religious tradition, age, age squared, income, sex, marital status, region, job status (full-time, part-time, etc.), size of community length of residence in current location, children under 18, and financial worry. The model is restricted to volunteers only.

Accordingly, the only comparisons made thus far have been across religious traditions and across levels of church attendance. Another key comparison, however, is across types of social organizations. Is the process by which churches facilitate volunteering a unique one or can it be generalized to secular voluntary associations? In other words, is there something inimitable about the social capital found within churches?

We can test whether church-based social capital has an effect on volunteering that is comparable to the social capital formed in secular organizations. To do so, we have operationalized participation in a secular voluntary association so that it is analogous to church attendance. The 1995 Giving and Volunteering survey allows us to do this because respondents were asked whether they were members of an array of voluntary associations, and then how often they attended meetings held by these groups. The resulting "meeting attendance" variable can then be compared to church attendance. Conducting this analysis requires us to change our dependent variable from that used in the models discussed above. There we were modeling the decision to volunteer; here we are modeling the amount of time spent volunteering. We have done this because of the suspicion that respondents would report attending club meetings as a form of volunteering. If that is the case, then a model predicting the decision to volunteer using meeting attendance would be tautological. However, even if someone considers attending a meeting as volunteering, using the total time spent volunteering allows us to consider time spent in voluntary activities *other* than meetings. Because the measure of time spent volunteering approximates the assumptions of Ordinary Least Squares (OLS) regression, that is the method employed for this analysis.

For each voluntary association with which respondents affiliate, they were asked to indicate how often they attend meetings, with options ranging from no participation to attending meetings every or nearly every week. The variable *meeting attendance* is the respondent's maximum level of participation in any single voluntary association. We believe this most closely approximates the church attendance variable, allowing for a meaningful comparison between the two variables. Table 6.7 contains the results of the analysis. Columns one and two demonstrate that participation in both voluntary associations and churches is positively associated with nonreligious and religious volunteering. As expected, participation in voluntary associations has a larger coefficient for nonreligious than religious volunteering, while the pattern is reversed for church attendance.

But what about the second-order effect of church attendance, that of channeling voluntarism into church-centered activity at the expense of voluntary activity outside the church? Is there an analog in secular organizations? Columns three and four suggest an answer. For these two models, the analysis was restricted to volunteers only. Again, we see the channeling effect: attendance at church correlates negatively with nonreligious volunteering, while attendance at association meetings has a negative correlation with religious volunteering.[23]

Table 6.7 Relative Impact of Secular and Religious Participation on Time Spent Volunteering

	Nonreligious volunteering All	Religious volunteering All	Nonreligious volunteering Volunteers only	Religious volunteering Volunteers only
Meeting attendance	2.41***	0.227*	2.706***	−0.247+
	(0.207)	(0.091)	(0.405)	(0.195)
Church attendance	0.411*	1.12***	−1.124**	1.963***
	(0.256)	(0.113)	(0.672)	(0.291)
Adjusted R^2	.101	.101	.067	.119

+p < .10   *p < .05   **p < .01   ***p < .001, one-tailed test

Source: *Giving and Volunteering 1995.* Calculated from a linear regression model which includes the following control variables: education, religious tradition, age, age squared, income, sex, marital status, region job status (full-time, part-time, etc.), size of community, length of residence in current location, children under 18, and financial worry.

These results suggest that the form social capital takes within a church community does not have appreciably different effects from that found within secular voluntary associations, at least in regards to voluntarism. This is similar to Nemeth and Luidens's conclusion in Chapter 7 that people who participate at least weekly in either religious or nonreligious organizations contribute equally to charity. As with the results reported above, the cause of the channeling effect remains a subject for future research: is it simply a function of a ceiling on respondents' time, or do attitudinal barriers inhibit involvement in secondary activities? If it is the latter, then it would seem that there is a divide among volunteers in America that reflects the cultural difference between the churched and unchurched.

CONCLUSION

Just as religion has been an important part of the early theoretical work in social capital, it ought to be considered—and considered critically—in any assessment of Americans' voluntarism. This chapter has shown an unequivocal relationship between church attendance and volunteering, and conjectured that the link between them can be found in the social capital created within a church community. Thus, the theory is that as networks of reciprocity are formed among churchgoers, they become more civic-minded. That civic-mindedness, in turn, leads to a willingness to engage in voluntary activity.

However, church-based voluntary activity is not always directed to the wider community. Rather, among volunteers, the more one attends church, the less likely one is to engage in non-church voluntary activity. A similar process can be observed in secular organizations—attendance at meetings leads to all forms of volunteering, but among volunteers only, participation in secular groups channels volunteering into nonreligious venues. Because comparable processes are observed in both churches and secular organizations, it seems plausible that at least in this one regard the social capital formed within them is comparable— that they are the same species, and not merely the same genus. Here we differ somewhat from Coleman in Chapter 3, who argues that religious and secular social capital should not be equated. We do not disagree with the sentiment; surely there are important differences between social capital formed within religious versus secular communities, and within different religious communities (as our own data on the channeling effect suggest). Notwithstanding these differences, however, it is also true that empirically there appear to be important similarities between these different sources of social capital. While we do not fully accept Warren's characterization of Putnam's definition of social capital as a "universal cultural resource, unaffected by the specific institutional settings in which it is embedded" (Chapter 4), we *are* compelled to note what is similar across churches and secular organizations.

If it is the case that, in at least some respects, churches and secular voluntary associations are more alike than different (and only further research will provide the answer), then the pervasiveness of religion in America bodes well for research into social capital. The study of churches need not be separated from the study of secular associations. Rather, research into religious organizations can contribute to building a *general* theory of social capital.

Chapter 7

The Religious Basis
of Charitable Giving
in America
A Social Capital Perspective

Roger J. Nemeth and Donald A. Luidens

Survey data collected over the past decade indicate that Americans are generous contributors to charities. More than two-thirds of all households contributed to charities between 1987 and 1995, with the average annual household contribution being about $1,000. This level of giving has not changed significantly over the past eight years. Similarly, the percentage of annual household income given to charities has remained at, or above, two percent over the same period of time (Independent Sector, 1996).

Over this same period of time, national surveys have revealed that membership in religious organizations has also remained strong. These surveys indicate that more than two-thirds of the American people report religious memberships, with Americans being more likely to belong to a religious organization than to any other voluntary organization. Moreover, these same data reveal that members of religious organizations are far more likely to contribute to charities, and to contribute greater amounts, than are those who report that they do not belong to such religious organizations.

Findings such as these raise the question of how best to explain the relationship between religious involvement and charitable giving. Is the relationship between religious involvement and charitable giving explained simply by self-interest? For example, is the difference in giving simply the result of members giving to their own churches and their own church programs? Or is the difference in charitable giving merely a reflection of the particular social and economic status of church members? Perhaps, however, there is something about the relationships among church members that helps to account for the differences in charitable giving. Maybe the relationships found in a church are such that they also encourage members to support the efforts of charitable organizations outside the church so as to improve the quality of life of the community more generally.

When viewed from a social capital perspective, religious participation in America can be expected to produce greater charitable giving, and not just for religious causes. One reason for this expectation is that charitable giving is a central part of the ideology of most religious groups (see Chapter 1 and its discussion of the potential role of ideas, ideology, and worldviews and the types of social capital they generate within groups). Giving, however, may also be influenced by the social structural characteristics found in congregations. Congregations and synagogues are groupings that are likely to exhibit attributes that should enhance charitable giving. Because they create norms and obligations for their members, and because they exercise formal and informal sanctions when these expectations are violated, congregations and synagogues regularly produce a "habit of giving" among their parishioners (see Hodgkinson, 1990b). Indeed, it could be possible that a parallel "habit of volunteering" accounts for the relationship between church attendance and volunteering reported by Campbell and Yonish in the previous chapter of this volume. This chapter examines the relationship between charitable giving and participation in religious and nonreligious voluntary organizations. By analyzing differences in financial contributions among these groups we hope to discern patterns that shed further light on how religious membership and participation might create some of the essential ingredients needed to produce social capital.

THEORETICAL FRAMEWORK

Social capital has the potential for being a particularly useful concept in exploring the structural basis of religious charitable giving. By focusing on Coleman's (1988, 1990) theory of how the relations embedded in a particular social structure facilitate the actions of individuals, the concept of social capital offers a social structural explanation for what may appear to be private, individual-level decisions. Certainly these decisions include, but are not limited to, economic decisions. Indeed, when he initially introduced the term, Coleman was attempting to link the economist's concept of rational choice with sociology's notion of socialization. To quote Coleman (1988, 98):

> My aim . . . is to import the economists' principle of rational choice for use in the analysis of social systems proper, including but not limited to economic systems, and to do so without discarding social organization in the process.

For Coleman, social capital is a feature of social organizations, and it is located at the group or organizational level. It is this conceptualization of social capital that we will employ in this chapter.

But how can the relations found in a particular social structure generate social capital? Coleman discusses a number of aspects of group relations that can facilitate the action of members. For example, the level of trustworthiness found among members can have a profound influence on what they are able to accomplish together. Likewise, group relations can shape the nature, extent, and effectiveness of obligations, expectations, and sanctions found operating among group members. But group relations are also important influences because of the social networks they offer members. Such social networks offer informational channels, and their importance varies depending upon whether they are closed (i.e., when all actors interact with each other) or more atomized (i.e., when there is little interaction among the network members). The social capital produced from social networks can also be heightened depending on whether or not such relationships are multiplex in nature (i.e., whether or not the information and resources from one relationship can be appropriated for use in other relationships).

The likelihood of social capital being created within churches is enhanced by the fact that most church members are likely to identify other church members as some of their closest friends (Olson 1989, 1993). Most members of a church are likely to share much in common. For instance, they are likely to be in the same general social class, live in the same community, have children attending the same schools, and have memberships in many of the same non-religious organizations and clubs. Consequently, the close and multiplex nature of their relationships can create trust among church members and facilitate a common sense of what is good or desirable, as well as facilitate cooperation towards achieving goals of mutual benefit.

An example of how church or synagogue membership might produce social capital is the influence members have on each other's recognition of community needs and their support of charities—charities such as Habitat for Humanity (HH). Relationships among church members are likely to influence how well-informed or how well-educated such members are about housing needs of families in their communities. Such needs might be identified by church leaders, or they may simply become known through informal conversations with other parishioners. Relationships among church members are also likely to increase the level of trust that members have in each other and in each other's assessments of the need and worthiness of families seeking HH assistance. The legitimacy of requests for housing assistance is often established by a church committee recommending the sponsorship of a family or by a respected member vouching for them. Church relationships also help to establish expectations by informing parishioners about whether or not other members are giving to HH, and if they are, to what extent they are supporting it. Thus, the level of trust in relationships evident among parishioners can greatly influence their giving to charities by helping to inform members of needs and by enhancing the legitimacy of requests for help.

Although a forceful and cogent argument can be made that religion creates social capital in the form of charitable giving, it is a bit more difficult to generate an empirical verification of such a causal relationship. One of the difficulties of studying social capital is that it cannot be directly observed. As a feature of a social organization that enhances coordinated actions, social capital only becomes evident by examining the intended outcomes of social action, and even then its influence must be inferred. In the present study, for example, revealing all of the numerous (and often unmeasured) means by which religion influences giving is impossible. Even if one were to control for a plethora of variables, the role of social capital in enhancing the charitable giving of church members would still have to be inferred because it is embedded in the relationships of the individuals being studied.

One approach to studying social capital is to compare groups on the basis of some outcome for which they can be expected to differ. For example, if religious membership is found to be associated with greater charitable giving, one might infer that greater religious participation increases the trust and relations that Coleman argues is at the basis of social capital, and the resulting social capital can then be translated into higher levels of giving. Thus, if it can be documented that frequent religious attenders are more generous givers than less frequent attenders, this would be consistent with how social capital is expected to work, and it would lend support to the theory. Exactly *how* such religious attendance influences giving, however, must still be inferred.

This chapter analyzes and compares the level of charitable giving among both religious members and non-members. By varying the presence or levels of other variables (e.g. income), we hope to find whether religious membership influences giving in any discernible way, and if it does, whether the patterns can be explained in terms of relationships that are likely to be found exclusively among religious members. That is, can the differing patterns be used as inferential evidence of the role of social capital in enhancing giving patterns?

DATA

Data for this study come from the *Giving and Volunteering Survey*, commissioned by Independent Sector and conducted by the Gallup Organization. These surveys are conducted biennially, and the data employed here are drawn from the 1989, 1991, 1993, and 1995 surveys. These surveys are designed to provide information on the levels of giving and volunteering evident among adult Americans, their motivations for doing so, and changing trends in such activities over time. These are the same data employed by Campbell and Yonish in the previous chapter of this volume. For our purposes, these data are used to address the following questions: What, if any, difference does religious membership have in fostering overall charitable giving? Does religious membership influence the likelihood of members giving to nonreligious charities? Do frequent church attenders contribute more of their income to charities than do those who do not attend or who attend less frequently? Does religious giving influence giving to other types of charities? And, if so, what are some of the possible reasons for this influence?

FINDINGS

The percentage of American households making contributions to religious organizations has declined slightly in recent years. Still, religious organizations are, by far, those charities most likely to have been supported financially. Indeed, in 1995, about one-half of all respondents reported making a contribution to religious organizations (Independent Sector, 1996). This was nearly double the figure for health-related charities, which ranked second in terms of the number of contributions made. Moreover, the average *amount* contributed to religious organizations far exceeded the average given to any other charity. The average annual contribution to religious causes in 1995 was over $400—more than five times the amount contributed to educational organizations, the next highest charity. In fact, the average amount contributed to religion is nearly double the level of giving to all other charities combined ($417 compared to $279)!

These figures, while revealing, simply confirm what has already been known from research on religious giving (see Hodgkinson, 1990a; Hoge, 1994; Ronsvalle & Ronsvalle, 1992)—namely, that religious organizations are the most strongly supported of all types of charities. Here, we seek to take the analysis one step further. In particular, we wish to ascertain whether belonging to religious organizations influences the likelihood of members contributing to charities in general, and to nonreligious charities in particular? Data that address these questions are presented in Table 7.1.

RELIGIOUS MEMBERSHIP

Displayed at the top of Table 7.1 are the percentages of religious members and non-members contributing to charities over the four surveys. While the percentages of members and non-members supporting charities appear to have dipped somewhat between 1993 and 1995, a significantly higher percentage of church members contributed to charities than did non-members in each of the years examined. Religious members are (by a margin of 20–25 percent) more likely to contribute to charities than are non-members, and this difference between the two groups has remained fairly steady over time.

But what about charities that are specifically nonreligious in nature? Perhaps

Table 7.1   Comparison of the Giving Patterns of Members and Non-members of Religious Organizations

	1989	1991	1993	1995
Percentage of houoseholds contributing to charities of all types by religious membership				
members	77%	76%	78%	71%
non-members	55%	55%	54%	49%
Percentage of households contributing to nonreligious charities by religious membership				
members	57%	59%	58%	53%
non-members	52%	52%	50%	47%
Average amount contributed annually by households to nonreligious charities				
members	$278	$265	$242	$257
non-members	$255	$190	$189	$208

differences between church members and non-members are somewhat inflated simply because church members give to religious causes? A comparison of households contributing to nonreligious charities is also presented in Table 7.1. As was the case with households contributing to charities in general, there appears to have been a slight drop-off between 1993 and 1995 in the level to which households supported nonreligious charities. However, in each of the four years analyzed, the fact remains that religious members are more likely than non-members to provide some level of financial support even for nonreligious charities. For each year considered, there is a 5–7 percent difference in the extent to which religious members, as opposed to non-members, provide support for nonreligious charities.

Finally, the percentages given at the bottom of Table 7.1 reveal that religious members are not only more likely than non-members to *contribute* to nonreligious organizations, but they are also more likely to contribute in *greater amounts*. While the gap between the two groups varies from year to year, the average annual amount contributed to nonreligious charities is significantly greater for religious members than for non-members. For example, in 1995, the most recent year for which we have data, religious members contributed about 20 percent more on average to nonreligious charities than did non-members ($257 versus $208 respectively).

Moreover, this pattern of religious members giving more than non-members to nonreligious charities is not simply explained by differences in income. This can be seen in the comparison of members and non-members presented in Table 7.2 which analyzes differences in giving between church members and non-members for each of five different income levels. These data reveal that church members give at least as much (and often more) to nonreligious charities than do non-members within each of the different income levels examined. Differences between the two groups are particularly pronounced at the low and high ends of the income distribution.

Table 7.2 Average 1995 Household Contributions to Nonreligious Charities by Income Level by Membership in Religious Organization

Religious Membership	1995 Household Income				
	< $20,000	$20–39,999	$40–74,999	$75–99,999	> $100,000
Member	$70	$160	$350	$700	$1490
Non-member	$25	$140	$275	$690	$1150
Members as a percentage of non-members	280%	114%	127%	101%	130%

Thus far the analysis has shown that religious members are: (1) more likely than non-members to contribute to charities in general and nonreligious charities in particular; and (2) likely to contribute more to nonreligious charities than are non-members, regardless of income level. It must be remembered, however, that these discrepancies in giving levels between church members and non-members would be further enhanced had giving to religious charities been included in the analysis. Clearly, religious membership influences giving to nonreligious, as well as religious, charities. But how, and by what means, does church membership encourage individuals to be more generous with their financial resources?

Religious Participation

If religion's influence on charitable giving results from relationships embedded in religious organizations (as the social capital model would suggest), then one would expect that those members who participate more in the life of their church or synagogue will be more strongly influenced by these relationships. In other words, we would expect greater religious participation to be associated with greater support of charities. Table 7.3 addresses this issue and examines the relationship between religious attendance and charitable giving to nonreligious organizations.

The findings revealed in Table 7.3 indicate that church attendance appears to have little effect on the likelihood of members contributing to nonreligious charities—except for weekly churchgoers. While over one-half of all church members contribute to nonreligious charities, it is only among those who attend church on an almost weekly basis that we find any significant increase. Roughly two-thirds of those who attend church on a weekly basis make contributions to nonreligious charities; in contrast, only 57 percent of those attending church less than one to two times a month do so. But this is exactly what one might expect with regard to social capital—the norms and expectations of a group are likely to be strongest among those who interact frequently and on a regular basis.

A very similar pattern is found when we examine the *amount* contributed to nonreligious charities. The giving pattern exhibited in Table 7.3 once again sug-

Table 7.3 1995 Household Contributions to Nonreligious Charities by Religious Attendance

	Not at all	Few times a year	Religious Attendance Once/twice a month	Almost weekly
Average amount contributed to nonreligious charities	$220	$222	$230	$310
Percentage of households contributing to nonreligious charities	55%	57%	57%	66%
Average percentage of 1995 income contributed to nonreligious charities	.42%	.35%	.31%	.53%

gests that church attendance has an impact on the amount contributed to non-religious charities only when such attendance reaches a weekly level; the only substantial difference in giving is found between members who attend less than weekly and those members who attend weekly. Those who attend religious services less than weekly give annually at an average about $220. But those who attend weekly contribute at an average of $310. The additional increase in the amount of financial contributions made by weekly attenders represents a one-third increase over that given by those who attend church once a month or less.

The relationship between church attendance and the percent of income contributed to nonreligious charities is also presented in Table 7.3. It is significant to note that the average percentage of income contributed to nonreligious charities for all members is less than one-half of one percent. The pattern revealed here, however, is similar to the one found in the previous two questions. The relationship between attendance and the percentage of annual income contributed declines slightly at each church attendance level up to the level of weekly attendance—though this drop of about one-tenth of one percent is not statistically significant and is best described as no change across these categories of lower levels of church attendance. But, once again, the only group that exhibits a significant increase in giving to nonreligious charities is found among those who attend church most frequently. With reported giving for nonreligious charities at about 0.53 percent of income, this group gives about 20 percent more of their income to nonreligious charities than the average reported for those who attend church less frequently.

The findings from Table 7.3 indicate that religious participation does not influence giving to nonreligious charities significantly until attendance reaches an almost weekly basis. Indeed, in each of the three comparisons made in the table, the only substantial difference in giving is between those who attend weekly and those who attend less frequently. This finding suggests that the social capital produced by the relations found in churches and synagogues is evident only among the most frequent attenders. Simply being a member or being an infrequent attender, it appears, does little to increase one's financial support for nonreligious charities.

Possible Reasons for Religion's Influence

If religious participation does produce social capital, which in turn is transformed into greater charitable giving, then what is it about the relationships of those who attend religious services frequently that affects their giving? Perhaps those members who attend religious services frequently have more and deeper (i.e. multiplex) relations among themselves than do less frequent attenders. If so, then perhaps the social capital produced in churches and synagogues can also be found among frequent participants in other types of voluntary organizations.

The 1995 Giving and Volunteering Survey asked respondents if they spent time with friends from their church or synagogue. The data and statistics presented in Table 7.4 indicate that there is a very strong positive relationship between attendance and socializing with friends from church. Eighty-two percent of church members who do not attend religious services also do not spend time with church or synagogue friends. This pattern is consistent with previous research findings (Olson 1989), and it is not too surprising given the fact that weekly attendance and ongoing fellowship with other church members, both within and outside the church, is at least an ideal norm in most religious traditions.

Table 7.4 Time Spent with Friends from Church/Synagogue by Religious Attendance

| Time Spent with Friends | Religious Attendance | | | |
	Not at all	Few times a year	Once/twice a month	Almost weekly
Not at all	442	298	94	144
	82%	45%	25%	13%
Few times a year	62	224	123	258
	12%	34%	33%	24%
Once/twice a month	22	109	117	340
	4%	17%	31%	32%
Almost weekly	13	26	41	339
	2%	4%	11%	31%
Totals	539	657	375	1081
	100%	!00%	100%	100%

Gamma value = .66
Significant at .001 level

Figure 7.1 Percentage of Members Participating on an Almost Weekly Basis

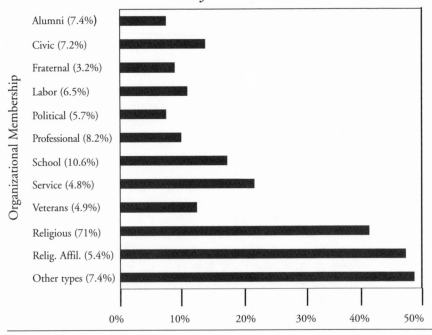

While high levels of church attendance and socializing among members of religious organizations is common (as evident in Table 7.4), how does this compare with members of nonreligious voluntary organizations? Figure 7.1 compares the percentage of members from 12 types of voluntary organizations who participate in their organization on a weekly or nearly weekly basis. Of all the types represented, three stand out as being particularly high in weekly participation. The first are those who participate in churches, which we have already examined. The second are those who participate in religiously affiliated organizations that exist outside religious denominations per se (e.g., B'nai Brith, Knights of Columbus), while the third is a residual group of organizations not included in any of the other eleven types. This third category includes sports and hobby clubs as well as nationality and ethnic groups. What is additionally important to note about Figure 7.1 is the percentage of respondents reporting membership in each type of organization. With over 70 percent of respondents reporting membership in religious organizations it is, by a very wide margin, the largest single category (see figures in parentheses). In comparison, the other two categories with high percentages of weekly participants (the "other types" category and the religious affiliated groups) include only about 11 percent and 5 percent of respondents respectively. Indeed, when all nonreligious types of organizations are combined, the percentage of weekly participants averages less than 15 percent. Thus, the high participation rates we observe among religious members is truly extraordinary when compared to most members of nonreligious voluntary organizations.

What effect does high participation in nonreligious organizations have on charitable giving of members? Based on the findings from religious members, we would expect weekly participation in nonreligious organizations to also have a "compounding effect" (i.e., we would expect weekly participants in nonreligious organizations to spend more time socializing with other members, to be more likely to give to charities, and to give in greater amounts than less frequent participants).

Table 7.5 compares the percentage of contributors to all charities broken-down by respondents' participation level and type of membership. In this table respondents are classified into one of four categories: (1) those who attend religious organizations less than weekly as well as nonreligious organizations less than weekly; (2) those who attend religious organizations less than weekly, but attend nonreligious organizations weekly; (3) those who attend religious organizations weekly, but attend nonreligious organizations less than weekly; and (4) those who attend religious organizations as well as nonreligious organizations on a weekly basis. The lowest level of contributing is found among those who participate on a less than weekly basis in either religious or nonreligious

Table 7.5 Participation Level in Voluntary Organizations and Charitable Contributions

Charitable Contributions		Participation Level in Voluntary Organizations	
	Type	Religious Organizations	Nonreligious Organizations
Percentage of households contributing to any charity 55%	1	less than weekly	less than weekly
81%	2	less than weekly	weekly
81%	3	weekly	weekly
94%	4	weekly	weekly
Percentage of household income contributed to all charities 0.7%	1	less than weekly	less than weekly
1.3%	2	less than weekly	weekly
2.3%	3	weekly	less than weekly
3.3%	4	weekly	weekly
Percentage of household income contributed to nonreligious charities 0.3%	1	less than weekly	less than weekly
0.9%	2	less than weekly	weekly
0.5%	3	weekly	less than weekly
0.9%	4	weekly	weekly

organizations (Type 1). Only 55 percent of this group reported any charitable contributions, and they contributed to charities at a much lower level than any of the other three types represented. Weekly participation in either religious or nonreligious organizations substantially increased the likelihood of giving to charities (Types 2 and 3). Indeed, weekly participants in *either* religious *or* non-religious organizations contribute to charities in nearly the same proportions. Finally, weekly participants in *both* religious and nonreligious organizations had the highest percentage of contributors (Type 4). At 94 percent, they were near-ly 13 percent more likely to contribute to charities than were weekly partici-pants in only one of the two types of organizations, and 39 percent more like-ly than less-frequent participants in both types of organizations. Thus, the level of participation in organizational life, whether religious or nonreligious in nature, affects the rates by which individuals contribute to charities.

But what about the level of such contributions? Also presented in Table 7.5 is the relationship between the percentage of income given to all charities and level of participation in religious and nonreligious organizations. The lowest percentage of income donated to charities was from those who do not partici-pate on a weekly level in any voluntary organization (Type 1). This group donates just slightly more than one-half of one percent of their income. Weekly participation in either religious or nonreligious organizations significantly increases the percentage of income contributed. Those who were weekly par-ticipants in nonreligious organizations (Type 2) gave on average about twice as much as those in Type 1. However, weekly participants in religion (Type 3) gave nearly twice as much of their income to charities as did weekly participants in nonreligious organizations (Type 2). Thus, the type of organization in which one is active does appear to influence levels of charitable giving. And, those who participate on a weekly basis in *both* religious and nonreligious organizations (Type 4) give a substantially higher percentage of income (about 3.3 percent) than do any of the other three types. Thus, it seems that active participation in any voluntary organization increases the probability of giving to charities and the level of giving, but active religious participation has a particularly strong influence on the level of such giving. Being active in both religious and non-religious organizations further encourages members to give to charities and to give more generously.

One final question remains: Does the influence of participation, and specif-ically religious participation, carry over to giving to nonreligious charities? The influence of weekly participation on the percentage of income given to nonre-ligious charities is found at the bottom of Table 5. It is important to note ini-tially the general level of giving to nonreligious charities: the overall average of giving to nonreligious charities reported by Americans is less than one-half of one percent of total income, and, as a result, the percentage of income donat-ed to nonreligious charities is less than one-half that given to religious organi-zations.

As was the case in earlier findings, those who are not weekly participants in either type of voluntary organization (Type 1) gave the lowest percentage of their income to nonreligious charities. Not surprisingly, those who are weekly participants in nonreligious organizations (Type 2) gave a much higher percentage of their income to nonreligious charities than did weekly participants in religious organizations (Type 3). Those who were actively involved in nonreligious, but not in religious, organizations (Type 2) contributed three times more of their income to nonreligious charities than did those who were not actively involved in either type of organization (Type 1). Moreover, such Type 2 respondents contributed nearly twice as much of their income to nonreligious charities as did those who were weekly participants in religious, but not in nonreligious, organizations (Type 3).

Still, high religious participation plays a role in giving even to nonreligious charities. The percentage of income given by those who are weekly participants in religious, but not in nonreligious, organizations (Type 3) is nearly double that given by individuals who do not participate on a weekly basis in either type of organization (Type 1). Thus, being highly involved in church or synagogue appears to encourage giving even to nonreligious charities.

It is also interesting to note that those individuals who were highly involved in both religious and nonreligious organizations (Type 4) gave nearly the same percentage of their income to nonreligious charities as did those who were actively involved only in nonreligious organizations (Type 2). This was true despite the fact that those who fall in the Type 4 category also gave a higher percentage of their income to religious charities than did less actively involved members. This suggests that the higher giving to churches by those who are highly involved in religion does not subtract from their giving to nonreligious charities. Rather, those in Type 4 were able to accomplish such giving levels only by the fact that they simply contributed a higher percentage of their income to all forms of charity.

This finding is particularly interesting, given the observation of Campbell and Yonish in the previous chapter that members who attend church regularly are less likely to engage in non-church voluntary activity. The difference in the impact of church participation on contributing money to, as opposed to volunteering in, non-church organizations could be explained by differences in the nature of the two resources. Perhaps church members simply have less "spare time" than "spare money" to contribute. Thus, the more time they spend volunteering in their church leaves less time for church members to volunteer in other charitable organizations.

CONCLUSIONS

Is there a religious basis for charitable giving in America? Does religious participation create social capital which, in turn, translates into greater charitable giving? Clearly, more Americans contribute to religious organizations than to any other type of charity, and they do so in substantially greater amounts. Furthermore, members of religious organizations are more likely than those who are not members of religious organizations to make contributions to non-religious charities and to contribute to these charities in greater amounts.

Our findings suggest that one reason for the increased giving of religious members is their relatively high participation levels. Compared to most members of nonreligious organizations, religious members are substantially more likely to participate on a weekly basis, and it is these frequent attenders who are primarily responsible for the increased giving among religious members. Moreover, when compared to less-active participants, we find weekly participants in all organizations to be more generous givers. This frequent involvement in the life of an organization may well create a basis for the trust and familiarity needed if relationships are to produce social capital that can then be transformed by an organization into fiscal capital.

Still, one must view the findings of this chapter to be largely preliminary in nature. Clearly, more work needs to be done, particularly with regard to the employment of control variables that might influence the relationship between religion and charitable giving. Nevertheless, the findings presented here indicate that social capital could well serve as a very useful theoretical framework in explaining this relationship.

From a social capital perspective, active participation in voluntary organizations leads to greater and deeper networks of relationships among members. From these relationships come greater social capital, possibly in the form of greater trust and respect among members and greater knowledge and trust in charitable programs. The social capital that is produced in these social networks, in turn, generates greater giving in both religious and nonreligious charities among those that are actively involved.

Chapter 8

Ties That Bind and Flourish
Religion as Social Capital in African-American Politics and Society

Fredrick Harris

When a large bank loaned one million dollars to a small, struggling storefront church in Queens, New York, to enable it to construct a new church building, many wondered why a bank would lend money to such a risky enterprise. The decision to grant the loan was influenced by the provisions of the Federal Community Reinvestment Act, a law stipulating that banks doing business in poor and working-class neighborhoods must reinvest in those neighborhoods. But the bank was also influenced by the intense level of cooperation evident among church members. Bank officials were impressed that the congregation had paid off a five-year mortgage on a vacant lot—the future home of the new church—in three years and that it had also retired the debt on the storefront two years ahead of schedule.

How did a small congregation, with meager material resources, accomplish such success? Congregants raised money for the church by selling fruit, sponsoring family outings, and making handmade items for sale. However, the most consistent means of raising church revenue was through tithing, the practice of believers giving one-tenth of their income to the church. The storefront minister described the giving habits of his congregation as follows: "Some folks who give, give their last mite . . . but they find such favor and love in what we are doing that they give what they have to give" (Eaton 1999, 20).

The concept of social capital fits well with common understandings of how religion fosters group cohesion. For those who harbor commitments that are

121

anchored in religious beliefs, religiously endowed social capital reflects a unique set of resources that enhances the possibility for successful cooperation. In contrast to theories of group cooperation that insist that material incentives are needed to induce individuals to cooperate with others, religious worldviews and practices—depending on their orientations—have the capacity to diminish the need for material incentives when group cooperation is anchored in religious beliefs. The mere act of joining a community of faith, and the socialization that comes with membership in a religious community, increases the possibility of cooperation among actors through the existence of institutionally derived networks, the creation of norms that promote rewards and punishments, and the nurturing of trust among actors whose relationships are cemented in shared beliefs and practices.

This chapter is devoted to assessing religiously endowed social capital in African-American politics and society as a case study. However, I first want to address briefly religion's overall capacity to nourish and sustain social capital. Scholars who either implicitly or explicitly examine the links between religion and social capital frequently focus on religion's contribution to the development of civic skills in religious institutions. While this aspect of religion's influence on the formation of social capital is important, as I will discuss in greater detail below, religion can create social capital in more subtle ways. One such subtle way it does so is through what I believe to be a unique feature of religion's contribution to the formation of social capital—namely, its ability to nurture and sustain reciprocity among actors.

After a brief discussion about religion's effects on reciprocity, the chapter examines the internal and external factors that shape black churches' involvement in political and social life. It demonstrates how historical forces and the institutional design of most black churches help to nurture the formation of social capital in black communities. The historical development of black churches in the United States and blacks' historic exclusion from mainstream political life provide some answers as to why black churches are more engaged in political and social affairs than their white counterparts.

To provide some context to that history, the chapter assesses the acquisition of civic skills in religious institutions, a process that is important because such skills are transferable to social and political activities outside the church.

Finally, in order to address the theoretical questions raised earlier, it examines survey responses to probe motivations behind church members' participation in church work. Exploring the motivations behind church work not only provides evidence of what types of incentives shape church activities, it also reveals how motivations may vary by race and ethnicity, indicating which groups have greater access to religiously endowed social capital, and, in turn, which groups have the greater capacity to mobilize religiously endowed social capital in behalf of social and political action.

RELIGION, RECIPROCITY, AND COLLECTIVE ACTION

This chapter considers religion's capacity to produce and nurture social capital. Religiously endowed social capital may well provide stronger ties for group cooperation than one would expect from social capital generated from secular sources. Secular forms of group cooperation may need to rely on material incentives to induce individuals to cooperate with others, but religiously oriented group cooperation may be able to induce collective action through nonmaterial incentives—such as a desire to do good works—that are often rooted in the beliefs of religious communities. (See also Chapters 1 and 6 in this volume.)

The idea that a divine actor(s) animates group cooperation complicates commonly held views on why individuals engage in collective action and questions fundamental assumptions about collective action. What happens, for instance, when social and political actors believe that their activism is guided by a sacred force? How do actors calculate the decision to cooperate with others when rewards for cooperation or sanctions for defection are promised in the hereafter, where the long-term benefits of cooperation outweigh the short-term personal costs to activism?

Reciprocity is important to group cooperation because it facilitates collective action through the belief that actors will ultimately benefit from their cooperation with others or will incur sanctions if they do not cooperate. Though religion's contribution to the operation of reciprocity has been overlooked in discussions about religion and the formation of social capital, religion has much to contribute to the study of collective action. Putnam (1993a, 172) identifies two ways in which reciprocity generates group cooperation. One way is through "balanced reciprocity," a process in which a "simultaneous exchange of items of equivalent value" takes place among actors, thereby nurturing and sustaining group cooperation among actors. Another way that reciprocity generates group cooperation is through generalized reciprocity. Generalized reciprocity affects group cooperation because the alliance among cooperators entails a "continuing relationship of exchange that is at any given time unrequited or unbalanced, but involves mutual expectations that a benefit granted now should be repaid in the future." For cooperators with belief structures that promise rewards or punishments in the hereafter, these expectations of deferred rewards may provide a stronger source of reciprocity than secular sources, since human actors do not possess the same power to reward and punish as does a perceived sacred force.

Thus, transcendent values assist in the operation of reciprocity because they provide actors with mutual expectations about whether rewards or punishments for their (un)cooperation will be granted in the future. Moreover, religiously induced reciprocity can relieve human actors—whose powers to reward and punish actors are inconsequential compared to the omnipresent powers of a perceived sacred force—from rewarding and punishing cooperators and defectors.[1] Examining religion's influence on reciprocity expands our understanding of social capital and highlights the complexities of group cooperation when religious values are considered.

THE FORMATION OF SOCIAL CAPITAL
IN BLACK CHURCHES

Both the history and the structure of black religious institutions serve to shape a defining feature of religion's contribution to social capital formation—namely, the development of civic skills. The involvement of black churches in social and political activities is affected not only by the institutional design of black churches, which are mostly Protestant, but also by the history of black exclusion from American mainstream political and religious institutions. These internal and external dynamics matter. In *Making Democracy Work,* Putnam (1993a) argues that historical circumstances determine whether political and social institutions will encourage group cooperation. He further argues that communication networks within social organizations determine the social capital needed for cooperative action and that the design of institutions influences the capacity of social networks to produce social capital:

> Some . . . networks are primarily "horizontal," bring together agents of equivalent status and power. Others are primarily "vertical," linking unequal agents in asymmetric relations of hierarchy and dependence (Putnam 1993a, 173).

Putnam found in Italy that horizontal linkages are associated with broader civic competence. Similarly, in the United States, African Americans gain civic skills through horizontally structured Protestant churches that are organized by congregants themselves rather than through a church hierarchy. These civic skills prove essential when church members decide to engage in political and social activities through church-sponsored activities as well as through activities outside the church.

History figures prominently in the engagement of many black churches in political activities. After emancipation, when newly freed black men had their first opportunities for electoral participation, religious institutions provided the organizational infrastructure for mass political mobilization (Foner 1988; Walker 1982). Reconstruction was not only a period of open political participation for African Americans, it was also a period of institution-building among black denominations. Black Christians organized autonomous Baptist denominations and joined the Northern-based African Methodist Episcopal Church, which fiercely competed with the independent Baptist churches for the religious loyalties of newly freed slaves (Walker 1982). White Protestant denominations in the South excluded blacks, especially from clerical leadership, and this exclusion, combined with the desire of blacks for self-determination, led ex-slaves to found and join mostly black-led denominations. These separate black religious denominations were, and still are, the largest black organizations in the United States.

Still, there were few "free spaces" for freed slaves. It was the churches that provided meeting space for political gatherings, and church leadership and laity were elected to state political conventions and to local and state elected offices. Black clerics were particularly prominent in Reconstruction politics. Eric Foner (1988, 93) estimates that "[o]ver 100 Black ministers, from every denomination from AME to Primitive Baptist, [were] elected to legislative seats during Reconstruction." Ministers used their churches as a political launching point, and "among the lay majority of black politicians, many built a political base in the church." Black religious institutions and organizations were strongest in the urban South: "[p]olitical mobilization . . . proceeded apace in southern cities, where the flourishing network of churches and fraternal societies provided a springboard for [political] organization" (Foner 1988, 110).

In his study of the African Methodist Episcopal (AME) Church, Clarence E. Walker (1982) explains how the laity and hierarchy of the AME church met the political and organization needs of the black male electorate. In some Southern states, local AME congregations became the center of black political organizing. Church missionaries, presiding elders, ministers, and deacons within the AME served as delegates to state constitutional conventions, as Republican presidential electors, and they were elected to Congress, state legislatures, and city councils.

Walker illustrates how the elaborate organizational infrastructure of the AME church politicized members:

> Methodism, with its units of class, society, and band, provided ministers with an organization structure they could use for political purposes. This was particularly true of the class, which in some ways corresponded to the organization of a modern political party. These meetings and regular church services provided the minister-politicians with the arena for the dissemination of their political and religious ideals (Walker 1982, 126).

With the end of Reconstruction, both religious and secular institutions "accommodated" to white domination in the South. As a result of the repeal of laws that legally protected black citizenship rights, black electoral mobilization came to a halt, leaving in its place severe sanctions against organized opposition. In the presidential election of 1876, the Republican Party, the party of the freedmen and women, sabotaged black political development by promising to withdraw federal troops from the South in exchange for Republican control of the presidency (Logan 1968; Franklin 1980, 285). Thus, during the last decades of the nineteenth century, the consensus of both major political parties to allow the erosion of black citizenship rights effectively kept African

Americans out of the American political party system. Within the Republican Party, "lily-white" Republican factions cropped up throughout the South, while black Republican groups, now demobilized, were relegated to separate "black and tan" factions that competed with Southern white Republicans on the national level for party patronage (Walton 1975). Rayford W. Logan (1968) aptly describes this period as the "nadir" of race relations in the United States. The growing exclusion of African Americans from voting and from party activity left a void that only black religious institutions could fill. In the South, whites promoted their political interests through the Democratic Party which, in many states, restricted participation to whites only. African Americans could participate in the American polity only through an ineffectual Republican Party.

After the Great Migration, urban party machines in the North attempted to include black migrants along with European immigrants, but such interracial coalitions were rare in the South. The populist Agrarian Revolt of the 1890s saw one such moment—both blacks and poor whites in the South mobilized against the economic domination of Bourbons and Northern Industrialists. But even then, the resulting Populist Party was organized around racially separate rural organizations. Lawrence Goodwyn (1978, 122–23) notes that during the Agrarian Revolt "white supremacy prevented black farmers from performing the kinds of collective public acts essential to the creation of an authentic movement culture." In fact, after the Populist Party's electoral defeat in 1896, one of its most prominent leaders, Georgia's Tom Watson, abandoned his ideals of interracial cooperation and became a defender of white supremacy (Goodwyn 1978). These events and policies intensified the development of racially separate political spheres, forcing African Americans to cultivate their own organizational resources for political mobilization. One of the most crucial of these was the black church, which would provide institutional resources for the civil right movement in the 1950s and 1960s.

THE PRACTICE OF CIVIC SKILLS
BY RACE AND ETHNICITY

Given this history, does the black church continue to foster the development and use of civic skills among its members? An analysis of the uses of civic skills in religious institutions suggests that black churches continue to influence the development of social capital in African-American politics and society. In his study of the political behavior of black ministers in the early 1970s, Charles Hamilton (1972) recognized the importance of African American religious institutions as resources for the development of civic skills. "Many blacks," he noted, "learned about organizations, acquired political skills and developed an ability to work with and lead people through the institution of the church" (Hamilton 1972, 117).

The vast majority of black churchgoers are Protestant. Indeed, more than half of black churchgoers are affiliated with one of the three major Baptist denominations.[2] Other black churches, such as the African Methodist Episcopal Church (AME), are organized more hierarchically,[3] although congregants have the opportunity to practice organizing skills within congregations and district associations. These predominantly black denominations, as well as majority black congregations affiliated with majority white denominations, give blacks the opportunity to learn organizing and civic skills through their participation in church work.

Does this history and institutional structure of black religious groups matter? In order to address this question, the practices and motivations of churchgoing African-Americans, Latinos, and whites were examined to ascertain the differences across the three groups. Because blacks and Latinos are alike in that they are minorities within American society and that they both exhibit lower educational and economic resources than whites, one might expect blacks and Latinos to differ from whites. But, while blacks and Latinos share these characteristics, they tend to differ in terms of the institutional structure of the religious congregations they attend. In contrast to the congregationally centered structure of black churches, the institutional design of Catholic congregations is more hierarchical. This difference is likely to contribute to lower rates of skill acquisition among Latino church activists, a majority of whom are Catholic. Since Catholic churches are hierarchically structured, and thus have comparatively fewer opportunities for lay involvement than Protestant churches, it was anticipated that Latinos would be less likely to acquire church-based skills.

In order to assess whether black churches continue to foster the development of civic skills, survey data from the Citizen Participation Study (Verba et al. 1995, Appendix A) were analyzed. Most surveys, given their sample size of 1500 respondents or less, include relatively few African-American or Latino respondents. However, the Citizen Participation Study was designed, in part, to provide a larger pool of both African-American and Latino respondents. The first stage of the study consisted of a 15,000-case random telephone survey of the American public. This stage involved the use of a relatively short interview to identify respondents in terms of their levels of civic participation and their race and ethnic background. From this survey, a longer, in-person interview was conducted with 2517 of the original respondents, weighted so as to produce a disproportionate number of the two minority groups. This follow-up survey, which involved measures of religious involvement as well as civil and political engagement, included 478 African-American and 370 Latino respondents. The study is therefore ideally suited to compare African Americans with Latinos and whites in terms of how religious variables might affect the acquisition of civic skills within their respective communities.

These data reveal that African Americans do, in fact, have more of an opportunity to develop civic skills in their churches than whites and Latinos. Nearly 40 percent of African Americans practice civic skills at their place of worship compared to only 20 percent of Latinos and 28 percent of Anglo-Whites (Verba, Schlozman, Brady, & Nie 1993, 477). Similarly, African Americans (38 percent) are slightly more likely than whites (35 percent) and substantially more likely than Latinos (16 percent) to hear political messages at their place of worship (Verba et al. 1993, Table 4, 485).[4]

The greater level of participation in church work among blacks has participatory consequences. Research shows that blacks receive a greater political boost from their participation in religious institutions than whites (Harris 1994). Again, blacks receive more church-based political stimuli because they are more likely than whites and Latinos to be a member of a congregation, affiliated with Protestant rather than Catholic churches, and to be exposed to political messages at their place of worship (Verba et al. 1993, 491–92; Harris 1994).

On the other hand, responses from the Citizen Participation Study reveal only slight variations in the practice of church-based civic skills by race and ethnicity.[5] While blacks are more likely to be active in the church, those who are active in church work, regardless of whether they are blacks, whites, or Latinos, practice skills roughly at the same rate. Figure 8.1 shows racial/ethnic variations in the practice of the four civic skills among believers who are members of a church and who attend worship services at least once a month. Blacks are more likely than whites to practice two skills—namely, attending church meetings where decisions are made (73 percent) and giving presentations (43 percent). Whites are slightly more likely than blacks to report writing letters as a part of their church work (27 percent), while both blacks and whites report giving presentations at their church at the same rate (37 percent). With the exception of giving presentations, Latinos who are active in their congregations are less likely than black or white church activists to write letters (20 percent), plan a meeting (32 percent), or attend meetings where decisions are made (51 percent).

Black women represent an overwhelming majority of congregants in black churches. As institutions that are central to black civil society, black churches are led by a male-dominated clergy yet sustained by a membership that is, on average, 70 percent female (Lincoln & Mamiya 1990). Because black women are more deeply committed to religious institutions than black men, we would expect them to acquire more civic skills through church work. A longitudinal analysis of patterns in church attendance and membership in church groups suggests that black women have the opportunity to learn and practice civic skills at greater rates than black men, white women, and white men. Using data from the General Social Survey (GSS), Figure 8.2 shows the distribution of weekly church attendance by race and gender over time, collapsed into five time periods spanning the early 1970s to the early 1990s.

Gender, more than race, affects whether believers attend weekly church services. A third of both black and white women report attending religious services at least once a week. This pattern in women's church attendance has been consistent for all five time-periods, suggesting that both black and white women

Figure 8.1 Civic Skills Practiced in Church by Race and Ethnicity

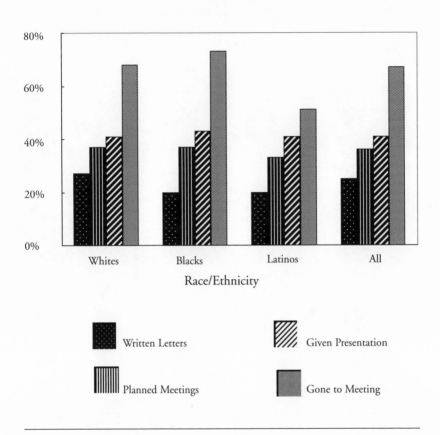

are exposed to situations where they practice and learn civic-enhancing skills. In contrast, regular church attendance among both black and white men has hovered around 20 percent, although white men have a slight edge in attendance over black men. What is surprising here is that the level of church attendance among black men does not differ greatly from that of white men, and, as a result, these patterns challenge assumptions about the "recent" exodus of black men from churches (Kunjufu 1994). But, while regular attendance at church services among black males has remained much the same since the early 1970s, black men do not attend church at the same rate as black women—suggesting that black men are less exposed than black women to the opportunities to engage in civic-enhancing skills in churches.

Figure 8.2
Church Attendance by Race and Gender, 1970s–1990s

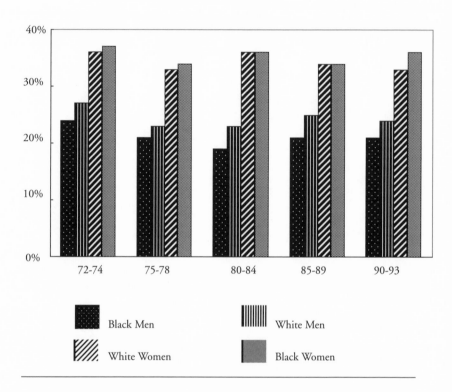

This gap in church attendance between black women and men may have consequences for political participation. Although statistical models from survey
data show no significant difference in reported voter participation between
black men and women, government statistics on voter turnout show a small
advantage to women. In almost every age category used by the Census Bureau
to estimate voter turnout, black women report higher levels of turnout than
black men. In the 1992 presidential election, the gap in voter turnout between
black women and black men was six percentage points, while the gap between
white men and women was two percentage points.

This relatively higher voter turnout among black women defies conventional understandings of who votes. Since the average income and education levels
of black women are less than those of white women or black men, we would
expect their voter activity to reflect their relatively low socioeconomic status.
Regular church attendance among black women may provide at least one explanation. And Jesse Jackson's 1984 presidential campaign, which relied on church

networks to mobilize black voters, is instructive. In that year's November election, the voter turnout rate among black women was substantially higher than among black men, especially in the age groups in which black women substantially outnumber black men in church attendance. For instance, in the 18-20 age category, the male-female difference in reported voter turnout among black voters was 11 percent. In the 21-24 age group, the gap was six points, while for the 25-34 and 35-44 age groups the gap hovered around ten percentage points. But the gap narrowed considerably in the age categories where black men's church attendance is highest: the gap in turnout was less than two percentage points for the 55-64 and 65-74 age groups.[6]

Black women gain not only from their church attendance but also from their extensive participation in church work. Not only does regular attendance in church services boost the voting turnout of black women, but so does their participation in church activities. Figure 8.3 shows the degree of participation in church-affiliated groups by race and gender from the 1970s to the 1990s. Black women are more engaged in church work than white women, black men, or white men. During the 1970s about 55 percent of all black women participat-

Figure 8.3
Participation in Church-Affiliated Groups by Race and Gender, 1970s–1990s

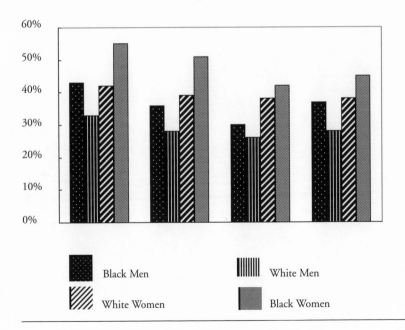

ed in church groups; by the early 1990s that rate of participation had declined to 45 percent. White women's involvement in church work remained relatively stable over the same period of time, hovering around 40 percent, but still noticeably lower than that of black women.

Although black men attend church less frequently than white men, they are nevertheless more involved in church-affiliated groups than white men. This greater level of involvement is probably explained by the patriarchal power they can exercise in these groups. Even so, the level of church involvement among black males appears to have eroded slightly since the 1970s, as their reported level of participation in church-affiliated groups fell from 43 percent in the mid-1970s to 37 percent in the early 1990s. These different levels of participation in church life may help to account for the fact that black women go to the polls at a greater frequency than one would expect on the basis of their income and education.

The idea that black men who are involved in church work gain more civic skills through the patriarchal power relations in churches is partly confirmed

Figure 8.4
Civic Skills Practiced in Church by Race and Gender

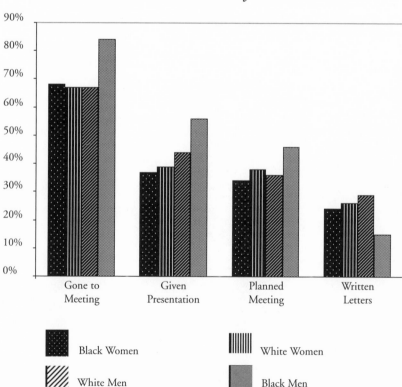

through data from the Citizen Participation Survey. Figure 8.4 shows that black men practice civic skills in churches more than black women, white women, and white men. This finding is surprising since black men are considerably less likely than black women to attend church weekly or to be active in church-based organizations. Yet, for the few black men who are actively engaged in church life, churches serve as a place for them to nurture their civic skills.

Black men who attend church practice civic skills at a higher rate than black women, white males, and white women—whether in terms of planning meetings (46 percent), giving presentations (56 percent), and attending a church meeting (46 percent); the exception was that of writing letters. On the other hand, differences in practicing civic skills are modest between and among those black women, white women, and white men who are active in their churches.

These findings raise questions about how the learning of civic skills is distributed among various groups within such churches. Although the institutional design of most black churches may provide blacks who attend church with favorable resources for social and political action, certain norms and values that regulate the participation of women in church life may reinforce ideas and practices of gender inequality. On the other hand, the higher proportion of black men practicing civic skills may simply reflect expectations for them to fill leadership roles, since relatively few black men attend church.

MOTIVATIONS BEHIND CHURCH WORK

Another way to assess religion's impact on social capital is by analyzing why believers become involved in church work. If believers are involved in religious institutions that foster the development of civic skills and if those institutions also nurture motivations that foster group cooperation, then religion provides even further ground for social capital formation. However, probing human motivations is a tricky enterprise, and it is difficult to know why, and under what conditions, individuals are moved to act. Nevertheless, assessing the motives behind churchgoers' participation permits an exploration of religion's contribution to the building of social capital. It allows us to reflect on whether the social capital produced by religious institutions is in any way different from that which one would expect to emerge from secular institutions.

If church members are active in their congregations because they want to receive material goods, then participation in church groups may not be any different from membership in any other benefit-extracting organization. On the other hand, if church members are moved to participate in church activities because of non-material benefits, such as the desire for social intimacy or for altruistic reasons, then religion's capacity to foster group cooperation would be different from that generated by most secular institutions.

Survey data from the Citizenship Participation Study supplies insight into how church members think about their participation in church activities. The survey asks:

> Here is a list of reasons people give us for being active in their (church/synagogue). Thinking about your activity in your (church/synagogue), aside from going to services, please tell me if each of these reasons is very important, somewhat important, or not very important in keeping you active.

Respondents were then asked to rate nineteen different reasons for their activism,[7] and their responses to these nineteen statements were assigned to four different categories that reflect religious, altruistic, material/egotistic, and social motivations for church participation.[8]

Table 8.1 shows the percentage of blacks, whites, and Latinos who report that these particular statements were "very important" reasons for their participation in church work. Not surprisingly, religious explanations were the strongest justifications for participation in church work, a finding that suggests that non-material incentives have strong effects on determining whether religionists participate in church activities. Church activists reported that affirming their religious beliefs (76 percent), learning about their religion (71 percent), receiving a religious education (59 percent), fulfilling religious duties (59 percent), and furthering religious goals (56 percent) were "very important" to keeping them active in church activities.

In addition to religious explanations, church activists were also highly motivated to participate by altruism and a desire for social intimacy. About three-quarters of church workers reported that lending a hand to people (78 percent) or making their community or the nation a better place (71 percent) kept them active in church work. Nearly half (46 percent) reported that "doing their share" influenced their church activism.

Considering the weight of social motives provides further evidence of religion's contribution to the formation of social capital. Social motivations are important because they entail what Putnam describes as social connectedness—a resource that facilities group coordination through the intensity of social interactions. More than half of the respondents reported that they were active because they wanted to "share their ideas with others" (61 percent) and "be with other people" (58 percent).

In contrast to religious, altruistic, and social motives that sustain participation in church work, considerably fewer church activists expressed a preference for material or egotistic motives for their participation in church work. Less than a third of church workers (30 percent) reported that they are active because of the services their church provides and one-fifth (20 percent) reported that they are active because of their church's recreational activities. Fewer than a fifth of church members reported that their activities are strongly affected by the opportunity to receive personal help from their church (19 percent),

Table 8.1 Reported Motivations for Activism in Church Life by Race and Ethnicity

Motivations	Whites	Blacks	Latinos	All
Religious:				
Affirm faith	73%	81%	85%	76%
Learn about religion	65%	85%	78%	71%
Religious education	57%	60%	73%	59%
Further religious goals	48%	75%	66%	56%
Duty as member	51%	77%	71%	59%
Altruistic:				
Lend a hand to people	71%	91%	94%	78%
To do share	38%	66%	56%	46%
Better nation	43%	86%	75%	71%
Material:				
Services	25%	47%	33%	30%
Recreational activities	15%	30%	34%	20%
Personal help	14%	31%	26%	19%
Recognition	7%	22%	23%	12%
Meet important people	5%	23%	17%	10%
Further career	5%	12%	20%	8%
Social:				
Share ideas	56%	74%	66%	61%
To be with people	52%	71%	60%	58%
	N = 556	N = 192	N = 69	N = 837

Percentages reflect responses of "very important" for each question about motives.

to get recognition from people they respect (12 percent), to meet important people (10 percent), or to further their career (8 percent). These responses to material and egotistic explanations further reveal religion's capacity to nurture non-material incentives for group cooperation.

Considering explanations for church work by race and ethnicity shows important distinctions. Group variations also suggest how mixed-motives—which entail a combination of material and non-material incentives for group cooperation—may influence members' participation in church work. Mixed motives are particularly at work among black and Latino church activists, who are more likely to report that material motivations keep them active in church work than do white church activists.

In Table 8.1 the black-white gap in reported explanations for church participation is particularly large for altruistic and social motives. Nearly all black church workers reported that lending a hand to others who need help is "very important" to their involvement in church activities (91 percent), while about three-quarters of white church workers (71 percent) considered that explanation important to their church work.

Similarly, black church workers are more likely to report that they are engaged in church activism because they are the type of person who "does their share" (66 percent) or because they want to make their community or nation a better place (86 percent). Less than half of white church workers thought that doing their share (38 percent) and making their community and the nation a better place (43 percent) are very important explanations for their involvement in church work. Moreover, black church workers were considerably more likely to report that their activism was generated by a desire for social intimacy. About three-quarters of black church workers reported that having the opportunity to share ideas with others (74 percent) and to be with others (71 percent) were important reasons for their participation, while white church activists were less likely to see those explanations as important.

The rather large differences between black and white church activists suggest that religion's contribution to some forms of religiously endowed social capital benefits black churchgoers more than white churchgoers. Since black church workers express a higher degree of altruistic motivations and a greater desire for social intimacy, possibilities for church-based collective action are, on the whole, greater for black churchgoers than they are for their white counterparts. However, black church activists also give explanations for their participation that reflect material and egotistic motives. Almost one-half of the black church activists (47 percent) report that the services their church provides are very important reasons for their involvement in church work, while a quarter of white church activists (25 percent) give that explanation. Similarly, black church activists are twice as likely as white church activists to cite that recreational activities offered by their church (30 percent) and the help they receive from their church for personal or family problems (31 percent) motivate their church work. Black activists are also three times more likely than white activists to report that receiving recognition from their peers (22 percent) and meeting important people are important reasons for their involvement in church work. Such expressions of materialistic motives probably reflect the greater material needs of black churchgoers, since black churches also tend to be more involved in providing social services than majority white congregations (Chaves & Higgins 1992).

Like black activists, Latino church activists also express higher levels of religious and altruistic motivations for their engagement in church work. Indeed, Latino activists are more likely than white and black activists to express that their activism affirms their faith (85 percent) or that they are active because they have a desire to lend a hand to others in need (94 percent). Unlike blacks, however, Latinos are slightly less likely to give materialistic/egotistic explanations for their church activism.

On the whole, responses to rationales for activism in church work indicate that non-material motives (religious, altruistic, and social) outweigh material motives as explanations for participation in church activities. Again, the greater frequency with regard to religious rationales for action is not surprising since believers' activism is rooted in their faith. Together, religious motivations and other motivations that are influenced by religious beliefs and practices (such as altruism and a desire for social intimacy) contribute to the formation of social capital by linking group cooperation to incentives that diminish the need for material incentives to produce the same result (Mansbridge 1991).

CONCLUSION

Several conclusions can be drawn from this chapter on the role of religion in the formation of social capital in African-American political and social life. First, this chapter suggests that religion has a capacity to generate the practice of reciprocity as a feature of group cooperation, an aspect of religion-as-social-capital that has been mostly overlooked in discussions about religion and social capital formation. Still, much more research needs to be done to undercover the links between religion and reciprocity, especially how rituals such as tithing may promote norms of reciprocity among believers.

Second, this chapter reveals that the nature of motivations that derive from religious commitments for collective action are likely to differ from motivations for collective action derived from non-religious bases, and that those religiously influenced motivations are likely to promote cooperation among a community of believers. Descriptive analysis of responses from the Citizen Participation Study indicates that altruistic and social motivations are cultivated in religious communities, suggesting that religious values can potentially soften the need for material incentives in inducing individuals to cooperate with others. Although material and egotistic motivations may be important to believers' participation in religious activities, findings from the survey indicate that church-goers are far more motivated by their faith, altruism, and their desire for social intimacy than by material interest.

Finally, this chapter reaffirms the important role of religious institutions in generating social capital in African-American communities. Although inequalities along gender lines exist within black religious institutions, African Americans—especially African-American women—develop civic skills that can be employed for social and political activism. The evolution of black religious institutions as centers of social and political life in the nineteenth century and the internal structure of Protestantism continue to make black religious institutions an important feature in the development of social capital formation in black communities. Given the history of black churches and the higher levels of altruistic and social motivations that blacks report for involvement in church activities, it is no surprise that black religious institutions have the capacity to generate and sustain social capital in black communities.

Chapter 9

Social Capital and Societal Vision
A Study of Six Farm Communities in Iowa

Janel Curry

Most discussions of social capital and the state of civil society focus on inter-personal relations and the behavior and beliefs of individuals. However, as Wuthnow notes in Chapter 12, this approach leads to an over-emphasis on small, informal, and voluntary settings, and it emphasizes individual moral resolve, trustworthiness, character, and altruistic sentiments. In so doing, it neglects both the study of institutions and the distinctions among different types of social ties and different types of associations.

Fortunately, more recent theorizing, arising out of the earlier work of Mark Granovetter (1973), offers some hope for addressing different kinds of social ties. Generally, this theorizing has focused on understanding the difference between stronger, more personal ties and those that are weaker and more out-ward-looking. Putnam refers to the kind of ties developed in close-knit com-munities with intimate familiarity as "thick" trust (Putnam 1993a, 171); thick trust is embedded in personal relations that are strong, frequent, and nested in wider networks. In contrast, the more outward-looking ties are based on "thin-ner" trust. He argues that this type of trust in "the generalized other" is even

This research was funded by the Pew Charitable Trusts Evangelical Scholars Program, the Center for Global and Regional Environmental Change at the University of Iowa, the Leopold Center for Sustainable Agriculture at Iowa State University, and the Anne U. White Fund of the Association of American Geographers.

more useful because it extends the trust beyond those whom one can know personally, giving even those one does not know the benefit of the doubt (Putnam 2000, 136).

The concepts of bonding and bridging social capital parallel these notions of thick and thin trust. Bonding social capital is necessarily inward-looking, reinforcing exclusive identities and homogeneity. Bridging social capital is outward-looking and encompasses a diverse group of people. According to Putnam, both have their place in the overall development of social capital. Bonding is good for developing specific reciprocity and building solidarity, while bridging networks are better for linkage to external assets and institutions as well as for increased information flow (Putnam 2000, 22). Without the cultivation of bonding internal to communities, actions might degenerate into mere rent-seeking.[1] Without bridging to outside institutions and resources, bonding social capital might be of little worth because it lacks the information and ability to mobilize outside resources to the benefit of the community (Gittell & Vidal 1998, 15–16). Thus, social capital is not valuable unless it connects someone with something new (p. 18).

Consider a rural town of 500 people I recently visited. By all measures of volunteer organizational membership, the town was high on social capital. It had more public space (Elks Lodge, hockey rink, Veterans Hall, Masonic Lodge, etc.) than any town of that size I have ever encountered. Yet this town suffered from high levels of alcoholism, sexual abuse, and an inability of its young people to survive outside the social circle created by this enmeshment. Associational membership was an end unto itself. In such a case, bonding was so strong that social enmeshment was the result; virtually no bridging took place. As a result, associational involvement was not directed toward any particular end nor was it used as a basis for bridging to outside institutions in any attempt to move in some particular direction.

This understanding of different types of linkages leads to certain paradoxes with regard to social capital: weak ties, often portrayed as a sign of the demise of civic society, are indispensable to communities. While strong ties among members of a group may lead to group cohesion, they can also lead to the ineffectiveness or inability of a community to move in any positive direction. In less dense networks with more indirect contacts, one's ability to manipulate networks, get ideas, influence structures, and gather information is enhanced—the fewer the indirect contacts, the more encapsulated is one's knowledge of the world beyond one's immediate friends. Thus, weak social ties, bridging in nature, are crucial (Granovetter 1973, 1370–71).

This study seeks to address whether religion plays a role in fostering a community's mix of bonding and bridging social ties. More specifically, this study analyzes religion primarily in terms of the particular religious worldviews associated with different religious faiths. Do such shared religious worldviews simply serve to increase bonding, while decreasing bridging relationships? Or, do different kinds of religious worldviews move their adherents in different directions with regard to fostering bridging relationships with those outside the religious community?

THEORETICAL FRAMEWORK

This study attempts to illuminate the relationship between religious worldviews and social capital, with social capital being further delineated into its bonding and bridging components. The focus is on those aspects of culture that people use to interpret their world—i.e, its symbols, language, values, and assumptions. This focus contrasts with the more typical topics often addressed in discussions of social capital—topics related to the interpersonal ties and relational networks in which people are embedded that are closely related to social structure (Wood 1997, 598).

As Edwards and Foley (1997, 671) point out, it is the sociocultural component of social capital that provides the context within which social capital acquires meaning—it provides the vision that can facilitate an individual or collective action not otherwise possible (Edwards & Foley 1997, 671). Herein lies the difficulty in measuring social capital: it cannot be assessed directly, but requires operationalization using specific indicators. Yet such indicators, like counting the number of voluntary associations in a community or the participation rates in those organizations, do not provide insights into the linkages between and among worldview visions, social capital, and outcomes (Wall, Ferrazzi, & Schryer 1998, 315).

Coleman (1990, 302) argued that social capital is nested in structures or relations between individuals and groups, but that is was not reducible to those structures, and while it could be appropriated by individuals, it was not simply an attribute of individuals (Edwards & Foley 1997, 670). Membership per se does not produce or even measure social capital. Even when social capital is treated in structural terms, operationalized as memberships, it is not simply membership per se that produces social capital. Not all memberships lead to the "something" that is social capital, because membership can lack a societal vision.

Social capital is also embedded in, and arises out of, shared societal visions. This study explores the relationships between social vision, as evident in religious worldviews, and social capital. It illustrates that social capital, in its bonding and bridging forms, cannot be understood apart from the religious worldviews that underlie communities. These religious worldviews are reflections of ultimate commitments and embody what people believe to be "just there," or what is so fundamental that it is not dependent on anything else for its existence, as all else depends on it (Clouser 1991, 16–19). Such worldviews are grounded in communities (Curry-Roper 1998b) and are associated with answers to fundamental questions of existence. What is the nature of humankind? What are the most fundamental problems facing society and ourselves. What is the nature of evil? On what do we place our hope for these problems' solution?

As noted in Chapter 1 of this volume, the answers to these questions, arising out of one's religious worldviews, affect the nature of one's associational life. Social capital has the capacity to foster the social and economic health of a community, city, or region. But the capacity of social capital to serve as a resource for such collective ends can only be appropriated by individuals in the context of a shared vision; without such a shared vision this capacity of social capital remains dormant.

THE STUDY

This study focuses on six Iowa communities, each of which is composed of a relatively homogeneous religious group. Iowa, like many other states in the Midwest, is a mosaic of relatively homogeneous ethnic/religious communities on which the prosperous agricultural economy of the region has been built (Borchert, 1987; Egerstrom, 1994). These particular communities were chosen for study based on the following criteria. First, there had to be some evidence that the religious groups have maintained a strong coherence of commitments to their particular theological positions. Second, these groups had to be located in communities whose population was less than 3000 people. Third, farming had to be dominant in the local economy. And, finally, ethnic homogeneity had to have been largely maintained.

Based on these criteria, the following communities were selected for analysis: Wayland (German Mennonite), Wellsburg (German Reformed), Cascade (German and Irish Catholic), Paullina (Anglo and Norwegian Quaker), Hull (Dutch Christian Reformed), and Lamoni (Anglo Reorganized Church of the Latter Day Saints). These communities provide an excellent context for the study of how religion shapes social capital because each exhibits a high level of face-to-face interaction. Given the religious homogeneity and small size of these communities, I expect to find a high level of social capital, particularly bonding social capital, already present.

Information and data were collected by three different methods. First, two discussion groups were organized within each of the six communities, one comprising farmers and another comprising their spouses. The groups were drawn from the churches that dominate the rural communities of the study, thus reflecting the community itself. In the group discussions, participants were asked to respond to a series of narratives set in farming contexts that presented situations or dilemmas related to the study variables. Content analysis was used to analyze the transcripts arising out of the discussion groups.

Second, participants within each discussion group were also asked to fill out a short questionnaire on themselves and their farms. Questions asking about farm organization membership and subscriptions to farm publications were also included in the questionnaire. In addition, they were asked to rank the strength of their agreement/disagreement with thirty value statements that discriminated among the relevant variables.

In the third part of the study, I personally interviewed four individuals from each social group in greater depth (N = 24). These persons were selected to represent different age groups and farming types. The core of the questions employed focused on what an individual sees as the most fundamental problems facing society and on how those problems can be solved—the human condition and its solution (Yinger 1969, 90-91).

FINDINGS

The six communities were ranked along two scales representing the bonding and bridging aspects of social capital. Bonding, the inward-looking aspect of social capital, was scaled according to the strength of a group's communal orientation. Communal involvement entails primary-group interaction at the level of family and friends among those who share a common religious and cultural heritage (Roof 1979), whereas associational involvement refers to an individual's participation in organizational, institutional, or congregational activities.

Communal orientation, rather than associational involvement, was used as a measure of bonding in this study.[2] The story used to tap one's communal orientation described a situation in which a farmer faced having to sell his farm due to development pressures. If he did so, however, he knew the whole community would have to follow suit because he owned the largest farm and also rented the acreages of others, which helped sustain the community. The dilemma in this situation relates to the tension between what might be good for one personally versus what would be good for the community as a whole. Responses to this hypothetical situation were placed along an individualistic-communal scale, and then refined through individual interviews and an analysis of questionnaires.

Bridging is the outward-looking aspect of social capital that encompasses a diverse group of people and is a form of social networking. This study measured bridging by computing the average number of memberships per person in farm organizations. Organizations were limited to those that were farm-related because these organizations serve purposes most clearly related to bridging characteristics such as serving as channels for information and avenues for influencing and understanding government policy. While they might have some social aspects to them, and thus represent some aspects of bonding, memberships in farm organizations are primarily bridging in nature.

The six communities, despite their similarities, exhibited discernable differences in their responses to this hypothetical situation tapping communal (bonding) orientations. The more individualistic groups focused on the continuation of the farm itself and on a minor part of the story—the condemnation of a piece of land for a road. Very little was said about the relationship between the farmer's choices and the community—even though this was clearly the dilemma. Instead, comments from the more individualistic groups centered primarily on the impact of development on the sustenance of family farm units rather than on the sustenance of the community as a whole. In contrast, the more communitarian groups generally focused their discussions on community concerns. The most individualistic in perspective were the German Reformed, Catholic, and Quaker groups, while the Dutch Reformed, Mennonite, and Reorganized Church of the Latter Day Saints (RLDS) groups were the most communal in their worldview.

These differences in worldviews were further confirmed in the in-depth interviews with four individuals from each group. When asked to address the most basic problem facing their individual communities, participants from the individualistic groups focused on the lack of participation of young people in the church, the lack of activism in the community, and the need for jobs for young people. The participants from the communally oriented groups talked instead of the need to maintain a sense of community, the need to include those who aren't like themselves, and the need for the church to reach out to the community. In addition, individuals from these more communally oriented groups showed much more satisfaction with how much cooperative life already existed—e.g., pride in building an apartment complex for the elderly or in their community's commitment to local businesses and schools.

These responses take on a pattern. In the individualistic communities, the communities' problems and solutions lay in getting others more involved and more committed and in attracting businesses that provide jobs. Among the communal groups, the problems and solutions are related to their own willingness to reach out to others and serve others. Similarly, responses to the most basic problem facing agriculture followed suit. The individualistic groups identified problems of low prices, labor costs, and the reduced profit margin. Reasons for this reduced profitability ranged from government regulation to corporate farming. The more communal groups also identified low profit margin as a problem, but made connections to the larger community. Low hog prices were connected to low teacher salaries, reduced church funds, and to the less vibrant local businesses. And, once again, the problem and solution lay more within themselves—the need to be more content with what they had; the need to put faith in God rather than in governmental intervention; and, the need for one to desire to have a neighbor more than to desire to have what that neighbor possesses.

Low-Bonding Groups

The individualistic groups—Quakers, German Reformed, and Catholic—all fell into a low-bonding, but high-bridging, category. The German Reformed and Catholic groups exhibited relatively similar characteristics, and their communities face similar problems in their efforts to mobilize members for some community need—perhaps reflecting the low levels of bonding within their communities.

The German Reformed group mirrored the cultural traits that have been reported among other East Frisian settlements (Rogers & Salamon 1983; Schnucker 1986, 87–88). Commitment to either the development of non-farm businesses or social activities has traditionally been weak in East Frisian communities (Rogers & Salamon 1983, 543). Thus, opportunities other than farming are often lacking, despite the fact that vertical integration, especially of the hog industry, and increasing farm size (and associated decreasing farm population) remain threats to the well-being of this particular German Reformed community.[3] One of the participants in the study commented on the difficulty in gaining support for local initiatives, including efforts of county social service agencies to start a "Meals on Wheels" program in the community. Responsibility for the well-being of the elderly, in this case, was believed to end at family boundaries.

The low bonding exhibited by the German Reformed group, in contrast to its Dutch Reformed counterparts (discussed later), may have its roots in the more "evangelical" and pietistic religious character of the German Reformed tradition (Curry-Roper 1998a, 23). Religious experience in the German Reformed community is focused more on the individual and individual expressions of piety such as personal Bible study and prayer (Leege 1988, 711). A dilemma created from this worldview was illustrated in a discussion that occurred with a group from the participating church. When discussing the tremendous increase in farm size and what this meant to their community (decreasing population), members of this religious community seemed paralyzed. Their generally evangelical and "American" worldview is associated with an emphasis on the social boundary of the individual farm unit and individual property rights. As a result, their traditional emphasis on a non-differentiated farm society has left them with few economic activities other than farm-related ones. Furthermore, their individualistic perspective and lack of any tradition of institution-building leave them with a great deal of work to be done if they hope to counter structural trends in agriculture that may lead to the demise of their way of life and community. Within this context, bridging activity remains largely one of individual farmers joining farm groups within the model of interest group politics.

With its similar high bridging and low bonding characteristics, the Catholic community of Cascade also has had trouble mobilizing community members. The history of the schools in the community gives an example of the difficulty of initiating community action. Catholics have valued hard work and passing on their farms to the next generation, but they generally have not been involved in the community. Historically, Cascade had two Catholic high schools; these merged in 1961. By 1976, when the high school was on the verge of closing due to financial problems, several individuals suggested that the town explore the option of forming a separate Cascade public school district. Protestant families in the community were especially interested because they had been busing their children to the next town to go to school. But no initiative was ultimately undertaken. As a result, the West Dubuque County School District bought the school building, and the area has become part of that larger school district by default (Aitchison 1994; *History of Cascade* n.d., 109).

Today, only one Catholic grade school remains in Cascade. Sixty percent of the parish members send their children to the Catholic grade school (McDonnell 1994), but parish members expressed some frustration over the lack of commitment on the part of Catholic parents in paying for the school. Tuition rates are extremely low, yet any proposed raise in tuition is met with resistance.[4]

There exists a fundamental paradox with regard to the Roman Catholic Church in the U.S. (Leege & Trozzolo 1985, 8). While the symbols of the Church are communitarian, the value of the culture, the economy, and the polity in which the Church is located tend to be much more self-centered and individualistic. While Catholics may have been more communal and less individualistic in orientation in the early 1800s, they are now part of the cultural mainstream of the nation when it comes to individualism (Leege 1988, 710–11).

The Quaker group, while falling within a low-bonding category, also exhibited a high level of bridging action. In fact, several members of the Quaker group belonged to more than ten farm organizations, including co-op boards. Certainly these Quakers fit the pattern of the more individualistic groups, but their level of involvement and the range of types of organization to which they belonged were quite different from the German Reformed and Catholic groups. While the Catholic and German Reformed farmers belonged to only traditional farm organizations and producer associations, the Quakers belonged to these groups and to alternative agricultural groups such as Practical Farmers of Iowa and the Leopold Center for Sustainable Agriculture.

The mix of low bonding of individualism and the extremely high levels of bridging can only be understood in the context of the worldview perspective of Quakers. Steere (1984, 3) identifies Quakers as rugged individualists. This individualism is found in the major Quaker doctrine of the Inner Light. From the very beginning, Quakerism has focused on the mystical witness of the Inner Light to the individual (Steere 1984, 16). Though not everyone chooses to call upon this power, Quakers believe it is available to all, thus reflecting a belief in the essential goodness of humans (Comfort 1959, 55-57). And since humans are seen as basically good, Quakers believe that some level of perfection of society is possible. In addition, the universality of their concept of grace means that this perfection can be extended to society and the world as a whole, leading to an intense desire to try to improve society (Comfort 1959, 58).

The high level of associational involvement and its relationship to a Quaker worldview were evident in the comments of the Quaker participants. They expressed concerns over population growth, the need to feed the world, and the need for social change. And the burden of those changes fell on themselves, undergirded by a strong sense of purpose and progress. As one participant stated, "I'm gonna hafta get to work . . . and as the light is . . . the goodnesses comes—and it will, if you keep working and believing." The Quakers thus modeled an individual activism stance. What separated them from the German Reformed and Catholic groups is that their activism went far beyond interest group politics, toward a larger vision of social change.

Still, these Quakers faced challenges similar to the other two groups exhibiting low-bonding, but high-bridging, characteristics. A great deal of hope was placed in education as a force in social change. In fact, their commitment to their children's education was itself creating problems for the future of the group. Many people within the Quaker group sent their children to a Quaker high school about six hours away. In addition, many Quaker children went on to college, often state universities or good liberal arts colleges. If they returned at all, it was often with a non-Quaker spouse. So the numbers of people involved in the Meeting was diminishing. And, in spite of their community involvement, the town of Paullina itself struggles with providing opportunities for non-farm families, and the school population continues to fall even after consolidation with an adjacent school district.

High-Bonding Groups

Communal visions of life arose throughout discussions within Dutch Reformed, Mennonite, and Reorganized Church of the Latter Day Saints groups. The Dutch group's response to the narrative focused on the community as a whole. Participants spoke of the desire of people in Hull to stay in the community. They spoke critically about the heirs of this hypothetical farmer who might, in the end, value money over the preservation of the community, and they noted the respect this farmer would surely enjoy in the community if he were to place the community's needs first. Similarly, members of the RLDS and Mennonite communities also discussed the need for the farmer to see himself as part of a larger communal whole.

The origins of these high-bonding or communal visions are diverse, and their subtle differences lead to variations in the outworkings of the visions. Each of the communal traditions, from those trying to build a society based on Christian institutions to those who withdraw from society to live out the Kingdom of God, is built on a communal vision of life that is quite radically different from that of mainstream American society. Decisions within these communities are affected by these most basic worldviews. And it is of no surprise that these groups, exhibiting the strongest communal perspectives, have strong educational institutions to pass on these visions to the next generation. The Dutch Reformed in Hull are strongly committed to their K-12 school system as well as their local college. A number of families in Wayland send their children to the Mennonite school system forty-five minutes away, and many young people go to Mennonite colleges. The commitment to distinctive religious education exists to a lesser degree among the RLDS. Participants in Lamoni lamented the demise of the common value system that once existed in the local public school system. In addition, concern was expressed over whether Graceland College was failing to portray their religious tradition positively. In spite of this, two-thirds of the students at Graceland College are from an RLDS background and the college remains the main employer in the town of Lamoni and the major RLDS educational institution.

These high-bonding groups ranged in their bridging tendencies, with the Mennonites exhibiting the lowest levels of farm association involvement, followed by the RLDS and then the Dutch Reformed. Religious worldviews underlying these particular groups again give insights as to their placement along this bridging dimension.

Mennonites have traditionally withdrawn from society into the security of the community, where life could more easily be modeled after Christ (Nafziger 1965, 188). This withdrawal is based on the idea that Christ initiated the first fruits of the Kingdom of God that now live in the hearts of believers. This Kingdom will come into its fullness with Christ's return, but in the meantime, believers are to live as if in the Kingdom, following closely the teachings of Jesus. They are to witness to the world through their alternative example of how to live—in nonconformity to the world and with an ethic of love that forbids military service, the use of violence, and any personal litigation or use of the judicial system (Nafziger 1965, 188). The Mennonite communal vision emphasizes personal piety and simplicity of life. Mennonites have always had a certain amount of suspicion of institutional structures, the accumulation of wealth, and formal education.

The Mennonite group, however, illustrates the limitations of our understanding of a religious group's social capital if we fail to take into account that group's religious worldview. At the surface, it would appear that this Mennonite community is an inward-looking community with strong internal, or bonding, ties but with little connection to the structures and institutions of the larger society. A closer look, however, reveals that this is not the case.

Wayland, the Mennonite community in this study, is a prosperous farm town, due partially due to its focus on turkey production and to strong historic cooperation that extends beyond community boundaries. Turkeys were first introduced in the community in the early 1930s as a result of cooperation among local hatcheries, growers, truckers, processors, and feed suppliers. By 1980, more than three-quarters of a million turkeys were marketed within a five-mile radius of Wayland. This spirit of cooperation was also expressed by several participants from the group who initiated a discussion of the possibility of giving ownership of land to the church while maintaining rights of usage for a lifetime, so as to ensure the passage of farms on to the next generation. This kind of discussion was only possible in Wayland and only due to the Mennonite communal worldview that is intertwined with an ethic of simple life and resulting suspicion of wealth. In addition, though Mennonites joined fewer farm organizations than did those in the other religious communities, those they did join included more alternative agricultural organizations. Their communal visions remain somewhat counter to the mainstream society.

The outworking of their worldview, however, has not necessarily been withdrawal in any sense that would negate the formation of bridging social capital. The Mennonite group in the study, typical of Mennonite communities, also showed strong connections and experiences in the larger world. As part of Mennonite tradition, many of the men in the participating congregation did alternate service in opposition to military service, and members of the congregation have also served with Mennonite Disaster Service or the Mennonite Central Committee, relief organizations established through the cooperation of all Mennonite denominations. This has led members of the Mennonite congregation to have experiences across North America and the world (*Sugar* 1971, 10; *Sugar* 1986, 33–35).

Bridging then was taking place through international Mennonite organizations, via the local congregation. This included a commitment to sending their children to Mennonite colleges, the most popular of which requires a semester abroad in a Third World setting. Personal, in-depth discussions revealed the influences of the "return information flow," personal experiences of the participants, and the sense of belonging that went far beyond the local community. Concerns over structural injustice in the area as well as the world was also quite evident.

This Mennonite case reveals some of the difficulty in drawing connections between differing levels of bonding and bridging. Some bonding ends at the local community, but some can also be part of a larger worldview that connects such trust into a larger institutional structure. It is not so much the shared ethnicity that serves as the factor influencing social trust; rather, it is the common societal vision based on a religious worldview. This common worldview created something related to the "thin" trust described by Granovetter, so important to the formation of social capital. Yet, in this case, this bridging social capital was clearly grounded in a localized "thick" trust at the local level. Just as Harris found with regard to his study of African Americans in this volume, Mennonites use their religious institutions as their main arena for expression.

The Reorganized Church of the Latter Day Saints (RLDS) group in Lamoni, Iowa, also exhibited strong levels of bonding that can be traced to their religious worldview. The settlement of the town and surrounding community was organized by a joint stock company associated with the RLDS (Launius 1986). Though the RLDS has its roots in the Mormon tradition, the group has historically identified more closely with mainline Christianity and, thus, is clearly differentiated from the Mormon culture and religion that developed in Utah. The RLDS identified with the original Mormon vision of the establishment of a perfect community of the saints—one that was to usher in the second coming and reign of Christ. However, this "Zion-building" emphasis has been tempered with a more spiritual interpretation of the initiation of the millennial Kingdom of God through personal righteousness and moral perfection (Launius 1986, 315). At one time the RLDS believed that one had to be at a particular gathering place to go to heaven, but now they believe that it "begins within us, and where we are, that is where we are to function, rather than all clamoring to this one special spot."

In spite of this change in interpretation, the vision of Zion remains strong in RLDS society. One participant left a university academic position in 1978 to return to the area as part of this vision. He indicated:

> My grandfather was walking—back in the 1930s—across the field to help my uncle and as he crossed over the hill just south of where our silos now are, the fear of the Lord was impressed upon him that it was his job, as a stewardship, to build up this area as an outpost of Zion. They (he and his sons) put it all together to form a group and it got to be three thousand acres. The idea of building this up as an outpost—our idea of Zion—was not something in the heavens, but the place of a Zionic condition, where people treat one another equitably and fairly and you work together in peace and harmony.

This same vision was also evident during the farm crisis in the 1980s. At that time, the RLDS church had a bishop in Lamoni who was concerned about the financial condition of a local bank. As a result, he took some of the regional church funds and invested them in the bank in order to shore up the bank financially. His argument was that this was a proper use of church money, as they were "storehouse resources" that could legitimately be used to try to build Zion. In the end, the bank survived, and the funds were safe. Nevertheless, while the communal vision may be clear, it still exists in tension with the larger American culture: despite the fact that church funds were not lost, the bishop was removed from office.

Why the RLDS community exhibited lower levels of bridging activity is difficult to explain. Commitment to the RLDS worldview seems to be reflected primarily as contributions of time and money to the RLDS church, which relies heavily on lay leadership. Failure to contribute time and money, when one has the means to do so, is viewed as a lack of responsible stewardship. This, in turn, limits the breadth of RLDS's vision for society as well as its influence within the now largely non-RLDS town and larger society.

The Dutch Reformed group exhibited higher levels of membership than the other high-bonding groups. Their membership levels, in fact, put them into a high-bonding and high-bridging category. Dutch Reformed communities have always been known for their maintenance of strong boundaries and internal bonding. Similar to other Dutch Reformed communities, the vision of this Iowa group has led to an economically varied and institutionally rich community—a community created by the desire to build a society that lives under the laws of God and institutions that are founded on Christian principles, but not controlled by the church. Here, young people desire to stay in the area, and they have more job opportunities than in most other small towns. As evidence of this desire to stay in the community, farm size has not increased as quickly as elsewhere in the state, and rural depopulation is not a problem. Farms have intensified as they continue to be passed on to the next generation (Curry-Roper 1998a).

For John Calvin, the major source of Reformed theology and tradition, redemption meant bringing all things, secular and sacred, into proper order (Gingerich 1985, 265). This entailed building a society where particular rules governing the conduct of life were to be obeyed literally, such as keeping the Sabbath (Bjorklund 1964, 228). But unlike the Mennonites who traditionally express suspicion of institutions, or the RLDS who focus status on contributions to RLDS institutions, the Dutch Reformed actively embrace institutional development, as well as engagement in societal structures. Part of this emphasis arises out of later immigrants to this Dutch community, influenced by the thought of Abraham Kuyper, a late-nineteenth-century Reformed thinker in the Netherlands. Kuyper believed that Christians and non-Christians understand the world in radically different ways (Stob 1983, 253). This perspective led to Kuyper's call for the development of independent Christian centers of higher education where religious insights could direct research. In addition, Christian schools, Christian labor associations, Christian agriculture societies, etc., have developed out of this vision (Stob 1983, 256; Paterson 1987). Institution- building, along with theological affirmation of larger societal institutions and structures, is part of the Calvinist worldview.

CONCLUSIONS

This study illustrates the complexity of the concept of social capital, even when differentiated into bonding and bridging components. First, relatively homogenous groups with high levels of face-to-face relationships are not all alike. They show great variability in levels of both bonding and bridging social capital. As a result, our discussions of social capital need to abandon the myth that, in previous generations, small towns in America existed in some golden era of social capital and, as a result, all we need to do to cure our social ills today is to rediscover ways of translating that experience into modern society (Newton 1997, 578; Minkoff 1997, 606–7). Let us put to rest the myth of small-town America—it was not, and is not, a monolithic place. Moreover, cities and even regions can exhibit the same range in societal vision, institutional capacity, and social capital that we find in small towns.

Secondly, the findings of this study illustrate how high levels of bridging alone, in the absence of bonding, are not enough to lead to healthy local communities with sustainable local institutions. Associational involvement per se does not somehow automatically lead to the trust so essential to social capital.

Newton claims that the recent growth in large, professionally organized, business-like associations that tend to be remote from their members and joined for the benefits and services they provide, have little impact on social capital (Newton 1997, 582). The findings presented here point in Newton's direction.

Third, certain measures of associational activity suggesting low levels of bridging can easily miss actual engagement with the larger society that falls within the definition of bridging activity. Religious worldviews encourage particular ways of engaging the larger society. Some of these philosophies of engagement, particularly those illustrated by the Mennonites in this study, encourage the development of institutional structures within their religious tradition that can serve as strong bridging forces—even though they may not be easily detected in formal surveys. This particular type of bridging seems to be associated with those with a stronger communal identity. And, in the end, such worldviews may affect social change to a greater extent than individually-based social engagement (Merry 1988).

Underlying the differences among the groups in this study are questions that are largely religious in nature. For what reason does one engage the world outside one's community? Is the engagement simply to enhance one's individual interests? Or, does the motivation arise out of some strongly grounded religious belief that calls one to act, not out of one's own interests, but in the interest of a larger vision of societal justice? And how does one participate within institutional structures—as an individual, or as a member of a religious tradition, grounded in a local group, yet part of a larger, international worldview group? Does one ground that engagement in an identity that reflects some local religious community, or in a religious identity that is much broader in scope? These are not easy questions to study, yet they are crucial for the further delineation of the concept of social capital. Religious worldviews may help in explaining group patterns of bonding and bridging in that, as noted in the introductory chapter, religious worldviews can shape the nature of one's associational life.

Associational activity, by itself, whether local or national, may not help us understand social capital formation. "Communities of commitment" (using Bellah's words), with their respective societal visions out of which associational activity arises, may be the places where we can better begin the search for understanding social capital. Understanding such communities and their worldviews could lead down a fruitful path toward a more nuanced explanation of social capital, its different types, and how it interacts and finds expression at the varying scales of institutional structure.

Chapter 10

Religious Involvement, Social Capital, and Political Engagement
A Comparison of the United States and Canada

Corwin Smidt, John Green,
James Guth, and Lyman Kellstedt

Democracy, as Tocqueville insisted, requires civic associations that are not specifically political in nature, yet ones that still function as sources of meaning and social engagement. As he took note of American life in the early 1800s, Tocqueville observed that the United States had a breadth and depth of group participation that appeared to be unmatched anywhere. For Tocqueville, associational life was essential for the protection of individual liberty and the overall well being of democracy; he argued that American democracy would not survive unless citizens continued to join with others to address matters of common concern.

As readers of this volume are well aware by now, more recent analyses of associational life, and its impact politically, have focused largely on what has been called "social capital," a framework of analysis that refers to features of social organization that facilitate working and cooperating together for mutual benefit (e.g., friendship networks, norms, and social trust). Accordingly, social capital can be viewed as a set of "moral resources" that lead to increased cooperation among individuals. In the words of James Coleman (1990, 302–4):

> Like other forms of capital, social capital is productive, making possible theachievement of certain ends that would not be attainable in its absence. . . . For example, a group whose members manifest trustworthiness and place extensivetrust in one another will be able to accomplish much more than a comparable group lacking that trustworthiness and trust.

Social capital may be generated through a variety of formal and informal inter-actions between people. But, it is difficult, if not impossible, for social analysts to observe the full range of such relationships between individuals directly—even if one limited one's analysis simply to those individuals who associate together with-in one distinct social network. On the other hand, it is possible to assess individu-al patterns of memberships in voluntary associations—and to do so across differ-ent national settings. Accordingly, considerable attention has been given to associ-ational membership as the "indicator of choice for examining the rate of forma-tion or destruction of social capital" (Stole & Rochon 1998, 48).

How do voluntary associations help to generate social capital? Generally speak-ing, it is argued that participation in voluntary associations fosters interactions between people and increases the likelihood that trust between members will be generated. Group activity helps to broaden the scope of an individual's interest, making public matters more relevant. In addition, it is argued that participation in organizations tends to increase a member's level of information, to foster leader-ship skills, and to provide resources essential for effective public action (e.g., Verba et al. 1995).

Moreover, such interactions with others can serve as an important stimulant of individual political activity. Thus, it is posited that involvement in voluntary asso-ciations stimulates people to become politically active—and that it does so over and beyond what might be expected simply on the basis of those personal charac-teristics that might be seen as predisposing individuals to such activity. Collectively, the result of such memberships in voluntary associations is an "increased capacity for collective action, cooperation, and trust within the group, enabling the collective purposes of the group to be more easily achieved" (Stolle & Rochon 1998, 48). Thus, the argument is that engagement in such civic associa-tions (1) helps socialize individuals, teaching them mores with regard to how one should think and behave—mores necessary for maintaining a healthy society and polity, and (2) fosters engagement politically through greater public awareness, broadened interests, and enhanced skills.

This chapter analyzes the relationship between religion and civic life in the United States and Canada. It does so largely through a "social capital" framework of analysis and by using what might be called a "most similar" strategy of compar-ative analysis (Lipset 1990, xiii). A comparative, cross-national study provides a stronger test of the posited relationship between religion and associational life than does an analysis within one cultural context. If religious life is related to the for-mation of social capital, then religious life and social capital should be interrelated at the individual level across both cultural contexts. However, if there are differ-ences in religious life across the two settings, then differences in levels of social cap-ital should also emerge across these two, "most similar," settings. Thus, by engag-ing in a comparative, cross-national study of the relationship between religion and civic life, relationships that may exist between the two should be clarified in terms of what is, or is not, unique to one particular setting, and, as a result, the analyst should be better able to identify those particular religious factors that may, or may not, serve to undergird associational life cross-nationally.

DATA AND METHODS

The chapter is based upon an analysis of a survey of 3000 Americans and 3000 Canadians conducted by the Angus Reid Corporation in the fall of 1996 (September 19 to October 10). This telephone survey was designed, in part, to address the issue of social capital and contained a variety of questions used to tap various components of social capital. As a result, the survey is ideally suited for the analysis proposed.

Statistical weighting was applied to the survey data to adjust the sample of each country in terms of its sex and age composition so as to mirror the distribution within Canadian and U.S. populations, and, in the case of the U.S. sample, in terms of the representation of African Americans as well. The U.S. sample also included a sample "booster" of 200 Hispanic Americans (including Spanish-language interviews).

Respondents were asked whether they were members of any voluntary organizations or associations. If they answered "yes," respondents were then asked whether they were members of any organization that fell within any of fourteen different categories of associations/organizations.[1] If the respondents indicated that they were members of any voluntary association related to that category, they were then asked whether or not they did any volunteer work for that particular group. Thus, with these answers, one can create two different variables— a composite index ranging from 0 to 14 for social memberships and a similarly constructed composite index ranging from 0 to 14 for volunteer activity.

The analysis presented in this chapter consists largely of an examination of the "lay of the land." The initial task is to determine whether or not religious life in Canada differs from that in the United States. If certain elements of religion do contribute to the formation of social capital, then variation in those elements of religious life across the two countries should lead to differences in the level of social capital within those two countries. Second, the relative level of social capital evident in the United States will be compared to that evident in Canada. Once the cross-national differences in patterns of social capital have been examined, the chapter will examine those factors that may help to account for any differential levels of social capital found across the two settings.

ANALYSIS

Religious Differences

Tables 10.1 and 10.2 examine religious patterns of religious affiliation, church attendance, and religious beliefs among Americans and Canadians. Table 10.1 presents the distribution of religious affiliation by country in terms of particular religious tradition[2] and pattern of church attendance. It is clear that the pattern of religious affiliation does differ significantly between the United States and Canada. First, there is a higher percentage of Americans (24.7 percent) than Canadians (11.1 percent) who are affiliated with an evangelical Protestant denomination as well as a much higher percentage of Americans than Canadians who are affiliated with a Black Protestant denomination (9.0 percent versus 1.1 percent, respectively), Conversely, there is a much higher percentage of Roman Catholics in Canada than in the United States (32.7 percent versus 20.4 percent, respectively),[3] while the percentage of mainline Protestants is fairly comparable in magnitude across the two countries, with about 20 percent of both Americans and Canadians tied to mainline Protestantism.

With regard to patterns of church attendance, Americans are much more likely than Canadians to report higher levels of church attendance. Following World War II, Canada has experienced a rather dramatic drop in church attendance; Gallup polls indicate that nearly two out of every three Canadians reported attending services weekly in 1946 (Bibby, Hewitt, & Roof 1998, 238). This erosion in attendance among Canadians is evident in the data presented here. While more than 40 percent of all Americans report that they attend church either regularly or frequently,[4] only about 20 percent of all Canadians report doing so. Conversely, nearly one-third of all Canadians (32.9 percent) report that they rarely attend church, while only about one-sixth of all Americans (16.7 percent) do so. Thus, Canadians differ from Americans both in terms of their patterns of religious affiliation and their patterns of church attendance.

Are such cross-national differences in affiliation and attendance also reflected in religious beliefs? It only takes a very quick examination of Table 10.2 to recognize that Americans are much more likely than Canadians to report "religious" answers to the various questions posed.[5] Regardless of whether one examines belief in God, specific beliefs related to the Christian faith, or relative significance of a particular religious faith, Americans were significantly more likely to provide "religious" answers to the questions than were Canadians. Thus, the first criterion necessary to link religion and social capital cross-nationally—namely, that there be important cross-national religious differences between the United States and Canada—has been met.

Differences in Associational Life

Now that it has been demonstrated that religious life in the United States differs in important ways from that in Canada, we can turn our attention to whether differential levels of social capital also appear to be evident across the two countries. If religion does contribute to the formation of social capital, then one might expect that there would be important differences between the two countries in terms of associational activity.

Nevertheless, other cultural factors could well still be at play. Lipset (1986), for example, has hypothesized that Canadians are less likely to be involved in voluntary associations than Americans in that Canadians exhibit stronger col-

Table 10.1
Religious Tradition and Church Attendance by Country

	Canada (N = 3000)	United States (N = 3000)
Religious Tradition		
Evangelical Protestant	11.1%	24.7%
Mainline Protestant	21.1	18.6
Black Protestant	1.1	9.0
Roman Catholic	32.7	20.4
Other	33.9	27.3
Church Attendance		
Rarely	32.9	16.7
Occasionally	29.6	23.2
Periodically	16.7	20.4
Regularly	13.6	21.4
Frequently	7.2	18.3

lective orientations—with Canadians being more disposed to rely on the state for solutions to social problems, and Americans being more likely to emphasize voluntary activity to achieve such ends. While Lipset (1986, 114) has linked these cross-national differences to "the defining event which gave birth to both countries,"[6] he has also emphasized that this stronger tendency toward volunteerism in the United States is tied to the greater sectarianism of American religion. Americans tend to be associated with denominations that couple a congregational form of polity with an emphasis on an individual relationship with God, while Canadians, on the other hand, have generally been affiliated with churches that are more hierarchically organized and that have served as state religions in Britain (Anglican) and Europe (Roman Catholic).

Previous findings with regard to comparative associational patterns in the United States and Canada have been somewhat mixed. One comparative study (Curtis 1971), based on data drawn from the United States in 1960 and Canada in 1968, revealed that membership in voluntary organizations across the two countries was basically equivalent in nature: when one excluded memberships in unions, 51 percent of Canadians and 50 percent of Americans reporting such memberships, with 31 percent of Canadians and 29 percent of Americans reported multiple associational memberships. On the other hand, Lipset (1986, 135), using data collected by the Center for Applied Research in the Apostolate (CARA) in 1982, contended that "Americans are much more likely to belong to voluntary associations than Canadians." These data revealed that only 58 percent of Canadians reported membership in some type of association (including unions), while 76 percent of Americans did so (including unions).

Such differences in findings result, in part, from definitional issues. As noted above, differences in the levels of associational membership can be a function

Table 10.2 Religious Beliefs by Country

	Canada % Agree	U.S. % Agree	Canada Mean	U.S. Mean	Eta
The concept of God is an old superstition	22.2	9.6	2.08	1.51	.22***
Human beings are not special creation	39.6	20.9	1.68	1.94	.24***
Salvation through life, death, and resurrection of Jesus Christ	63.1	84.3	3.50	4.32	.28***
Jesus Christ was not the divine son of God	19.2	11.9	2.08	1.62	.18***
Bible is the inspired word of God	65.2	83.3	3.54	4.24	.25***
I have committed my life to Christ	35.4	59.9	2.54	3.44	.28***
One doesn't need to go to church to be a good Christian	82.6	68.0	4.15	3.62	.18***
All great religions are equally true	66.6	54.6	3.55	3.15	.12***

of the fact that some studies may include union membership as a form of voluntary associational membership, while others do not. But, an even more important factor potentially affecting levels of associational membership is whether or not church membership is included in the domain of associational membership. The 1982 study employed by Lipset employed church membership as one form of associational membership, while the earlier study did not. Thus, given the religious differences between the United States and Canada as revealed in Tables 10.1 and 10.2, it is not surprising that differences in patterns of voluntary association across the two countries emerge when church membership is taken as one form of associational membership.

But what patterns were evident in 1996, nearly a decade and a half later—particularly when membership in "religious or church related groups" is used instead of church membership per se as a reflection of associational activity?[7] Table 10.3 begins to address this question. The data reveal that Americans were more likely than Canadians to report some form of associational membership (52 percent to 45 percent, respectively), with Americans also being more likely than Canadians to report memberships in two or more such associations (48 percent to 40 percent, respectively).

While the level of associational membership in the United States exceeds that of Canada in this 1996 survey, the level to which Americans are involved in voluntary associations may have declined over the past three decades.

Consistent with Putnam's contentions that America has exhibited a decline in associational membership over the past several decades, the level of associational membership in the United States revealed in this 1996 survey, with 52 percent of Americans reporting such memberships, stands lower than the 62 percent reported by Americans in a major survey conducted in 1967 (Verba & Nie 1972, 176). On the other hand, while fewer Americans today may be members of some voluntary association, those who are members appear to be more broadly involved than Americans three decades ago. Only 39 percent of Americans reported that they were members of two or more such organizations in 1967 (Verba & Nie 1972, 176), but 48 percent of Americans did so in 1996. Thus, whereas fewer Americans may be involved in voluntary associations today than in the past, those who are so involved appear to be more extensively involved than their counterparts several decades ago.

Do the religious differences noted earlier between Canada and the United States become evident when one examines involvement in "religious or church related" associations? Not surprisingly, Americans are much more likely than Canadians to report membership in such groups (33 percent of American compared to 20 percent of Canadians). But, the frequency with which Americans and Canadians reported membership in such groups is much higher than that found in some previous surveys of membership in religious groups. For example, the Verba and Nie study of 1967 found that only 6 percent of Americans reported membership in "church-related groups, such as women's auxiliary,

Table 10.3 Patterns of Associational Membership in Canada and the United States, 1996

	Canada	U.S.
Associational member		
Non-member	55%	48%
Member	45%	52%
Number of associational memberships		
None	55%	48%
One	5%	4%
Two or more	40%	48%
Membership in "Religious or church-related group"		
No	80%	67%
Yes	20%	33%
Pattern of association membership outside of "church-related" group		
Non-member	56%	49%
Member of some association outside the church	44%	51%
Report of volunteering in associational group		
Non-member	55%	48%
Member, but no volunteering	4%	4%
Member, plus volunteering	41%	48%

Bible groups" (Verba & Nie 1972, 42). During the past several decades, there has been a growing emphasis on "small group" ministry with many Christian churches. Whether this increase in membership in such "church related" groups is a reflection of such an emphasis is unclear from these data, but certainly such an increase is consistent with that particular strategy of church ministry.

Given these differences in membership with regard to "religious or church related" groups across the two settings, are the overall associational membership differences between Canada and the United States simply a function of differences in membership related to "religious or church related" groups? If one were to eliminate membership patterns with regard to such religious groups, would the differences across the two countries diminish or disappear? Simply stated, the answer is "no." As can be seen in the lower half of Table 10.3, cross-national differences continue to be evident even when membership in "religious or church related" groups is eliminated from the analysis—51 percent of Americans and 44 percent of Canadians report memberships outside such groups.

Finally, Table 10.3 displays the extent to which respondents not only report membership but report volunteering activity within such organizations as well. Obviously, membership in a voluntary association does not reveal whether or not such a member engaged in any activity related to that association. The bottom portion of Table 10.3 addresses this issue, and the data reveal that relatively few Canadians and Americans limit their associational activity to membership alone. The overwhelming majority of those who report some form of associational membership also report engaging in some volunteer work related to the association of which they are a member. For both Canadians and Americans, associational membership also entails volunteer work; the two, regardless of context, go hand-in-hand.

Table 10.4 presents the specific kinds of associational memberships broken down by reported levels of church attendance, while controlling for the country of residence. As noted earlier, respondents were asked about membership with regard to fourteen different types of groups, and level of reported membership is presented according to whether the respondent reported a low, medium, or high level of church attendance.[8]

What is striking about Table 10.4 are the relatively consistent patterns that are evident. First, the likelihood that membership with a particular associational group increases as level of church attendance increases is generally consistent across the two countries. As level of church attendance increases, the reported level of membership tends to increase as well—regardless of the particular types of associational category analyzed. There are only three exceptions to these otherwise consistent monotonic patterns across the two countries. One exception relates to environmental groups, where medium church attenders are modestly more likely to be members than are high church attenders. The other two exceptions relate to "community or neighborhood" groups and "support or care" groups, where differences between medium and high church attenders tend to be more marginal in nature.

Second, the percentage of respondents reporting membership in some group within each particular category is generally consistent across the two countries as well—even when one controls for level of church attendance. For example, only 5 percent of low-church-attending Canadians reported membership in a "religious or church related" group, whereas 55 percent of the high-church-attending Canadians do so; the comparable figures are 7 percent for low-church-attending and 59 percent for high-church-attending Americans. Rarely do the percentages found in comparable categories across the two countries deviate by a few percentage points.

What about volunteer activity beyond mere group membership? Are those who exhibit high levels of church attendance also likely to engage in high levels of voluntary activity as well? Do those from different religious traditions tend to exhibit different patterns of voluntary activity? And, finally, do those who belong to "religious or church related" groups tend to confine their associational memberships and involvement to such groups?

Analysis revealed that levels of church attendance, both in Canada and the

Table 10.4 Pattern of Membership in Voluntary Associations by Level of Church Attendance Controlling for Country

Membership in Voluntary Association Group Category	Canada Church Attendance			U.S. Church Attendance		
	Low N = 1866	Med. N = 497	High N = 619	Low N = 1193	Med. N = 609	High N = 1185
Professional or job-related group	17%	27%	26%	20%	27%	27%
Social service group	8%	14%	15%	8%	11%	18%
Religious or church-related group	5%	36%	55%	7%	35%	59%
Environmental group	6%	10%	5%	9%	11%	8%
Youth work group	7%	16%	16%	11%	17%	23%
Health-related group	14%	29%	22%	17%	25%	26%
Recreational group	7%	16%	12%	7%	12%	16%
Senior citizen group	16%	26%	24%	13%	20%	20%
Veterans group	5%	11%	18%	6%	8%	18%
Women's group	3%	4%	4%	7%	9%	11%
Political group	4%	9%	14%	5%	11%	16%
Support or care group	5%	9%	8%	7%	12%	9%
Cultural or educational group	11%	23%	33%	13%	20%	31%
Community or neighborhood group	15%	26%	22%	20%	27%	26%

United States, are related to volunteer activity—even when such volunteer activity is confined totally to those groups that are not specifically "religious or church related" groups. Thus, for example, a majority of high-church-attending Canadians and Americans not only report membership in voluntary associations outside the church, but report engaging in voluntary work with such groups as well (57 percent of high-church-attending Canadians and 55 percent of high-church-attending Americans—data not shown).

Since both organizational membership and involvement are tied to political participation, it is likely then that those factors that affect variation in political participation will likely be associated with variation in these measures of social capital as well. Thus, the lower levels of social engagement in Canada may be a function of differential levels of other factors (e.g., education and race) that have been found to be associated with levels of political participation as well—rather than to religious differences across the two settings.

Table 10.5 examines the relationships between several sociodemographic variables (specifically, sex, race, age, and education) and a single, combined additive index tapping both memberships in social organizations and voluntary activity within them (which, for the ease of reporting, may be occasionally referred to as the index of civic engagement). The same table also examines the relationship between this combined index of civic engagement and two variables tapping religious characteristics of the respondent (specifically, religious tradition and church attendance).

The values of eta reported in Table 10.5 reflect the variation in the sociodemographic categories rather than variation cross-nationally. The value of eta for cross-national differences related to the index of civic engagement is .10 (data not shown). Thus, if one wishes, for example, to assess whether differences in some particular sociodemographic variable outweigh "cultural" differences between the two countries, then the value of eta for that variable as presented in Table 10.5 needs to exceed .10 for this civic engagement index.

With regard to variation in levels of civic engagement, significant differences emerge between males and females—with females being much more likely to report membership and voluntary activity than males in both settings. But while such gender differences persist within both cultural contexts, these differences are not nearly as great as the national differences evident. Likewise, national differences persist across both racial categories. Regardless of whether respondents are white or not, those respondents who are from the United States were much more socially engaged than those from Canada. Thus, both country and race are associated with differential levels of social capital (as measured by civic engagement).

Generally speaking, organizational membership and voluntary activity is curvilinearly related to age—those younger than 35 and those 55 or older are less likely to be socially engaged than those who are 35 to 54 years of age. National differences are not as strongly related as age to civic engagement. Nevertheless, national differences persist in civic engagement across all three age categories.

Table 10.5

Mean Scores on Index of Membership and Volunteer Activity by Social and Religious Characteristics Controlling for Country

| | Index of Membership and Volunteer Activity | | |
	Canada	U.S.	Eta
Sex			
Male	2.83	3.56	
Female	3.23	4.35	.07
Race			
White	3.04	4.10	
Non-white	3.03	3.61	.01
Age			
Under 35	2.14	2.96	
35-54	3.64	4.84	
55 plus	3.35	4.06	.16
Education			
HS or less	2.01	2.01	
Voc. tech.	3.02	4.27	
Some college	3.26	4.38	
College graduate	3.64	5.25	
Post-grad	5.36	6.33	.29
Church attendance			
Rarely	1.67	2.00	
Occasionally	2.50	2.85	
Periodically	4.47	4.13	
Regularly	4.41	4.60	
Frequently	5.65	6.33	.32
Religious tradition			
Evangelical Protestant	4.40	3.94	
Mainline Protestant	4.13	4.85	
Black Protestant	1.96	5.00	
Roman Catholic	2.65	3.65	
Other	2.37	3.31	.16

Education is strongly related to levels of civic engagement—those with higher levels of education are much more likely to report increased levels of organizational membership and involvement. But the impact of country on this relationship is less consistent; it is only among those who report more than a high school level of education that Americans begin to exhibit greater civic engagement than their educational counterparts in Canada.

Church attendance is also strongly related to civic engagement; higher levels of reported church attendance are monotonically and strongly related to higher levels of organizational membership and activity. And, once again, national differences continue to persist with regard to the relationship between church attendance and civic engagement; generally speaking, across almost all levels of reported church attendance, Canadians are less likely to report civic organizational membership and activity than their religious counterparts in the United States.

Finally, Table 10.5 presents the relationship between religious tradition and civic engagement within Canada and the United States. The United States is home to large numbers of those who belong to churches tied with the evangelical Protestant and black Protestant traditions. Previous analysis of these data (Smidt 1999) revealed that Roman Catholics tended to exhibit relatively high levels of social trust compared to those within other religious traditions, while black Protestants exhibited the lowest such ranking of social trust across the religious traditions analyzed. Yet, despite their relatively high levels of reported social trust, Roman Catholics tended to be relatively unengaged socially in the United States—ranking only ahead of those who fall into the "other" category in terms of religious tradition. Likewise, despite their ranking lowest in reported levels of interpersonal trust, those affiliated with the black Protestant tradition ranked the highest in terms of social organizational affiliation and involvement. Cross-national differences, moreover, were not always consistent. Evangelical Protestants in Canada tended to be more civicly engaged than evangelical Protestants in the United States.

Associational Membership and Political Engagement

Obviously, people vary in the number of associational groups with which they may be involved, the particular kinds of associations of which they are a part, and the extent to which such associations may be organized. Civic engagement may well generate trust, foster habits of cooperation, and enhance political participation, but do greater levels of civic engagement necessarily tend to foster higher levels of social trust, habits of cooperation, and increased political participation?

It was shown earlier that a variety of sociodemographic factors are related to one's level of civic engagement. Are then the relationships between the religious variables and one's level of civic engagement simply a function of sociodemographic variation across such religious categories? And, does national residence have an independent effect upon various measures tapping civic engagement? In order to assess the relative effects of these religious variables as well as region itself, a Multiple Classification Analysis (MCA) was run. For the purposes of this analysis, the index tapping civic engagement is used as the dependent variable, while the index tapping social trust is used as an independent variable, positing that increased social trust leads to increased levels of civic engagement. In addition, education, church attendance, religious tradition, and national residence also serve as independent variables, while three sociodemographic variables, specifically, age, race, and gender, are introduced as covariates or control variables in the analysis. The results of this analysis are presented in Table 10.6.

Multiple Classification Analysis is based upon the extent to which the mean values of the dependent variable within different categories of the independent variables deviate from the grand mean, once controls for the various covariate variables and other independent variables have been introduced. Several important points emerge from this analysis. First, education continues to be strongly related to levels of civic engagement, with increases in education being associated with higher levels of such engagement. Even after controls have been introduced, the relationship between the respondents' level of education and level of civic engagement continues to be monotonically related, with the resultant beta for education ranking relatively high at a value of .27.

Second, it is clear that the two religious variables (i.e., church attendance and religious tradition) have an independent impact on civic engagement even

Table 10.6
Social Engagement: A Multiple Classification Analysis

Grand Mean = 3.52	N	Unadjusted Deviation from Grand Mean	Eta	Adjusted for Indep. and Co-Var	Beta
Education					
HS or less	2119	−1.50		−1.40	
Voc. tech	1109	−.04		.11	
Some college	976	.49		.27	
College grad	1031	.93		.88	
Post-grad	751	2.53	.29	2.36	.27
Church attendance					
Rarely	1477	−1.73		−1.70	
Occasionally	1573	−.85		−.82	
Periodically	1103	.77		.61	
Regularly	1038	1.02		1.07	
Frequently	751	2.65	.32	2.69	.31
Religious traidtion					
Evangelical Prot.	1038	.58		−.22	
Mainline Prot.	1185	.97		.72	
Black Protestant	304	1.15		.74	
Roman Catholic	1582	−.49		−.63	
Other	1833	−.72	.16	.08	.11
Social trust index					
Low	758	−1.00		−.76	
2	827	−.47		−.13	
3	1339	−.64		−.56	
4	1556	.47		.38	
High	1462	.86	.15	.57	.11
Country					
Canada	2965	−.47		−.06	
U.S.	2976	.47	.10	.06	.01
Multiple R					.456
Multiple R squared					.208

after controls have been introduced for education, level of social trust, race, age, gender, and national residence. Consistent with the findings of Campbell and Yonish in Chapter 6, church attendance has a stronger impact on such engagement (beta = .31) than does the particular religious tradition with which the respondent is associated (beta = .11)—the mean score for social engagement not only monotonically increases with increased church attendance, but the adjusted mean score jumps considerably as one moves from those who attend church "regularly" to those who attend church "frequently" (from 1.06 more than the grand mean to 2.69 more than the grand mean). And, consistent with the findings of Campbell and Yonish, church attendance rivals, if not exceeds, the importance of education in fostering civic engagement, as the beta for church attendance (.31) exceeds that for education (.27). One important point should also be noted with regard to religious tradition. Specifically, it is clear that, once controls have been introduced for the other variables included in the analysis, the level of social engagement among black Protestants far exceeds the average level of such engagement (the grand mean) and mirrors the level exhibited by mainline Protestants. This pattern is consistent with the findings and contentions of Verba, Schlozman, and Brady (1995) that religious involvement, particularly among those who lack the resources of money, imparts civic skills and engenders civic involvement. On the other hand, it is also clear that, once one controls for the various sociodemographic variables (as well as variation in church attendance across such traditions), the expected level of civic engagement declines among evangelical Protestants and Roman Catholics.

Third, the data in Table 10.6 reveal that increased levels of social trust are positively associated with increased levels of civic engagement. While these two variables are likely to be reciprocally related, it is also true that, once one has controlled for various sociodemographic and religious variables, the "independent" impact of social trust on civic engagement continues to be evident and relatively strong. The beta value for the index of social trust (.11) is the same as that for religious tradition.

Finally, it is also clear from Table 10.6 that national residence no longer has much of an independent impact on civic engagement once controls for the various other variables have been introduced—the beta value for place of residence diminishes to .01.[9] Nevertheless, even after differential levels of church attendance, religious tradition, education, and social trust have been addressed, the mean score for Canadians on the civic engagement variable still resides below the grand mean—suggesting a residue of cultural differences.

Obviously, religious factors help to shape patterns of civic engagement for both Canadians and Americans. But, do religious factors make a further important contribution to political participation, as one shifts from involvement in civil society to involvement in the political sphere? In other words, do religious factors contribute to political engagement beyond what is evident with regard to civic engagement?

In order to address this question, we again conducted a Multiple Classification Analysis but this time employed an index of political participation as the dependent variable. Once again we used education, church attendance, religious tradition, and national residence as the independent variables and age, race, and gender as the three covariates or control variables in the analysis. But, in assessing difference in these reported levels of political participation, we included the index tapping civic engagement (i.e., the additive index tapping both affiliation with social organizations and voluntary activity within such organizations) as an independent variable. The results of this analysis are presented in Table 10.7.

Several important points emerge from this analysis. First, it is clear that civic engagement is closely tied to political participation. Our measure of civic engagement has a strong and monotonic impact on levels of political participation. Scores on political participation not only monotonically increase with each increase in civic engagement, but the adjusted mean score jumps considerably as one moves from those who are "low" in their levels of civic engagement to those who are "medium" and "high" in such engagement (from a value of –.06 below the grand mean to 1.13 more than the grand mean). This strong relationship is reflected in its beta value of .43 as well.

Second, education continues to be moderately related to levels of political participation, with increases in education being associated with higher levels of such participation. Even after controls have been introduced, the relationship between the respondents' level of education and level of participation continues to be evident, with the resultant beta for education ranking relatively high at a value of .15.

Finally, it is clear that the two religious variables (i.e., church attendance and religious tradition) have little direct impact on political participation, once levels of education, civic engagement, country of residence, age, race, and gender have been taken into account. Church attendance continues to have some impact on political participation (beta = .07), but the impact of religious tradition all but vanishes (beta = .02).[10]

Thus, whereas church attendance and religious tradition helped to shape levels of civic engagement, they are less robust in terms of moving people directly into the political realm. But civic engagement has a direct, and profound, impact on political participation. Thus, many of the effects of church attendance and religious tradition on political participation are more indirect, through their particular contribution to civic engagement, than direct in nature. Accordingly, any assessment of the role religion plays in helping to shape political engagement must take into account religion's important contribution to political engagement by means of its indirect influence in shaping differential levels of civic engagement.

Table 10.7
Political Participation: A Multiple Classification Analysis

Grand Mean = 1.14	N	Unadjusted Deviation from Grand Mean	Eta	Adjusted for Indep. and Co-Var	Beta
Education					
HS or less	2105	−.33		−.19	
Voc. tech	1097	−.01		.03	
Some college	971	.08		.02	
College grad	1026	.20		.12	
Post-grad	702	.61	.27	.30	.15
Church attendance					
Rarely	1469	−.25		−.05	
Occasionally	1563	.08		−.02	
Periodically	1094	.22		.14	
Regularly	1031	.08		−.06	
Frequently	745	.24	.17	−.09	.07
Religious traidtion					
Evangelical Prot.	1034	.10		.04	
Mainline Prot.	1180	.12		−.04	
Black Protestant	303	.06		.05	
Roman Catholic	1565	−.06		−.01	
Other	1818	−.10	.09	.01	.02
Index of assoc. membership and volunteer activity					
Non-member	3015	−.42		−.36	
Low	1099	−.06		−.07	
Medium	1051	.47		.40	
High	735	1.13	.48	1.02	.43
Country					
Canada	2945	−.13		−.09	
U.S.	2954	.13	.12	.09	.08
		Multiple R			.529
		Multiple R squared			.279

CONCLUSION

Several conclusions can be drawn from this analysis. First, Americans and Canadians differ in their levels of religious involvement and civic engagement. Americans are more religiously involved and civicly engaged than Canadians.

Second, while the aggregate levels of such involvement and engagement differ across the two countries, the nature of the relationship between religious involvement and civic engagement tends to be identical within both countries. The likelihood of associational membership, almost regardless of the particular nature of such association, increases with growing levels of church attendance reported by Americans and Canadians alike. Increased levels of church attendance, regardless of country, are also associated with increased likelihood of volunteer activity—even when such associational membership and voluntary activity are confined to associational groups that are not specifically religious in nature.

Third, these patterns of association and volunteer activity are related, in part, to the religious traditions with which the respondent is affiliated. Regardless of country, mainline Protestants tend to be the most engaged, and Roman Catholics tend to be less engaged than Protestants as a whole. Because Canada has a higher percentage of Roman Catholics than does the United States, differences in associational activities between the two countries can be attributed, in part, to differences in the distribution of religious traditions across the two settings.

Finally, church attendance and religious tradition help to explain differences in levels of civic engagement well beyond that which can be explained by education, age, gender, race, and differences in social trust alone. On the other hand, such religious factors only help to explain differences in levels of political participation indirectly through civic engagement itself.

Chapter 11

The Language of God
in the City of Man
Religious Discourse and Public Politics
in America

Rhys H. Williams

Religion's place in contemporary American political society is by no means self-evident. We have a religiously and socially pluralist society with an ostensibly secular polity. In such a situation, how does, and how should, religion fit in? This volume has offered, en toto, one answer: religion forms a vital part of civil society and, at least partly through the generation of social capital, helps provide for a richer and more democratic public sphere. As a general response I am in complete agreement. But such a response does not exactly delineate *how* religion should be active when it enters the public sphere— and public politics— directly. One criticism of Putnam's formulation of the concept of social capital is that it does not consider religion as an overtly political force (see Edwards & Foley 1997). And yet such a presence is unavoidable. Religion has too much to say about the shape of social life to sit by and only exert its influence indirectly. Sometimes it simply *must* be political.

I use this chapter to explore religious language and how it works as a discourse of public life. First, I articulate an understanding of "culture" that differs from its common-sense versions. I then examine religious language as a cultural form in-and-of-itself, defining what counts as religious language in terms of making public political claims, and contrast it with other cultural resources available for such purposes. Finally, I consider the ways in which religious lan-

I thank Clarke Cochran for comments on an earlier draft of this chapter.

171

guage has particular advantages, and some disadvantages, for fostering a democratic public politics. These are crucial issues in understanding religion's "cultural power" in American politics (Demerath & Williams 1992; Williams & Demerath 1991, 1998), and its capacity for creating the conditions for democratic participation and a strong civil and political society.

My focus here is on religious language, and it makes a contribution distinct from that of Robert Wuthnow in the following chapter in which he offers an "institutionalist" understanding of religion and social capital that my culturalist focus on language is meant to complement. Similarly, in contrast to Cnaan, Boddie, and Yancey (Chapter 2), Warren (Chapter 4), and Wood (Chapter 5), I am concerned here less with the associational and organizational supports for civil society than I am with the symbolic forms that support democratic life. I believe those associational supports are absolutely essential, and the study of them crucial. However, the cultural forms with which the content of public life and public politics is discussed also matter a great deal. Some public languages open civil society to more voices and democratic debates, others close it. I am interested here in how religion thus participates. Finally, much like John Coleman's chapter in this volume (Chapter 3), I am interested in what makes religion unique as a public language; implicitly I am suggesting that our national life would be impoverished without its contributions— even as I note that not all of its contributions are necessarily *ipso facto* beneficial.

Thus, I present a different approach to religion that both complements and contrasts with what might be termed the "social structural" concerns of the religion-as-voluntary-association perspective that informs much of the work in this collection. I suggest that we think of religion as a "cultural resource" (Williams 1995) that is available to people interested in affecting the workings of public politics. While I do not use the term "social capital" as directly as many of the other authors included here, I assume both its existence and importance. Rather, I ask what happens once religiously motivated people want to influence public politics directly; what languages can they use to express their commitments and their agendas, and with what consequence for the body politic?

RELIGION AS A CULTURAL RESOURCE

To call religion a part of "culture" seems painfully obvious, but it can entail an important shift in analytic perspective. Culture can be conceptualized as more than the beliefs, attitudes, and values held by individuals. Certainly individuals' beliefs and values influence their behavior, thus affecting politics. But our understanding of culture need not be so restricted.

Culture can also be thought of as a type of "symbolic currency" that is used to express, interpret, and justify our actions to others as well as to ourselves. Language, including religious language, is a "cultural resource" that political actors use to engage in public affairs. Cultural resources, like material resources, can be used or misused, and are differentially distributed within society. Certainly there are differences between symbolic currency and material resources, and these differences are important in understanding how political culture works.[1] But the important point for my argument here is that culture is a public phenomenon—a collection of symbol sets to which many different actors have access. Consequently, the impact religion has on democratic politics in terms of its being a cultural resource is distinct from its impact with regard to voluntary associations and organizations.

This is so, at least in part, because religious cultural forms—unlike organizational memberships—are not necessarily confined to those who are active participants in religious institutions. Religious language, as a particular embodiment of culture, may originate within a specific confessional tradition. But when it becomes public—which it must if it is to influence politics on a cultural level—it cannot remain overtly sectarian. Once religious language crosses social boundaries, its interpretations, meanings, and impact are open to variation and contestation (Williams 1999b). This is, in essence, what it means to be public. Those who originate cultural messages cannot control them completely, nor control who else may choose to adopt and use them. Religious language can transcend any particular organization or social group and have a truly public presence.

Thus, questions as to whether religious *language* opens or closes space for democratic participation are distinct from the associational issues of social capital. Much religious language, particularly within Christian traditions, is universalizing and, at least in principle, opposed to the exclusionary sentiments found in nationalism, nativism, or other forms of social distinction. It forms a rationale for what in this volume is often referred to as "bridging" social capital—that is, social capital that creates relationships across social boundaries. And yet, religious language is not always a call for inclusion; a deep theme in American religious and political culture is the divide between the elect and the unregenerate, the saved and the damned, the morally pure and the unworthy. What is sometimes called "bonding" social capital comes into play here—the strengthening of internal ties within a social group, but at the expense of closing out (or even creating) outsiders. There is in religious language, therefore, the potential for simultaneous contributions to opening and closing political society.

RELIGION'S RELATION TO THE STATE
AND POLITICAL SOCIETY

An important distinction with regard to my understanding of religious language in public politics is that between and among the terms "state," "political society," and "civil society." The distinction is theoretically important (e.g., Casanova 1994) and can be shown to have important societal consequences (e.g., Demerath 1994; Demerath & Straight 1997). Briefly, the state is still use-fully conceptualized in Weber's terms as the set of organizations that have the legitimate monopolization on the means of coercion for a given territory. A state "church" or established ecclesia is the obvious model of religious involve-ment in the state, and as such the church's position is impervious to changes in governmental administration.

Political society, on the other hand, is the complex of organizations and social groupings that compete for political power, but are not incorporated into the stable institutions of the state. Religious involvement in political society could involve the sponsorship of political parties, institutionalized interest groups, or lobbying organizations. The distinctions among the state, political society, and civil society are not always perfectly clear, of course. For example, social movement organizations that are formal, bureaucratized, and operate with denominational backing (such as the National Right to Life Committee) would be a dimension of political society; however, more ephemeral social movement activity that draws many of its resources from religious communi-ties, targets "cultural" change, and is loosely organized might well be considered part of civil society.

Religion's relations to the state in the U.S. are quite different from those to political society. In formal terms, the United States is a structurally "secular" state, with a constitutionally mandated disestablishment and prohibitions on state interference with free exercise. The details of church and state relations are more complicated than that, of course, but are not at issue in this chapter. More important here is the historical fact that, in a culture and society as religious as the U.S., a total absence of religion from political life is impossible. Religion is both deeply and broadly relevant to American public life, but more so in cer-tain forms than in others. Religion may not be a formal part of the state appa-ratus nor may the state use religious tests as qualifications for citizenship or interfere (unduly) in the exercise of religion by individuals. But religion is a constituent building block of civil society, and it is a key link between civil soci-ety and the state through the institutions and practices of political society. Thus, if we are to understand how religious social capital can influence public life, we must examine the ways in which religion affects political society. Given that concern, I turn to a consideration of religious language and its particular properties as a cultural resource for public political discourse.

RELIGION AND RELIGIOUS LANGUAGE

Asking whether religion in the abstract is an acceptable component of demo-cratic politics leads attention to the differences among actual embodiments of "religion." There is no unified "religion" in a pluralist society; even as a concept, religion is highly differentiated and contested. Even the "same" religion, based on doctrinal, ideological, or denominational categories, is not a unified whole in different contexts. This goes beyond the obvious recognition that not all Catholics, Jews, or Muslims have identical political attitudes, or that contemporary "liberal" Protestantism is made up of several groups who, a century ago, were labeled "evangelical" Protestants. It calls notice to the fact that the phenomena and processes that constitute "religion" are sometimes a matter of public contest. Is theism necessary for religion? Is an institutional home necessary for religion? Is an organized community of believers necessary for religion? These are more than matters of academic definition—they haunt Supreme Court decisions on conscientious objection, holiday displays on public property, organized school prayer, and legitimate drug use. In fact, several Supreme Court decisions have treated any form of belief that *may function* for the *individual* as a religion, to be equivalent to any traditional religion (Demerath & Williams 1992). Within a pluralist society what counts as religion itself cannot be completely neutral politically.

Thus, there are cultural issues in understanding religion and public life that are separate from the study of religious organizations and institutions. Religious language has its own distinct relationship to public politics and the public sphere. In an age of mass politics, national campaigns, social mobility, and electronic media-driven communication, politics depends on language—its symbolic embodiments—for its enactment. Politics is less about social networks and bounded societal groups than it once was, as we now live in a political world in which language is the symbolic currency for identity, coalition building, and the tracking of political victories and defeats. Understanding how religious language works in this mix is important. Of course, culture has always been important for politics. Social structures exist in cultural terms, political life must always be interpreted, and power without meaningful authority is notoriously unstable.

But there is a good argument that our public politics is increasingly "mediated." Michael Schudson's book *The Good Citizen* (1998) makes this point through an examination of the historical development of American definitions of the meaning of "citizenship." We currently live in an age characterized by a "politics of information," where being a good citizen involves knowledge of many issues, candidates, and policies. In this hyper-informational political culture, the sheer task of knowledge mastery is almost impossible; hence, the forms in which information is presented become crucial. Attention to media and language has never been more important to the processes of both governing and trying to change government. The implicit shared culture that binds citizens together in a more homogeneous society is now absent in the United States. Language-based politics must present ideas and issues explicitly, being less able to rely on shared assumptions; the symbolic currency of language now carries more of the informational and political load. There is a certain irony in the fact that our increasingly pluralist society is increasingly reliant on mass media and shared symbolic repertoires to govern our national life. It makes the understanding of religious language all the more imperative.

Parallel to the rise of an informational political culture is concern with the organizational health of religious institutions. A good case can be made that cultural institutions control less and less of our collective life. Voluntarism has expanded from a principle of institutional organization to a cultural norm that celebrates individual autonomy and discretion (see Williams 1998). Nowhere is this truer than in contemporary religion, where there is a proliferation of churches and religious options. This proliferation is celebrated as a healthy plu-ralism by advocates of a religious open market (e.g., Finke & Stark 1992), while it is bewailed by critics worried about the splintering of institutional authority and societal inter-connectedness (e.g., Bellah et al. 1985; Hammond 1992; Roof 1993). Our organizational pluralism may or may not be a sign of institu-tional crisis. But, regardless, we live in an increasingly "media-ated" culture in which language has a central political role; religious language is one important medium for collective action, and *the* major medium for public religious expression.

What Is Religious Language?

What makes a language religious rather than secular? What makes a language religious rather than merely "moral"? It is plausibly argued that a constitutive characteristic of American religion is its focus on morality (e.g., Thomas 1989). Indeed, religious conflict in the U.S. has more often been about contested morality than about theological disputes. And the moral consequences of changed lives is taken, in popular culture, as the hallmark of religious conver-sion. Moreover, all ideological language is moral in that it posits an ideal world that "should" be and counterposes it to the tainted world that "is" (Williams 1996). A symbolically constructed "good society" is the prescriptive goal of ide-ologically sponsored political change (Williams 1995). Thus, if all moralized political language is considered to be religious, there would be no real nonreli-gious political language. While this may reinforce parts of Weber's "Protestant ethic" thesis—in that it notes the extent to which American culture is saturat-ed by desectarianized religious themes—such a conflation is not helpful for the problems posed in this chapter.

As a definitional matter, I assume that to be religious, a political language must ground its public claims in a transcendent authority outside society. Beyond just a moral base, it must be a transcendently anchored authority. Moreover, that transcendent authority must be hooked to some sort of supreme or divine source. I do not want to go so far as to demand theism, but mere calls to "natural law" are not enough to make a language religious. Natural law lan-guage may draw upon a transcendent, externally generated authority, but it need not be so grounded. The apocryphal story in this regard is that of the French astronomer who was explaining the mathematics of star movement to Napoleon. "And where is God in your scheme?" Napoleon is reported to have asked. The telling reply, "I have no need of that hypothesis."

To my mind this illustrates why natural law language was useful to the framers as a mode of expression. It captured the deist sympathies many shared and, in that sense, it was a faithful representation of their understanding of the relationship between humans and their creator. However, natural law language had the political advantage of being importantly vague on traditional religious questions. As a language form, natural law was generic enough to finesse most potential quarrels that might have arisen from the use of a sectarian language. By refraining from any particular faith's expression, the framers did not invite adherents of that faith to counter with their own interpretation of religious authority; nor did they goad those of other faiths to dissent. Natural law rhetoric legitimated action through a trans-societal authority but did not invoke specific identities, or the potential for constraints coming from those specific identities. In sum, natural law language is a moralized language for political action, and is available for religious interpretation, but it is not in itself religious.

Jasper (1992) divides political rhetoric into what he calls "instrumental" and the "moralist" modes. The former is a rhetoric of politics grounded in natural law or universal truths; these are *in principle* revealed truth. Moralist rhetoric, on the other hand, is that which invokes specific transcendent warrants—usually a version of "God"—as the authority for action. While both sources of authority lie outside society, natural laws, by their very law-like character, are predictable once discovered. In that way, instrumental rhetoric is a rhetoric of control. Moralist rhetoric, according to Jasper, is more often proscriptive and rigid than prescriptive and contingent. As a result, moralist arguments form a rhetoric of obedience that draws clear boundaries between the righteous and the fallen.[2] The difference between natural law's promise of potential control, and religious language's ultimate dependence on obedience is, in my view, crucial for understanding the differing political consequences of the two rhetorical forms.

Both natural law and religious language can be used to preempt political debate. They recognize and call upon absolute goods—values that are irreducible to any other values. Both rhetorics center their claims outside society and human teleology; they are "metasocial" warrants (Jasper 1992, 318)—or as Kenneth Burke calls them "god terms." In that way, both are antithetical to the pragmatic, compromise style of liberal politics.

But their different modes for apprehending their truths and their differing relationships to the "right" course of action are significant. Natural laws are discoverable and predictable, a knowledge potentially without limit. Religious language—that language with a transcendent authority that in some way embodies "God"—by contrast contains the potential for its own limitations. The source of authority is only discoverable, not humanly created; and the authority is something beyond impersonal law-like principles. Religious language thus stops short of the ultimate manifestation of its own implications. The limits of human knowing—not just in practice but in principle—put ultimate brakes on what human political actors can claim. That is, natural law limits humans in that there may still be undiscovered laws, but there is no necessary limit on human capacity to know the truth. On the other hand, humans cannot with certainty know the breadth and depth of the divine mind "that passeth all understanding." And, thus, religious truth is ultimately a logic of obedience. Science, with its principle of potentially limitless knowledge, makes all things possible to human society and institutions; religion, in principle, puts brakes on those ambitions of power and control.

RELIGIOUS LANGUAGE AS POLITICAL DISCOURSE

I reiterate that I establish this particular definition of religious language insofar as I am concerned with politics and the public sphere. How people define their religious commitments to themselves and others is my concern only when those definitions are used by people acting as citizens in public affairs. I am saying nothing about the intrinsic character or reality of religion itself, nor do I deny that people may find religious significance in natural law or human potential. What constitutes religious language (and I recognize that the analytic distinctions I have delineated are often difficult to discern empirically) matters because of the ways in which religious language works as political discourse. In this section I want to consider several characteristics of religious language as political discourse that distinguish it from other forms of political language.

Religious Language is Democratically Available

As a form of political claimsmaking, religious language is democratically available. Given the pluralism in American religion, perhaps I should say that religious *languages* are available. However, not every religious language is available to every person—some are differentially available by tradition. But, when considering the wide identification with religion in American society, and the presumptive legitimacy that religion generally enjoys both legally and culturally, there is only one other public discourse—"rights talk" (Glendon 1991)—that can rival religion as a medium for public claims.

Consider several other forms of political language. For example, in contrast to the language of "identity politics," religious discourse is authoritatively available to people across ethnoracial, gender, or class lines. While all people may in principle be able to use gender or racial position as part of a political claim, such status is eminently contestable as a source of political authority. In fact, whether one is even allowed to claim such an identity as a source of moral authority is restricted. This is so because the lines of dominant/subordinate status are clear when one considers race or gender, and those divisions privilege or obstruct certain groups from authoritative claimsmaking. Historically, racial minorities and women were denied public authority based on identity. And, among some social movements using identity politics today, one must be able to claim the subaltern status in order to speak authoritatively to its injustice. In either case, access to the moral authority of ascriptive identity is never universal.[3]

A second common discourse of public politics, scientific expertise, is also differentially distributed within society. Not only are some people trained in science while others are not, but access to such training is socially stratified. This world of professional expertise is so circumscribed socially and culturally that it can be considered to have a distinctive politics (e.g., Brint 1994). But, beyond the political demographics of such knowledge, the very core of "expertise" as a knowledge form is premised on the idea of restricted access. The extent to which technical expertise is readily available or easily comprehensible is the extent to which it is less valued. It is only as a type of "priesthood" that expertise has credence, something that stands in marked contrast to the "priesthood of all believers" that animates most American religion.

Finally, interest-based constituency representation is also, by definition, a scarce resource. Any constituency can have only so many authorized representatives, and, to the extent that their interests are organized, access is even further restricted. The essence of formal organization is restricting authority along a hierarchy. "Organizations" usually imply "leaders," and formal organization in a bureaucratic society is usually justified by legal-rational authority. The entire point of institutionalization, one might argue, is to centralize and consolidate decision-making power. Thus, the ability to claim to represent the interests of a constituency is limited directly by the extent to which those interests are defined, articulated, and organized.

Still, this type of political discourse—namely, the direct, manifest claim to represent the interests of a particular segment of society—is less commonly heard in the U.S. than in many other societies. In American politics, public actors often claim to be pursuing a disinterested, universal "public good" rather than the narrow interested perspectives of a particular constituency (Williams 1995). Even claims by groups such as labor unions are framed at a higher level of generality, such as the abstract "working families." Thus, our political culture is more open to the articulation of values than to interests, and many different moralized languages get used for public claims, including both natural law and religion.

Bergesen (1984) points to structural reasons for this tendency within American public politics. In other places, I have offered culturalist arguments for its existence, one of which is the historical importance of religion and religious identity in American life (Williams 1999a). Certainly the widespread use of "social movement" style politics in the U.S. contributes to this trend, as groups try to avoid being labeled "special interests" by calling for an abstract "public good." Whatever the source of this phenomenon, it strikes me that this aspect of U.S. political culture is distinctive from the political cultures of most European or Latin American countries where corporatist forms of political organization have some history or legitimacy.

In contrast to these alternative forms of discourse, the logic of American religion is, generally, universally available. This is admittedly a culturally contingent dimension of religion. Access to sacred words, and specifically to liturgical truth, is often restricted (Fenn 1982). But the United States' heritage of Reformed Protestantism, leavened by Arminian doctrines of Baptist-oriented denominations and the social experiences of a frontier society, have democratized and individualized access to religious authority (see Hatch 1989). Indeed, many portraits of American religion portray it as a general progression toward individualism in authority and experience (e.g., Hammond 1992; McLoughlin 1978; Roof & McKinney 1987).

This observation about American religion has some affinities with a current critique of American culture and individualism. That critique portrays the difficulties inherent in our "therapeutic culture" (Bellah, et al. 1985), one that prizes individual self-expression above communal ties. Even those who find greater value in the individualistic culture of "personalism" (Lichterman 1996) note that such a culture has a tendency to consider the only true authority to be that which emanates from individual experience. When applied to religious authority, such a perspective means that anyone with the requisite subjectivized individual experience has the authority to pronounce religiously on public issues. As a claimsmaking device, this is effective because such subjectivized experience and authority are unassailable by others. Unlike received tradition or even formal scholarship, others cannot counter claims based on existential experience—even when they are connected to public affairs. While claimsmaking rhetoric based on religious experience as the basis for religious authority is not common, its logic remains in place.

One result of this individualization and experiential emphasis is that religious language is hard to "organize" politically. Organization, by definition, is an ordering, often hierarchical, with a functional division of labor. Its advantages in public politics include the prioritizing of interests, efficiency of expression, and the easy manipulation of resources. Organization helps produce boundaries by creating "members" through its restricting access and making distinctions. But religion's democratic nature makes it difficult to "organize" in the same way, which means it is more available for democratic use.

This is not to say that authority within religious institutions or the authority to speak for organizations is democratically available. Rather, what I am contending is that individualized forms of belief and experience have undermined the religious authority of institutionalized leaders of religious organizations and have attenuated their ability to speak for a constituency or society (see Chaves 1994). Personal autonomy and the authority of personal experience have broadened the realm of who can speak religiously; they have also broadened the range of political actors who can use religious language to ground their public authority. Whether this "democratization" of access to religious authority, however, has diluted its public authority and efficacy is an important, and related, empirical question—one that will be considered below.

Religion as a Primary Group Attachment

As noted above, there is no unified "religion." Many religions have a universalizing message, potentially applicable to all people at all times. This is particularly true for Christianity and Islam, both of which have become worldwide ideologies. Both religions have warrants, deep in their founding stories and scriptures, that point to an ability to transcend the divisions of the world.

On the other hand, religion also has the common effect in public life of producing an exclusionary social world marked by symbolic boundaries. In part, this is in the nature of all identifying language. Defining what or who one is, is simultaneously a process of defining what or who one is not. Identity proceeds through differentiation. Producing distinctions is a form of "cultivating differences" (Lamont & Fournier 1992) and, as a political form, is important to the production and reinforcement of inequality. In this sense, religious identity is necessarily a part of religious and social differences.

Thus, religious language in public politics is often put in the service of reactive, discriminatory, and "organic" forms of nationalism, and in this way stands in tension with political tendencies toward universal expansion and inclusion. In the U.S. today, the organic form of religious exclusion is more often articulated as a civil religious "Americanism" rather than as a call for narrow sectarian exclusion. But the form is nonetheless related to the "primary group" identification of most religious commitments. Religion emanates from family, clan, blood, and the primary group attachments where personal and social identities are first formed. These tend to be ascriptive characteristics that people are less free, or willing, to relinquish. More than beliefs or attitudes are at stake when such commitments are challenged; a natural reaction is to close ranks, expel outsiders, and reassert difference.

This primary group connection reinforces what is, for many, the essential religious division—that between the saved and the damned, the elect and the unregenerate. This sectarian and often Manichean distinction is available in the religious understandings common in American culture, whatever the universal and inclusive dimensions of our heritage. The Reformed Calvinism that inspired Puritans to establish a "New Jerusalem" has been filtered through Arminian and voluntaristic tendencies so that the symbolic differences between the community and outsiders have been translated into bright lines dividing the worthy from the undeserving. Those outside the community of saints are often the charges or wards of the elect, in that their conversion—or at least their social control—is a political and moral duty of the community (Williams 1999a). Religion has been integral to creating the category of the "undeserving," whether it be welfare for the poor or social services for gay men suffering with AIDS. What is termed elsewhere in this volume as "bonding" social capital can be reinforced by religion—one is "with us" or "against us" and that distinction is moralized. Concomitantly, the fact that religion is considered by many to be a voluntary commitment and identity means that religion may be less exclusionary relative to other forms of identity talk. The prospect of regeneration and salvation is, at least in principle, available to all—it can be an "achieved" and not just an ascribed status.

Religion as Motivating Ideology

It is by now an obvious observation to note that religion is a superb motivating force for political involvement. Far from the simplistic nineteenth-century understanding of religion as a pillar of the status quo—whether through a legitimating hegemony or otherworldly quiescence—religion has been at the forefront of many movements for political and social change. The advantages that religious organizations provide for political organizing were noted above. The culturalist dimensions of religion as motivation are also important. This motivation has often been analyzed at the personal or interpersonal level; for example, people for whom religion is important are likely to become politically engaged when they believe that their commitments or values are threatened, or when they understand their religious duty to involve political action.

Beyond that analysis, however, religion can be understood as an ideological form in itself. Religion has great advantage as a movement discourse. It can provide the sense of *injustice,* the sense of *agency,* and the sense of *identity,* that collective action requires (see Williams 1996). That is, religious language points to the wrongs that need to be righted, but it also helps convince people that they are on the side of the right and can do something about the problem. In this way, religious language can reach out to those who are not personally religious, using widely recognized symbols and understandings to make action seem both justified and efficacious. It can do this because religious language can contain both the cognitive and affective components that make political action both possible and committed. Religion is both "ideology," an articulated vision of how the world should be, and "culture," a template for understanding the world, oneself, and their relations. If we think of culture as having cognitive, moral, and emotive components (Jasper 1997, following Parsons), religion is clearly implicated in all those dimensions, both as a force for change as well as for stasis.

However, as a political framework, religious language may produce a trade-off between the depth of the passion people bring to their causes and the breadth of their concerns. This is particularly true in institutionally differentiated societies where religion is regarded as having a "separate sphere" or a home domain. For many Americans, the "private sphere" is seen as religion's particular purview and great passion can be summoned for issues relevant to that domain. One need only see the extent to which particular issues, policies, and legal decisions regarding gender, sexuality, and family relations have galvanized religiously based political groups in the U.S. These matters have widespread resonance as "religious" or "moral" issues. Concomitantly, mobilized concern with international politics, economic justice, or other fundamental social structures is limited to small groups at the ideological edges. Despite the diligent attempts by activists on the Right to moralize those domains of policy, their messages have not produced the passion associated with "family values." And religious movements of the Left, while having had some success with peace and disarmament issues, have not been able to focus public attention on other public societal issues. Cochran (1990) notes that religious language is important in that it connects public and private life. But, it does not connect the passions of private life equally to all elements of public politics.

Religion as Resonant Rhetoric

The three factors listed so far go some distance, in my view, toward explaining religious language's attractiveness as a medium for political expression. They focus on what might be called "internal" properties of the language—on the characteristics that make it available and useful to public actors. In a sense they focus on the language itself as well as on issues of access to religious language.

A distinct question is that of the power or efficacy of religious language—its impact on publics and issues outside of the actors who are wielding the rhetoric. This can be called an issue of "resonance," where resonance refers to the receptiveness audiences have to public claims. Political actors are free to use whatever rhetoric they think might appeal to their supporters, bystanders, or others. But, some rhetorics resonate better than others—they "work" better, so to speak. Resonance occurs when particular claims align with the previous experiences, narratives, or cultural worldviews of the people who hear the claims.

The key paradox for any public claim is that it must resonate with both the group using it to express its public concerns/agenda and with groups outside that particular collective actor. Any message that is too internal, parochial, or self-referential will fail to connect—at the most extreme it can seem unintelligible to those across group lines. Thus, a public language must emerge for a truly public politics to be possible. The language that will resonate most effectively in a public setting must be available widely enough to reach across group lines, even while it maintains a particular content for particular groups. But the very public-ness of such a language means that claimsmakers cannot control completely the interpretations others put on their rhetoric (Williams 1995, 1999b).

Both the historical legacy of religion in the U.S. and the continued widespread religious commitment among Americans make religious language widely resonant among a variety of populations. Further, there are religious themes deeply embedded in American political culture (Williams 1999a). Our nation and its polity have been understood as deeply connected to a divine plan. One need not believe that a full blown "civil religion" exists in order to recognize the intimate intertwining of U.S. political history with religious understandings. As a result, the use of religious language places political actors within a legitimate tradition, providing legitimacy for both *participation* in public life and for the particular *claims* (the identification of problems *and* solutions) being made.

In sum, there are both "production"-oriented reasons (democratic availability; primary attachment; motivating force) and "reception"-oriented reasons (cultural resonance) for public political actors to adopt religious language. Whatever language political actors choose, it must recruit new supporters to join the cause, persuade bystanders who are not active on the issue that the cause is legitimate, and neutralize opponents' attacks. Religious language expresses and mobilizes the commitments of those already engaged with an issue; moreover, religious language is widely available and can express concern with regard to many different kinds of issues, whether for stasis or change. Thus, those "producing" a social movement can find religion useful (Williams 1996). And religious language resonates across many publics, is easily understood as a cultural lingua franca, and is presumptively legitimate—therefore making it an effective language for "reception"-oriented reasons. Political challenges that might not be accepted if based on secular justifications—because of the issue involved or because of the social status of the group making the challenge—can be articulated with religious languages.

THE SPACE FOR DEMOCRATIC PARTICIPATION

For both production and reception reasons, religious language is an available and attractive discourse with which to frame calls for social change (or resistance to change). The next question to be addressed, and one central to the current concern with religion and social capital, is the extent to which this discourse affects public life by opening space for democratic participation. Which *kinds* of religious language facilitate either the expansion or contraction of this political and cultural space?

First, consider how religious language opens the participatory field. I begin with the basic observation that religious language is a cultural resource for those social groups that have few conventional political resources, such as money, votes, or insider connections. Religious language can circumvent these obstacles. Political outsiders can use their cultural resources to "moralize" an issue (Williams & Demerath 1991); this is particularly effective when the issue goes public. Public religious language can reach across group boundaries to offer a widely available rationale for change. In order to use this resource, the religious language must be available for use. This does not mean that religious *truth* or institutional authority must be democratically available, only that the rhetoric of religious duty, transcendent authority, and moral order must be available and articulated. Given the general preference in American religious culture for individual authority and experience, that has not been a difficult bar for many religious languages to leap.

Next, religious language with an inclusive component complements the mass democratic impulses of contemporary politics. A universalizing message that is potentially applicable to all persons and all times can include all people in the relevant moral community. This makes their interests and values worthy of attention and respect. When combined with a language of redemption and reconciliation, this can produce a political culture that attempts to encompass and transcend differences—even across other structural cleavages such as class or ethnicity.

Finally, the contribution to opening space for participation in American politics comes not just from the structure of religious language, but from an important dimension of the way religious language envisions the *content* of the good society. A central language of American politics is that of individualism and rights; this is our classical liberal heritage, a cultural vocabulary drawn from the economic metaphors that undergird such concepts as the "social contract." According to critics from both Left and Right, this language is too often the hegemonic vocabulary of American politics. And, indeed, one can argue that the language of rights is the most universal and available language in American politics, even more so than religion. However, in many versions of social contract theory, rights are available only to "citizens," or members of the polity. Those outside the political community can be denied rights. Many of the applications for citizen status in American history, such as the civil rights movement, have been framed in religious terms; the argument is, in effect, that there is a set of principles that predate and preempt the idea of citizen rights.[4]

Whether or not the rights talk of liberalism is our fundamental discourse, language based on the liberal assumptions of the social contract and predicated on the protection of individual rights as the hallmark of a good society is a powerful cultural theme in our politics. It has certainly helped open the cultural space in the public arena for the participation of a variety of disenfranchised groups. But, importantly, it is not a rich language for expressing social relationships. In liberal rights talk most social relations are reduced to the logic of the economic contract—individualized, rational, self-interested, and ultimately provisional. Further, the notion of justice that is associated with such language is almost entirely procedural, with attention focused on the means by which justice is administered, rather than the ends or substantive outcomes.

Certainly there are religious languages that have some of these characteristics. Capitalist individualism and Protestantism certainly grew up together. However, many religious languages are fundamentally "relational"; they center not on the self-interested autonomous "man" but rather upon a series of relationships, between the divine and humankind, between the people of God and other peoples, and between the individual and the community. As Bromley and Busching (1988) point out, this relational logic is often "covenantal" and in contrast to the contract language of liberalism. In effect, such religious language in public politics provides another vocabulary for those whose lives are not captured by the dominant terms of debate. Whether this alternative language is effective is an important, if distinct, issue; nonetheless, the relational character of religious language is potentially counter-hegemonic.

However, there is a counter dynamic to these processes of democratic participation. Religious rhetoric on political issues often assumes the forms of "god terms"—terms that require no justification beyond themselves and serve to close debate rather than open it (Jasper 1992). An unquestioned source of moral authority, providing nonambiguous answers to social problems and articulated in the form of pronouncements, preempts public debate and eliminates alternative formulations. Further, the moral content of such language is often portrayed as uncompromisable, removing it completely from the necessary work of policy formation (see Williams & Demerath 1991). In other words, actors who have framed their claims as moral imperatives cannot easily "ratchet down" their demands to accept less on the grounds that it is a necessary compromise. To do so amounts to the selling out of a moral principle and "deal making" in the worst sense of the word. So, while religious language may get actors without conventional political resources to the public table, it may also lock them into strategies that cannot succeed completely.

When religious and moral language is used by persons with institutional claims to religious authority, such as clergy, two processes can have the effect of closing political debate. First, claimsmakers use their expertise to shut off rival interpretations; if those with specialized religious knowledge claim that there is but this one "religious position," a challenging claim is more difficult. Second, expertise in any field, including religion, has the effect of "de-politicizing" issues (Edelman 1977). Issues are removed from the realms of debate, compromise, and explicit articulation of values, and remanded to the specialized areas in which technical experts have a monopoly on authority. It turns a political issue about public life into a technical issue for "administration." Thus, the question as to whether religious language enhances the democratic processes of the public sphere is, in part, a question of the extent to which religious language opens or closes space for other types of languages—most crucially for the art of the compromise and the engagement with practical politics.

THE PUBLIC SPHERE AND RELIGIOUS LANGUAGE

In his influential work on the public sphere, Jürgen Habermas (1989) describes the public sphere not as a place as much as a realm of practical activity. The practices that compose the public sphere involve open debate, rational "speech-acts," and attempts at achieving a mutually emancipatory collective life. Habermas decries contemporary liberalism as having reduced the public sphere to a realm of mere "procedural" justice in which substantive visions of society cannot be heard. Nevertheless, his understanding of a truly democratic public sphere involves debate, reason, and process.

In a similar argument, Tipton (1993) claims that the truly American solution to the paradox of religion within America's secular polity is the discourse itself about what that place should be. For him, both classical liberals and communitarians have each illuminated only one side of the necessary dialogue. Communitarians have emphasized the important solidarity functions of religion in public life, warning against the anomie, divisiveness, and unchecked power that can arise from a completely secularized political life. Classical liberals counter that individual rights are paramount and that freedom is constituted by liberty from the external imposition of nonvoluntary obligations; religious freedom is thus only possible when the government is completely separated from any religious expression. Tipton notes that communitarians slight the importance of guaranteeing freedom for religious minorities, while liberals are insufficiently concerned with how public life is affected by the lack of a shared ethos. As with Habermas's conception of the public, Tipton argues that only when the dialectic is allowed to engage both understandings is the polity truly in balance.

These understandings of how a democratic public life is created clearly have room for the participation of religious voices. Indeed, one can make the stronger claim that religion must be included to have democratic politics. For reasons enunciated above, religious language has many qualities that contribute to democracy and social inclusion. However, there is a potential counter-argument to this inclusive vision. Habermas's formulation of the public sphere, and Tipton's call for the inclusion of religious voices into a give-and-take dialogue on public life, imply that only some forms of religious language can truly be legitimate. Forcing religion to conform to the demands of the liberal polity in order to be legitimate may well limit legitimacy to "liberal religion"—that is, religion that is willing to be tentative with its certainty, to compromise on moral issues as well as on forms of polity, and to accept its status as but one player in a multi-party game. Cochran (1990) recognizes this dilemma and notes that, as religious ideas are translated in the terms of American political discourse, they lose something of their distinctiveness:

> To speak only in terms accessible to public reason is to make the border area irrelevant. In this case there would be no religion-political interaction, only *political* argument (1990, 90; emphasis in original)

The resulting political argument could too easily be reduced to merely winning and losing particular issue battles and thereby forfeiting exactly what can be religion's particular contribution—a moral vision of the greater good of the community. On the other hand, if that substantive vision is offered in terms that brook no open debate or practical adjustment based on the values and interests of contending parties, how can a religious language contribute to the practices that compose the public sphere? Is there a deep irony in liberalism—

that for it to work properly it must react illiberally to positions that reject tolerance?

Such a conclusion about liberal democracy reduces, crucially in my view, the space available in the public sphere. It saves democracy by restricting it. And it misses crucial dimensions of religiously motivated political actors and their institutional situations, and of religious language and its cultural character. Sociologically, religiously motivated actors are not only that. They are also people who occupy class positions, ethnic and gender identities, and political statuses. Impulses for nondemocratic action that might arise from religious commitments are often hemmed in—if not completely counter-balanced—by these other structural features. This is, in part, a function of the ways in which institutions work. Institutions defuse the ability of any one social group to have its way totally in collective politics. Institutions have routines, rules, and unintended consequences that can be maddening, but that often means that outcomes are seldom the direct expression of inputs. Thus, even the most undemocratic expressions of religious truth have only the most marginal opportunities to become actual policies. Indeed, the more common consequence of dogmatic religious expression is to galvanize social movement mobilization among groups who oppose the initial religious expression (see Williams 1997).

Alongside institutional dynamics, there are cultural reasons why even nonliberal religious language is important to democratic public life. Religious language, like any other political language but perhaps more centrally than some, is multivocal. Certainly religious language has assumptive privileges in American culture. But, it is truly public and, thus, truly open for interpretation. The hopes and ambitions of speakers cannot always be matched by the interpretive understandings of those who listen. The translation between production and reception is a general dynamic of all cultural systems. But it seems particularly relevant in a culture dominated by a Protestant religious culture and a history of religious innovation. Access to scripture and the primacy of individual conscience and experience have put an emphasis on interpretation. Thus, the meaning propounded by movement leaders is not necessarily the interpretation received and recreated by others—even movement "followers." Religious language's function of drawing people into the public sphere invariably affects the messages and rhetoric they can use once they arrive there.

CONCLUDING THOUGHTS

In recent writings, I have been critical of what is generally called the "culture wars" argument (Williams 1997). Much of the war, I believe, is rhetorical, generated by some of the demands of effective mobilizing language that I have mentioned here. But I also object to overly cavalier dismissals of the symbolic aspects of politics as "mere rhetoric." Language creates, as well as reflects, social reality. Too many analyses of our cultural politics as "war" are not healthy for either political dialogue or our national future.

Thus, I am concerned with what kinds of religious language gain currency in our political culture—the language of God can have destructive effects on the social arrangements of the city of "man," particularly when that city is unalterably pluralistic. When the "truth" is spoken with such conviction that a considered response is not possible, the distortions of power and privilege can rival the effects generated by any worldly ideology. And, yet, this is precisely why religious language must be an active participant in both civil and political society. It is only when religious language is fully engaged with the problems, issues, and challenges of organizing human life that it is capable of contributing to emancipation as well as to righteousness, to justice alongside morality. Religion is best not used as a direct tool of the state, but it is wasted and political life impoverished when it cannot find a seat at the table. The American "experiment" has not always found the perfect balance among religious freedom, democratic politics, and social order. But the ongoing attempt to do so remains vibrant, and the body politic is the better for it.

Chapter 12

Can Religion Revitalize Civil Society?
An Institutional Perspective

Robert Wuthnow

Assessing the role of religion in revitalizing civil society requires addressing four questions: What is civil society? What are the marks of its vitality or lack of vitality? Is there compelling evidence that some or all of these particular marks have declined? And how might religion contribute to the strengthening of those aspects of civil society that are declining or prevent their further erosion? I shall argue that recent scholarly literature on the first three questions is quite divided, meaning that the answer to the fourth cannot be straightforward. But I also suggest that a reasonable argument can be made for greater attention being paid—both by scholars and by policy makers and religious leaders—to the complex institutional realities of which contemporary society is composed and that doing so provides additional insight into religion's contributions to the preservation of American democracy.

To anticipate my argument, it is notable that most discussions of civil society—and especially those that emphasize social capital—focus on interpersonal relations and the behavior and beliefs of individuals, especially in small, local, or informal and voluntary settings and in ways that privilege the moral resolve, trustworthiness, civility, character, and altruistic sentiments of individuals. Many of these discussions pay homage to Alexis de Tocqueville's remarks about Americans' voluntary spirit in the 1830s, while others feature data from recent surveys asking about individual membership in local organizations, voting, neighborliness, or views about fellow workers and neighbors or the personal characteristics of particular community leaders or public officials (Tocqueville 1969; Putnam 1995a, 2000). I do not challenge the importance of these kinds of activities and beliefs for understanding civil society; however, to concentrate exclusively on them is to miss a great deal about the way contemporary social life is organized. One has only to consider some of the following to indicate what is missing: the public and private system of elementary, secondary, and higher education—virtually none of which was present when Tocqueville visited—that currently shapes the values and lifestyles of nearly all Americans; the massive system of federal highways and transcontinental airlines that has emerged in the past half-century and on which much of the population's ability to interact with one another depends; and the thousands of watchdog agencies, political action committees, party officials, think tanks, law firms, research scientists, and community organizations that are formally separate from government but that receive funding from government and ostensibly serve the public interest (Boyte & Kari 1996; Schlozman & Tierney 1986). Examples such as these point to the fact that the yawning gap between government and private individuals that many analysts describe as civil society—precariously filled only by good-hearted people participating in town meetings and bowling leagues—neglects almost everything that actually constitutes civil society and that has long been of interest to social scientists who specialize in the study of institutions.

Although my argument is meant to emphasize the nuances and complexity of civil society (and can thus be read in various ways), it is most pointedly directed against recent arguments about social capital (especially that advanced in Robert Putnam's widely read and highly controversial *Bowling Alone*) in which all aspects of contemporary society sometimes appear to be reduced to a single factor—a factor that privileges the moral worth of gregarious people who happen to be well-connected to friends and neighbors through membership in middle-class clubs, associations, churches, and bowling leagues (Putnam 2000). To be sure, there is reason to be interested in such people and perhaps even cause for concern if such people are no longer as active as they once were. But interest in social capital, and indeed the revived usage of the term "civil society" (which was more common among political philosophers two centuries ago than it is among social scientists today), runs serious danger of being a step backward in social theorizing, not a step forward. For good reason, much of the best social theorizing of the last half of the twentieth century emphasized the structure and functions of *institutions*. This emphasis needs to be rediscovered in order to move beyond the present, often simplistic, discussions of social capital and civil society.

WHAT IS CIVIL SOCIETY?

Discussions of civil society[1] have emerged during the past decade despite the fact that relatively little use of the term was evident in nearly a half century of extensive social theorizing and empirical research. The reasons for this reappearance remain obscure, but are often associated with political developments in Eastern Europe, where the term was still more prominent in social theory and where the collapse of the Soviet Union opened new possibilities for democratic government and thus necessitated examination of the social bases on which democracy might be established. In the United States, discussions of civil society grew in popularity as criticisms of the federal government mounted, at first because of the military expansion and deficit spending in which the Carter, Reagan, and Bush administrations engaged in efforts to end the Cold War by outspending the faltering Soviet economy, and increasingly by public officials and business leaders who worried that rising tax rates in the United States and the soaring national debt were diminishing domestic firms' capacity to compete effectively in international markets. After the collapse of the Soviet Union, fewer arguments could be made compellingly for strong, centralized government programs in the name of national security, and associationalist theories of democracy, such as those of Tocqueville (or James Madison) reappeared.

Contemporary discussions of civil society reflect some of the anti-federalist, associational thinking that was prominent in the context in which they began to reappear in the late 1980s and 1990s. Most discussions of civil society emphasize the following. First, it is defined negatively as that which is not formally governmental, meaning that it is composed of the civilian population and does not depend on coercive powers of government as the primary means by which conformity to social norms is enforced. Second, it is also defined negatively as excluding those aspects of individual behavior that may be considered private, such as matters of intimacy, sexuality, and other relations within the family, or the leisure activities of individuals, or many of their personal convictions, beliefs, and opinions. Third, it is defined positively as the secondary groups, associations, and organizations through which citizens develop and express their collective aims and aspirations, and through which they either enlist the government's assistance to realize their aims or successfully pursue them on their own.[2] Fourth, because the aims of civil society are taken to be public or collective goods that require cooperation or the tempering of self-interest in favor of the good of all, purely economic activities are generally excluded, as are organizations oriented toward these activities (especially for-profit firms). And, finally, civil society also presupposes and includes a certain kind of individual or civic person, particularly one who can instinctively or through training behave responsibly and civilly toward fellow citizens, make informed decisions, participate rationally in public discussions about collective goods, and conform to conventional norms of moral decency and public propriety (Sinopoli 1992).

Although there is general agreement on each of these points, their exact meaning is deeply contested. Indeed, the principal debates about civil society hinge on disagreements about a central term in each of these five points: the meaning of coercive enforcement with reference to government, the distinction between private life and public life with respect to individuals, what sorts of mediating associations to consider, the inclusion or exclusion of certain economic activities, and the nature or importance of morally responsible individuals.

The question of coercive enforcement is vital because it forms the basis for arguing that a vibrant civil society must be a voluntary society; that is, one in which people are free to choose how to lead their lives, free from the fear of intervention by an oppressive or totalitarian government, and voluntarily engaged in helping others and working for the benefit of their communities. Yet the line between coercion and freedom is in practice difficult to distinguish. One particularly difficult issue is the role of law—and by extension the active or passive forms of government regulation that are generated to operationalize the law. Some writers on civil society insist that a strong system of fair and equitable laws is necessary for the functioning of civil society and should be regarded either as a component of it or as an aspect of government that pervades civil society. Another is the de facto coercion that may not come directly from government but be the result of social arrangements or customs that restrict the exercise of individual freedom, such as poverty or racial discrimination. A third issue pertains to those organizations in civil society that depend on the coercive powers of government, such as tax-exempt organizations whose economic viability rests on government's willingness to tax others. And there are perennial issues concerning the interpretation of constitutional guarantees, particularly the First Amendment, aimed at preserving freedom but in the process imposing certain limitations on these very freedoms. While voluntarism or the absence of coercion is an important aspect of civil society, then, it needs to be regarded more as a quality of behavior or as an aim to be preserved in social life, rather than as a clear line that can be drawn between government and civil society.

The issue of privacy, while at first glance focusing attention on public behavior as the essential characteristic of civil society, raises difficult questions about what exactly to exclude or include, as recurrent debates over the gendered connotations of these terms illustrate ("public man" and "private woman"), or as discussions of the relevance of sexual behavior to the public's evaluation of government officials or the role of community organizations in strengthening families suggests. Although the idea of civil society emphasizes the civic duties of citizens, it is by no means clear that any of the activities or beliefs of individuals can easily be excluded, especially if intimate sexual relations are relevant to public ethics or if personal religious sentiments are regarded as relevant items for protection by the courts.

The positive inclusion of secondary associations and other mediating groups as components of civil society raises questions about whether all such groups—even militant survivalists and hate groups—contribute to civil society or whether some should be excluded from consideration. More perplexing are questions about how large or small and about how formal or informal such groups need to be. Discussions of social capital—as the norms and networks that promote cooperative behavior in civil society—emphasize face-to-face interaction such as participation in local fraternal orders and ladies auxiliaries or attendance at neighborhood dinner parties (Coleman 1990; Putnam 1993a). Yet involvement in large-scale and relatively impersonal organizations, such as trade unions and political parties, may also warrant consideration. And if so, it becomes harder to know why bowling leagues and dinner parties should be regarded as an important component of civil society, while the American Association of Retired Persons (or, for that matter, the Democratic Party, the American Banking Association, and the World Health Organization) should not be given as much attention.

The exclusion of economic activities and organizations from civil society raises equally difficult questions. On the one hand, if the reason for their exclusion is concern about self-interest and materialism or competitiveness, then many nonprofit organizations and informal groups would have to be excluded as well. On the other hand, discussions of the informal social capital that occurs in firms or their contribution to social trust would suggest reasons why they might be included in discussions of civil society.

The issue of civil society depending on a certain kind of civic-minded, morally responsible, or virtuous person is also problematic. Although few would deny the importance of individual actions and decisions, social scientists insist that moral behavior is itself learned in and reinforced by social relations to such an extent that it cannot be examined in isolation from these relations. Thus, some social arrangements may be able to withstand a great deal of uncivil or amoral behavior, while other social arrangements may depend heavily on individuals behaving themselves. In short, people may be virtuous, but how they express their virtue depends on the fact that they live within institutions.

My reason for raising these conceptual issues is not only to suggest the difficulty faced in trying to delimit relevant aspects of civil society (although that difficulty is present in all discussions of the alleged decline of civil society); it is rather to suggest that discussions of the health of civil society are unlikely—if pressed to their logical extreme—to be very different from treatments of society in general. For example, the failing of public schools and rising crime rates can be (and often are) taken as indications that civil society is in danger, even though by some interpretations these problems may be the result of shortfalls in government spending on schools or police programs (and thus have more to do with taxation or administrative effectiveness than interpersonal networks). Similarly, it is difficult to separate concerns about participation in civic organizations from the family-leave policies of corporations or the private leisure activities of individuals that might create time for or compete with such participation. Put differently, what is to be gained, we might ask, by speaking of civil society as comprising only some kinds of groups and activities, as opposed to including all of society and asking if it is organized in ways that promote democracy?

This observation is one basis for suggesting that discussions of civil society may usefully be refocused by taking more explicit account of institutions. In sociological studies, institutions are generally regarded as complexes of organizations and related activities bound together by a common social function, mission, or focus.[3] Education, health, communication, government, family, and religion are examples (and, as these examples suggest, it is more common in everyday language to think of institutions than it is to understand what civil society may mean). Within each of these domains, connections are evident between individual needs and activities, such as schooling or receiving medical treatment, on the one hand, and the most collective or policy-oriented activities, such as national educational and health policies, on the other hand. The intervening levels of social organization are understood to include a wide range of social networks, patterned responses of individuals, firms, and movements, rather than only a few forms of voluntary participation. Although these organizations vary in economic and legal structure, no arbitrary distinctions need be drawn that exclude or include organizations strictly on the basis of how voluntary they are or whether they distribute or do not distribute profits. Thus, it need not be assumed that society functions better or worse simply because people happen to interact frequently with their neighbors or hold membership in voluntary associations (although such activities are likely to be of interest). Furthermore, discussions of social capital shift from ones that emphasize only the number of relationships individuals may have to ones that include the institutional settings in which these relationships occur. Insights can nevertheless be drawn from the literature on civil society to suggest particular aspects of institutional life that need to receive attention.

MARKS OF VITALITY

Acknowledging the role of institutions in contemporary social life suggests the importance of assessing the vitality of civil society by focusing on particular attributes or capacities of these institutions, rather than restricting attention to social capital or to specific activities such as participation in informal gatherings. Of greatest concern is whether or not democratic social arrangements are in place that maximize collective input into the discussion of common issues and values and whether these arrangements ensure the preservation of democracy itself (Taylor 1995). Among the marks of a vital democratic society, the following warrant special consideration: social capital, rights, communication, confidence in institutions, altruism, economic justice, integrative mechanisms, and higher-order values.

Social capital is a relevant consideration, but not the only one. Its relevance is as a way in which people can become aware of common problems, discuss them informally, establish trust, and develop ties that can be of use in mobilizing larger or more politically oriented efforts. To the extent that large numbers of people may be isolated or have nobody with whom to discuss problems or on whom to rely for securing advice and assistance, the likelihood of democracy functioning effectively and being preserved is diminished. Yet it should also be evident that these ties can be of many varieties: frequent interaction with next door neighbors may be helpful for expressing concerns about local zoning ordinances, whereas long distance phone calls or participation in Internet chat groups may be better at generating ideas about national health policy. Work place conversations may be a better source of information about many of the problems that concern people than participation in athletic teams.

Social Capital

An institutional approach to social capital highlights the fact that institutions both facilitate and restrict opportunities for social interaction. Institutions are in many ways arrangements that ensure the accomplishment of tasks without having to rely on first-hand interaction or social networks (Granovetter 1973, 1974). For example, employees of large companies seldom need to be in direct contact with the president of the firm because structures of authority, coordination, and responsibility exist at intervening levels of management. Besides making social capital unnecessary, institutions are often structured in ways that counteract inequities between people who have more or less social capital. For instance, legal norms governing institutions may reduce the role of social capital, as in fair hiring laws that increase the chances of qualified people getting jobs despite being excluded from social networks because of racial biases, gender, or physical disabilities. The primary consideration with respect to social capital is thus not how much of it exists in absolute terms, but whether enough is present both within and across institutions to help people express grievances or accomplish tasks that may require changes in institutions.

Individual Rights

As the fair hiring example suggests, legal norms that uphold respect for the rights of individuals are important to the vitality of civil society, both in ensuring the right to associate freely or to speak openly and in guarding against having to have ample social networks to receive equitable treatment. To the extent that public discussions and the law assert the importance of individual rights, civil society is stronger than when abuses of these rights are countenanced. Although it is also clear that social obligations and responsibilities must accompany rights, many of these obligations pertain to the extension of rights to groups who have been disadvantaged or focus on questions of how to balance the rights of competing groups. Rights are especially important in the context of institutions: where there are no institutionalized mechanisms for securing cooperation, responsibilities may need to be emphasized more than rights; but when institutions ensure that people behave responsibly most of the time because of rewards and hierarchies that encourage them to do so, it may be more important to define individuals' rights in relation to these institutions.

Communication

Another mark of vitality is the extent to which institutions and laws encourage the flow of information and open communication about social issues. Although social capital can enhance the exchange of ideas from person to person, it is only one component of larger and more complicated systems of communication. This is why many recent discussions of civil society have focused on journalism and other uses of mass media, asking questions about freedom from arbitrary government restrictions, potential violations of individual rights, responsibilities for accurate and fair reporting, and possible biases as a result of economic incentives or exclusion. In addition to these frequently discussed questions, attention also needs to be given to intra-institutional communication and to alternatives to the mass media. Schooling as a means of disseminating information is important, as are organizational newsletters, motivational speeches, and procedures for filing grievances. Indeed, one of the important roles that institutions play is providing access to a different kind of information than may be possible through the mass media, such as technical information, practice in organizing people, opportunities to participate in group discussions or on committees, and links to people with complementary skills or influence at different levels of society. These kinds of information may be as present in for-profit organizations as in voluntary associations.

Confidence in Institutions

An emphasis on institutions necessarily draws attention to public confidence in institutions as a topic of special concern for assessing the vitality of a society. Recent discussions of social capital (Seligman 1997) have emphasized generalized propensities to trust other people as a requisite for (and a by-product of) civic participation, but attitudes toward institutions are likely to be as important as those toward people in general. A person who for whatever reasons may find it difficult to trust strangers is still more likely to seek effective medical treatment if he or she has confidence that doctors and hospitals are well organized to provide care. It is nevertheless difficult to say categorically that high levels of confidence in institutions are indicative of a stronger society than lower levels, especially if high levels are unwarranted. Some degree of skepticism about institutions is in fact evident in most opinion studies, and for this reason relative declines become worrisome because they suggest that institutions are not perceived to be functioning as effectively as they once were.

Altruism

Because institutions develop to suit the interests of people most capable of shaping them, and because many of these institutions are dominated by economic considerations, discussions of altruism and the willingness of people to voluntarily help others remain important. Altruism can be assessed in terms of personal values, such as giving priority to helping others, or in terms of actual helping behavior (Monroe 1996). The latter, however, suggests the need to assess altruistic behavior in relation to institutions that may encourage or restrict it. Charitable organizations, the helping professions, and nonprofit or community agencies are especially valuable because they create ways for people to express altruism. Alternatively, organizations that require people to work long hours so that they have little time to help others, or that market self-gratifying forms of leisure, may discourage altruism from being put into practice (Schor 1992).

Economic Justice

Most understandings of democracy acknowledge that even the good intentions of altruistic individuals are insufficient to guarantee the equal access to rights and opportunities that may otherwise be compromised by power arrangements and economic structures. Checks and balances within government, as well as constitutional provisions, are one means of ensuring such guarantees, and knowledge of these aspects of government, voting, and other forms of political participation are thus important (Nardulli, Dalager, & Greco 1996). Redistributive mechanisms, such as progressive tax systems and inheritance laws, organizations that champion the rights of the poor, and movements concerned with economic justice are also worthy of consideration.

Integrative Mechanism

The fact that institutions are unstable must also be taken into account. Corporations fail or are forced to lay off workers, new economic opportunities require people to move to new communities, natural disasters leave people without homes or jobs, personal trauma or public scandals cause people to break ties with organizations, and so on. The dynamic character of institutions suggests that a strong society needs ways to reintegrate people who have been marginalized and left without means to be self sufficient. Old age assistance, aid to needy children, workmen's compensation plans, and emergency food relief are examples of such mechanisms. Besides these, movements and organizations also provide emotional support and ways for people to form new social bonds. Small support groups, self-help movements, relocation and job placement agencies, and community centers help fulfill these needs (Borkman & Parisi 1995; Chesler 1991; Wuthnow 1994a).

Higher-Order Values

Finally, the focus of most institutions on accomplishing routine tasks suggests that social vitality needs to be assessed partly in terms of citizens' willingness to consider higher-order questions, such as the meaning and purpose of life, the characteristics of a good society, what parents want most for their children, preserving the environment, and making the world a better place. These questions may not be answered clearly or consensually, but they require periodic reassessment. Opportunities for discussing them provide the occasions for legitimating social programs and for redirecting them as well as moments for renewing personal commitments and gaining greater understanding of people with opposing views.

IS CIVIL SOCIETY DECLINING?

The foregoing discussions provide criteria in relation to which an assessment of concerns about the decline of civil society can be made. These concerns have been expressed repeatedly as general statements about the United States and in terms of specific problems, such as alleged problems in morality, virtue, family loyalty, and commitment to communities (e.g., Bennett 1995; Bradley 1995; Elshtain 1995). They are nevertheless worth considering cautiously because arguments about decline are evident in every era and they are often voiced by propagandists interested in promoting causes and political agendas as well as by reformers interested in prompting consideration of the need for social renewal (Sandel 1996). Empirical information is more readily available about some aspects of the foregoing arguments than others.

Social Capital

Social capital has received considerable attention because of the accessibility of certain kinds of data on social ties and memberships. These data suggest that decline has occurred during the past twenty-five to thirty years in such activities as visiting neighbors, attending dinner parties, joining fraternal orders, and participating in bowling leagues (Putnam 2000).[4] Some of these declines may be attributable to shifts in leisure interests, but they also suggest that loyalties to local neighborhoods and long-term participation in highly structured voluntary activities (such as fraternal orders) are probably waning (Charles 1993). At the same time, participation in short-term, task-oriented, and sporadic social activities (such as occasional volunteering), as well as social ties in the work place, long distance phone calls, participation in major rituals such as weddings and funerals, and interaction via computer have increased or remained constant (Brown 1995; Fischer 1982). On balance, it is clearer that the nature of social capital is changing than it is that social capital is simply declining.

Individual Rights

Legal protections of individual rights and public attention to such rights appear to have increased in recent decades, rather than diminished; at least critics have focused on the so-called rights revolution, and definitions of rights have expanded to cover a larger number of special groups, such as the elderly, children, women, and homosexuals, and a wider variety of issues, such as the right to meaningful work or freedom from sexual harassment (Fukuyama 1995; Etzioni 1993). Although discussions of rights have emphasized the need for caution in extending rights that may infringe on the rights of others, even discussions of contested issues, such as homosexuality or affirmative action, suggest continuing support for the principle of rights.

Communication

There is little doubt that the flow of information and the availability of communication has increased over the past few decades, rather than diminished (Caplow, Bahr, Modell, & Chadwick 1991). A fourth major medium of mass communication—the Internet—has been added to print, radio, and television; more newspapers reach national audiences; the publishing industry has expanded, as has the number of cable television channels; and a larger share of the public than ever before attends secondary schools, colleges, universities, and continuing education programs where they are exposed to specialized and technical information. Some evidence suggests that television viewing is not as effective a medium for encouraging civic involvement as newspaper reading (which has declined); and many discussions emphasize concern about the quality and accuracy of public information and whether it is too much influenced by large corporations (Jackson-Beeck & Sobal 1980; Putnam 1995b; Norris 1996). Yet studies also suggest little relation between the number of corporations in media markets and the heterogeneity of messages communicated, while other research suggests that people select and filter information and are influenced by exposure to combinations of mass media and personal relationships.[5] On balance, there is perhaps more concern about too much information being transmitted than about a decline in information.

Confidence in Institutions

Confidence in institutions, like generalized trust in other people, appears to have eroded in the past three decades (Smith 1996; Taylor 1996). Fewer people than in the past express high levels of confidence in the leaders of major institutions or in the overall effectiveness of these institutions. Yet pollsters suggest that several qualifications need to be kept in mind. Particular institutions have been damaged by public scandals involving their leaders, rather than there being an across-the-board erosion of confidence in all institutions. Another qualification is that confidence varies with economic conditions, suggesting that trends are linked to actual performance and are cyclic rather than long term. Yet another is that relatively few of those who lack confidence in institutions appear to be so alienated that they are willing to engage in violent or extremist activities.

Altruism

Trends in altruism are harder to assess empirically. Many discussions suggest that Americans are more self-interested than in the past or that self-interest has been redefined in ways that contribute less to the public good and more to the expression of emotions and impulses (Bellah et al. 1996; Capps 1993; Lasch 1979; Leinberger & Tucker 1991; Nolan 1997). But few of these discussions rest on systematic evidence, while other studies suggest complex possibilities for combining self-interest and altruism. The clearest trends are in statistics on volunteering, which indicate pronounced increases over the past twenty-five years (Wuthnow 1998). And, although some critics worry that this increase may largely be attributable to rising numbers of civic-minded elderly people with time and energy to volunteer, it is also related to greater emphasis on community service in schools, to the attractiveness of the helping professions, and to growth in the numbers of nonprofit and charitable organizations (Hall 1992; Jenkins 1987; O'Neill 1989; Salamon 1992; Weisbrod 1988).[6]

Economic Justice

Redistributive programs and other efforts to promote equality suggest a less optimistic pattern. Although progressive tax policies, old age insurance, and many anti-discrimination practices remain in effect, federal social welfare expenditures have been reduced, linked to tighter eligibility requirements, and devolved to state and local jurisdictions. Most important, the past two decades have witnessed a widening gap between the income and assets of the wealthy and those of the poor, and larger numbers of the poor are concentrated in inner cities where jobs are unavailable, crime is high, social services are few, and racial segregation persists (Bound & Freeman 1992; Cohen & Dawson 1993; Gramlich, Laren, & Sealand 1992; Massey & Eggers 1990; Wilson 1987, 1996). Some evidence suggests that widening income disparities are common to all advanced industrial societies and are due to an expansion of low-wage service industries and the broadening of international labor markets, but research also suggests that these problems could have been mitigated by stronger labor organizations and more responsive government policies (Western 1995).

Integrative Mechanisms

Studies indicate that social dislocations, including job layoffs, career changes, domestic migration, and immigration have been increasing and that relocating and reassembling mechanisms have been slow to respond (Byrne 1994; Zeff & Lyons 1996). Some of the decline in memberships in traditional civic organizations results from these organizations' over-reliance on stable populations; some of it may also be attributable to greater time pressures in single-parent families or to the more general disruptions associated with divorce or geographic mobility (Cherlin 1992; Furstenberg 1996). Still, self-help groups and recovery groups have grown rapidly and emergency relief organizations have expanded their efforts.

Higher-Order Values

Questions about trends in higher-order values are perhaps the hardest to address. Most Americans continue to value family relationships and ties to loved ones, their personal freedom, opportunities to develop and utilize their talents, and chances to serve others, and many say they think often about what is truly important in life and desire more time to focus on basic values. Yet it is evident that Americans are materialistic and heavily influenced by advertising and consumerism (Wuthnow 1994b). To compound these problems, some observers suggest that Americans are embroiled in a culture war that may undermine commitment to democracy (Hunter 1991; see also Williams, Chapter 11 in this volume). Other observers express greater concern that America has adopted a live-and-let-live attitude to such an extent that people are reluctant to engage in serious debates about basic values (Wolfe 1998).

These considerations, then, do not suggest that American democracy is flourishing in all significant respects or that it is only declining. Even if the erosion of social capital that worries some observers were halted, other aspects of democracy, such as its need for mechanisms to uphold rights and its requirement for redistributive programs and ways to reintegrate the marginalized, would warrant concern. Nor do these considerations suggest that heightened levels of social capital would necessarily contribute positively to the resolution of these other problems. Indeed, it has often been the parochial attachments to "old boy" networks and "in group" favoritism that has required efforts to extend legal protections of individual rights and to create new settings within formal institutions for discussing and affirming basic values.

THE ROLE OF RELIGION

My emphasis on institutions and on the multiplicity of issues related to questions about the vitality of civil society is intended to redirect thinking about the ways in which religion may contribute to civil society. Standard thinking in recent years has been governed by an assumption that (a) civil society is indeed declining and thus needs to be *revitalized,* and (b) revitalization must come about through reform movements, especially at the grassroots level, and by focusing on the moral rejuvenation of individuals and families. Against this view, an institutional perspective suggests that religion's role in civil society needs to be considered in relation to the *maintenance* of vitality as much as to revitalization or reform, and that religion as an *institution* needs to be emphasized, including its organized and routine relationships with other institutions, rather than focusing only on moral rejuvenation.[7]

Social Capital

The role of religion in generating social capital is, in one sense, relatively incontestable: people who participate actively in congregations make friends with other congregants and are often more likely to interact with neighbors and hold memberships in other civic organizations.[8] Some evidence suggests that different religious traditions vary in the kinds of social capital they encourage—for example, liberal mainline Protestants appear to have wider ties with other civic organizations while evangelical Protestants focus more of their ties within their congregations—but there is little doubt that religious participation is conducive to social capital in some form or another. But the institutional character of religion suggests a need to go beyond social capital. Religion has effects because it provides employment for clergy, sponsors debates, generates special interest groups, and pays for lobbyists as well.

Individual Rights

Religion's role in protecting individual rights has received little emphasis in recent discussions of civil society, but this role is significant. Despite the fact that emphasis has been given to countervailing norms such as community responsibilities and moral obligations, religious organizations have been consistent advocates of human rights. Of course they have disagreed on whether to extend these rights to homosexuals or to apply them to questions about ordination and church discipline, but the social statements of most religious groups are framed in a language of rights. Moreover, rather than defending rights only in legal terms, these statements feature the divine rights of individuals and the relationship between spirituality and human development. Continuing to champion rights is one of the ways that religion can contribute to the preservation of democracy.

Communication

Religion's role in furthering communication is perhaps less clear. Mass communication is largely a product of the secular for-profit media, leaving open the possibility that religion's role in this area is relatively minimal. One exception to this generalization is the significant role that television preachers, especially Jerry Falwell and Pat Robertson, played in creating conservative reform movements in the 1980s (Lienesch 1994). Televangelism is perhaps weaker than it was in that decade, and yet its potential for raising money and attracting followers remains strong. Interest has also been generated in exploring ways in which media coverage of other religious issues and activities might be improved. What has been relatively neglected are the ordinary ways in which religious institutions promote communication. Most denominations provide news magazines and other printed material for their members, a growing number have web sites that include social statements and resolutions, and weekly sermons and religious education courses continue to reach millions of members. Although some research suggests that these media are not used as effectively as they might be, exposure to them does appear to influence congregants' values.

Confidence in Institutions

Confidence in institutions can be assessed partly in terms of attitudes toward religion itself, where a majority of Americans continue to express relatively high rates of confidence. Although some erosion occurred in the late 1980s as a result of the televangelist scandals, confidence has remained fairly constant, as have levels of attendance and membership. Those who express confidence in religion, moreover, are more likely to register confidence in other institutions. Still, there are some worrisome indications. Despite the fact that clergy are regarded as honest and ethical, many people do not consult the clergy on matters of serious personal concern, such as job-related or end-of-life issues, and many seem to be guided by popular and eclectic treatments of spirituality. Observers are divided about the possible effects of declining confidence or participation in organized religion. Some argue that democracy requires people who are firmly rooted in a particular faith tradition, while others suggest that in the future democracy may be more compatible with spiritual practices that strengthen individuals' capacities to live comfortably among several traditions.

Altruism

Altruism has been reinforced by religion in the past and is likely to be in the future, although the contribution of religion must increasingly be assessed in relation to secular nonprofits that fulfill some of the traditional service functions of religious communities. Regular participants in religious organizations are generally more likely than nonparticipants to value helping the needy, and many do engage in volunteer activities. Some evidence shows that participation reinforces the effect of religious beliefs on charitable activities, suggesting that beliefs will have less effect on altruism in the future if people are no longer as involved in their congregations (Wuthnow 1991). Comparative research suggests that the United States' high level of volunteering relative to that in other countries stems from its high rate of religious attendance, but observers are divided as to whether the United States will remain at this high level or gradually come to resemble other advanced industrial societies (Greeley 1997b). Comparative research also suggests that other societies have been able to develop significant numbers of nonprofit agencies through government and corporate sponsorship, rather than from a religious base. This research suggests that the United States might be able to maintain a strong nonprofit sector in the future even if religion were to decline. At present, religious organizations are increasingly working with secular service agencies to find arrangements that benefit from the finances and volunteers that congregations can provide but avoiding a duplication of efforts (Ammerman 1997). Examples of such interaction include congregations sponsoring independent nonprofit organizations, such as soup kitchens and homeless shelters, or participating in community-wide coalitions to finance low-income housing projects.

Economic Justice

Religion plays a potentially important role in promoting equality and redistributive efforts to help the poor.[9] Although sermons and social statements about economic justice appear to have a limited impact on parishioners' behavior, these issues are often mentioned by clergy and religious leaders and they do have some influence. In fact, one of the striking facts about contemporary religion is that it has been able to uphold alternative views of economic justice at all. For-profit firms increasingly deny responsibility for correcting social ills and government policy appears often to be driven by winning elections rather than adhering to social principles; clergy also experience pressures to say little that may offend parishioners, but seminaries and denominational agencies are sufficiently insulated from having to be popular that they can sometimes take principled stands on social issues. As government devolves responsibility for social welfare to local agencies, religious organizations have been working with these agencies to supply volunteers, meeting space, and leadership (Cisneros 1996; Cnaan 1997). Few proponents of these religious activities argue that they can take the place of government programs and policies, but religion's enlistment of middle-class people in efforts to help the poor may awaken consciences to support more progressive social policies.

Integrative Mechanisms

Religion also holds possibilities for helping people who have been marginalized by institutional change to become reintegrated into the society. Most of the support-group movement in recent years has been related to religious organizations, either formally or by meeting in church basements and drawing on religious networks for recruits and leadership. More broadly, the voluntary tradition in American religion encourages a great deal of switching from congregation to congregation or between faith traditions, and religious organizations have adapted to this situation by making it easier for newcomers to join and become integrated in congregational activities. Some evidence suggests that megachurches and other large congregations may be especially effective in doing this because they have many specialized groups with which to attract newcomers as well as opportunities for service in the wider community.

Higher-Order Values

Above all, religion provides opportunities for reflection about higher-order values. It is often difficult to demonstrate that exposure to specific sermons or participation in religious activities has a strong effect on the public's values, and some alleged effects are due to differences in who decides to participate in the first place. Yet the presence of religious institutions in the society maintains possibilities for discussions about values that could not occur were these institutions to disappear. There is a strong relationship in international studies between the strength of religious institutions and a nation's likelihood of believing in God, and belief in God is in turn related to such values as helping others, feeling that promises should be kept, looking to God for moral guidance, and valuing commitments to family and community. Such evidence suggests that religious organizations contribute to the vitality of civil society simply by providing the sermons, classes, and opportunities for worship that are the heart of their self-proclaimed mission.

CONCLUSION

Revitalizing civil society should not be thought of mainly in terms of looking for a charismatic leader to proclaim new ideas about how to find God or behave more responsibly toward one's neighbors. Nor should it be regarded as the work of reform movements that win votes for new candidates or launch third parties, or even as depending on lobbyists bringing different pressures to bear on national leaders. Those images of revitalization stem from the rare occasions on which religion has made an extraordinary difference in society, such as the civil rights movement in the 1960s or the Moral Majority and Christian Coalition movements in the 1980s and early 1990s. They sometimes appeal to certain evangelical, pietistic, or sectarian traditions in American religion that in essence believe established institutions are likely to be evil and that rejuvenation can come only from a remnant of zealous believers with special insight about divine purposes. Such views need to be tempered by a clear understanding of social institutions; otherwise, they are likely to be ineffective.

Clear thinking is needed about what exactly needs to be revitalized, rather than simply assuming that civil society is in decline. Questioning arguments about decline should not be regarded as tacit approval of the way things are. But hand-wringing can too easily be a way of escaping the hard, specialized work that is needed to ensure the well-being of society or to improve it. There is particular danger in focusing too much on decline and revitalization in relation to questions about religion because religion's languages of a fallen world and of the need for repentance can reinforce views that overlook the complexity of social institutions.

An institutional perspective does not disavow the need for revitalization, but emphasizes that it often occurs within institutions and because of them, as well as from the actions of charismatic leaders and social movements. Indeed, most charismatic leaders and social movements are more effective when they utilize the resources of institutions. More important, the preservation and improvement of civil society depends to a large extent on the judicious uses of funds, influence, knowledge, and administrative structures in institutions.

The contribution of religion to civil society needs to be understood in these terms. American religion is a well-established institution. At present it takes in more than $50 billion annually from charitable contributions, a figure that comprises more than half of all such contributions from individuals; it is more than three times the amount donated to educational causes and more than five times the amount donated to health-related organizations (Bureau of the Census 1995, Table 622). This income, together with that from the sale of goods and services (such as fees for weddings and funerals, seminars, and music lessons), is sufficient to cover the employment of approximately 371,000 full-time clergy (Bureau of the Census 1995, Table 649). In addition, approximately $12 billion is donated to religious organizations each year as volunteer time (Hodgkinson & Weitzman 1994, Tables 1.5 and 1.6).

Questions can be raised about whether the strength of American religion is waning and whether its resources are being used most effectively. But its contribution to civil society should not be considered only in terms of numeric or financial strength. Its role is better understood in terms of its overall presence, including the fact that this presence is highly pluralistic. White evangelical Protestants have shown the greatest vitality in recent years, and they have often supported political candidates who promised smaller government and more conservative policies on abortion and homosexuality. But evangelicals are religiously and politically diverse. Catholics often express disagreement with official church teachings on social issues, and participation at religious services among Catholics has declined, yet the church remains one of the nation's largest voluntary organizations, it supports a vast network of schools and hospitals, and its offices provide opportunities for deliberation about a wide range of public issues. Mainline Protestant denominations have declined in membership, yet these churches offer some of the most consistent support for liberal causes in American politics, ranging from greater public support for social welfare to nuclear disarmament to rights for homosexuals. Black churches, Latino churches, new immigrant churches, mosques, temples, and fellowship halls are often among the few organizations that provide services in inner city neighborhoods (see, for example, Wind & Lewis, 1994). And Jewish congregations contribute to a diverse array of causes and political issues as well as providing social capital and volunteer efforts (Sochen 1980).

The answer to the question of whether religion can revitalize civil society is nevertheless "no," at least if religion is regarded only as beliefs and convictions that somehow operate independently of other institutions. The possibility of revitalization from religion is not so much that religion will make a distinct moral or political contribution but that it is true to its own purposes and integrated with other institutions through the activities of individual members as well as formal alliances. For people who may wish to contribute to civil society through their congregations, energetic engagement in religious activity itself or in volunteer work in the wider community may be especially attractive. But it is also valuable to recognize the contributions that can be made through working in education and the media, by gaining and utilizing professional skills, and by being attentive to the political process.

Chapter 13

Religion, Social Capital and Democratic Life
Concluding Thoughts

Corwin Smidt

Over the past two decades, the concept of social capital has drawn a great deal of scholarly attention among social scientists, and it has fostered considerable research related to its presence, its availability, and its consequences. Not only has scholarly interest been generated, but considerable scholarly debate has emerged as well.

This volume adds to that discussion and debate, though it does so by focusing on a particular kind of social capital—social capital that is tied to religious life—and the kinds of consequences that flow from its presence. The authors of these chapters have addressed different issues and have presented assorted observations, analyzed particular data, and offered various explanations. Together, these chapters have helped to enhance our understanding of the complexity and richness of the interplay among religion, social capital and democratic life.

WHAT HAVE WE LEARNED?

As was noted in the introductory chapter, the social capital framework of analysis stresses the socialization of individuals that results from participation in associational groups and how this socialization serves to instill certain shared norms and encourage cooperative societal action. Advocates of the social capital framework posit that associational life functions to produce the trust, foster the extended social networks, and establish the social norms that sustain and enable healthy democratic systems (Foley & Edwards 1998, 12).

Those analysts who are skeptical of the social capital account of democratic life generally contend that the framework is too simplistic and that it neglects or downplays the important role that institutional structures play in fostering democratic life. They contend that the state is not simply a recipient of the social capital generated through associational life, but instead frequently plays an important role itself in the formation and continuation of associational life. Thus, according to such critics, the process of social capital production has both social and structural antecedents.

While most chapters of the volume did not address this particular theoretical issue directly, the previous chapter by Robert Wuthnow stands as a clear exception. Wuthnow does not dispute the important role that social capital may play in shaping civic engagement, but he does challenge any focus on the role of social capital that suggests it constitutes the only, or even the primary, factor in shaping the character of civil society or democratic life. Efforts to comprehend and foster vital civil societies and healthy democracies need, according to Wuthnow, to give particular attention to the role of social institutions, and not simply social capital, in the forging of such societies and democracies. Wuthnow's caution shifts the focus of analysis and the kinds of questions to be addressed because it places greater emphasis on institutions and the particular context in which social capital is forged: different institutions can foster, color, and restrict patterns of social interaction differently. But, Wuthnow's chapter also complements, in many ways, the discussion and analyses of social capital in the other chapters. His caution reminds us that the role of religion in fostering vibrant civil societies and healthy democracies is broader than that of social capital generated through religious means.

Other chapters of this volume address this theoretical issue more indirectly. The chapters by Warren and Wood point, in part, to the important role of institutions in civil society. Warren's analysis of the differences in the success of IAF in organizing Roman Catholic and African-American communities indicates that the institutional structures of a religious community have important consequences in fostering civic engagement beyond the consequences associated with the social networks fostered within those religious communities. Likewise, Wood's comparison of religiously and racially generated social capital highlights the importance of institutions in mobilizing individuals for civic engagement, pointing out that different institutions occupy different structural positions in the public arena that shape their abilities to project and advance power in a democratic fashion.

Generally speaking, most analysts have contended that the social capital generated through religious institutions varies in relation to the ecclesiastical structure of such religious institutions: congregationally based ecclesiastical structures are more likely than hierarchically based structures to foster greater organizing and civic skills because of their higher levels of lay participation in church work (e.g., Verba et al. 1995). Accordingly, Harris contends in Chapter 8 that African Americans gain civic skills through the horizontally structured Protestant churches they typically attend; were they as a group to attend more hierarchically structured religious institutions (e.g., the Roman Catholic Church), as most Latinos do, they would be less likely to acquire such civic skills. And Harris's analysis of data related to civic skills practiced by race and gender indirectly support these expectations.

However, Warren's analysis in Chapter 4 points to greater complexity with regard to this matter: parishioners within Roman Catholic parishes tended to be mobilized more readily and exhibit leadership more frequently than did parishioners within African-American congregations. To emphasize too strongly the hierarchical nature of the Roman Catholic Church within the American context may be misleading; such differences may be more relative, than qualitatively different, in nature. Both Warren (in Chapter 4) and Coleman (in Chapter 3) note that, at least in the American context, the Catholic Church in the United States places greater emphasis on lay leadership than was true previously. This shift can be attributed to various factors—including a shortage of priests, the emphases of the Second Vatican Council, and the cultural values of American society within which the church finds itself. Moreover, as Warren notes, there may be particular ways in which more hierarchical structures can prove to be advantageous in fostering and generating civic skills among the laity within a congregation or parish.

When one turns to the conceptualization of social capital, one finds that the chapters of this volume reflect current differences in scholarly perspectives with regard to the nature and location of social capital. The issue of whether social capital is something that individuals can possess and, thereby, transport from one social context to the next or is simply embedded in particular relationships tends to divide scholars who analyze social capital. The work of Putnam, a political scientist, has led many political scientists and economists to focus on associational membership, social trust (and other related attitudes), and the acceptance of and adherence to social norms—qualities that individuals can possess and transport from one social context to the next. Those who follow Putnam's lead seek to ascertain the ways in which variation in any or all of these particular individual level variables may affect social, economic, and political outcomes (at the individual and, at times, the collective level).

Other social scientists, mostly sociologists, have adopted versions of the social capital concept that are more in keeping with the understanding advanced by Coleman (1990), a sociologist. Coleman viewed social capital as a structural variable, something that exists only between and among unique individuals within specific relationships. In so doing, Coleman emphasized how such embedded social capital served to foster individual advancement or collective action.

For the most part, those authors of the chapters in this volume who are political scientists tended to follow Putnam, while those who are sociologists tended to follow Coleman in their conceptual understanding of social capital.

Those who hold social capital to be more a social structural than an individual variable generally emphasize the importance of context. When social capital is treated as a quality that individuals can possess and transport from one setting to another, the analyses that flow from such a perspective tend to focus on how social capital varies in terms of individual, rather than contextual, qualities. But for those who follow the more sociological approach, context counts—and counts crucially. Thus, for those who follow Coleman, one's level of trust as well as one's acquiescence to norms of reciprocity vary from relationship to relationship, and social capital is accordingly viewed to be rooted in the specific context in which it is found.

While sociologists do not deny the importance of individual differences, they generally view "the whole as being greater than the sum of the parts." As a result, sociologists tend to view aggregated, individual-level characteristics as poor reflections of properties of collectivities. Thus, studies of social capital that focus on associational membership, attitudes of social trust, and other-regarding norms can be productive, if the focus of such analysis is limited to its proper level of analysis. But those who follow Coleman's lead are quick to criticize those who treat social capital as some national-level measure that can be tapped by aggregating survey responses into a "grand mean," and thereby treat individual-level qualities as reflections of differences in collective attributes that distinguish one political culture from another (Foley, Edwards, & Diani 2001, 267, 271).

Still, such criticisms do not, by themselves, invalidate research that treats social capital as a quality that individuals can possess. For example, cross-national research that focuses on the generation of social capital among individuals across such different settings is seemingly exempt from such criticism. Such analyses do not treat social capital as an aggregate characteristic of a nation's political culture, but rather examine those factors that may, or may not, serve to generate such qualities cross-nationally (see Chapter 10). Likewise, the conceptualization of social capital as an individual quality does not preclude investigations of contextual differences in the generation of such social capital. Each approach to social capital (i.e., Putnam's and Coleman's) can generate important insights and understandings and provide valuable information about the causes and consequences of social capital.

Yet, one might also anticipate that different approaches may lead, at times, to somewhat different findings and conclusions. The issue of where social capital is to be found does affect one's decision about the particular methodology by which it should be studied. As noted in the introductory chapter, those who follow Coleman tend to study social capital through more ethnographic techniques of personal observation and participation. But, this adoption of different methodological approaches that flow from differences in conceptual understanding is not neutral in its effects, as is evident in findings reported in different chapters in this volume. On the one hand, those studies by Campbell and Yonish (Chapter 6) and by Smidt, Green, Guth, and Kellstedt (Chapter 10), which relied on survey research, downplayed the importance of religious tradition in relationship to religious attendance in explaining the levels of volunteer activity or levels of civic engagement. On the other hand, Warren (Chapter 4), who employed participant observation methods, emphasized the importance of religious tradition and religious institutions in efforts at community organizing. Such differences in findings may be a function of the particular methodology employed.[1] Certainly, participant observation tends to alert the analyst to unique qualities of the particular context under examination, while survey research seeks to find more general patterns that emerge across particular individuals and contexts and, in so doing, it downplays the uniqueness of particular individual cases under investigation.

When one turns to some of the empirical issues related to social capital, it is clear from this volume that not all associational memberships (nor all small communities) are necessarily alike. There are different kinds of social ties, and even the distinction between bonding and bridging social capital does not fully capture the variation that is evident in such memberships. Moreover, as Curry (Chapter 9) notes, even in the more intimate settings of small town America, in which face-to-face relationships are commonplace and where one knows one's neighbors, one finds variation in the level to which bonding social capital is generated.

Generally speaking, the social capital approach tends to value, at least at the societal level, the tempering of individual self-interest that occurs through association with others. Such associations foster broader, more commonly shared concerns and endeavors, and such relationships with others foster "reciprocity" in the form of mutual expectations. In addition, the notion of "bonding" social capital suggests that strong, personal relationships with others, relationships in which people are bonded together, are valued and advanced. Yet, it is also true that such "bonding" must be tempered in certain ways; bonding social capital without bridging social capital can be counter-productive. Thus, bonding social capital may be viewed as a necessary, but not sufficient, condition for a healthy community. Moreover, certain forms of weak ties or weak social bonds are also likely to be indispensable to the life of communities.

Nor are different associations likely to foster social capital in the same ways or to the same extent. Even religious communities that share the same faith tradition, where members are employed largely in similar professions (farming) and are located in similar contexts (small towns in Iowa), tend to generate different kinds and levels of social capital. The issue, then, becomes what kinds of association tend to generate interpersonal trust, to foster habits of cooperation and norms of reciprocity, and to forge expanded social networks, and under what circumstances, and with what effects for the polity?

In part, it appears that differences in the generation and forms of social capital are likely to be tied to the nature of the shared goals, values, and societal visions arising from the worldviews of those who affiliate with different associations or live within different communities. According to Curry's more ethnographic study of several rural Iowa communities, the social capital found within those communities, in both its bonding and bridging forms, cannot be understood apart from the particular worldviews expressed by members of those communities. And, because these worldviews are reflections of ultimate commitments, they tend to be religious in nature.

This brings us back once again to the normative issue of whether the renewal of civic associations, without moral renewal, is sufficient to foster the renewal of democratic life. Is the development of "civic character," with its readiness to join with others, sufficient to renew democratic health? Or will an increase in civic activity that fails to include the inculcation of "democratic" and moral values also fail to restore "health" and vitality to civic life?

The chapters of this volume do not directly address this issue. However, it is likely that most, if not all, of these authors would contend that, while the development of "civic character" may be a necessary condition for democratic renewal, it is not a sufficient condition for such renewal to occur. Certainly, religiously endowed social capital could be a vehicle by which some aspects of democratic renewal can occur. However, religion can be a positive as well as a negative force in democratic life. Its effects depend on the particular religious values that are promoted and advanced, the ways in which such religion is practiced, and the means by which religious people seek to advance their values through public policy. Thus, not all religiously endowed social capital may necessarily be healthy for democratic renewal. It simply "depends." Yet, as Wuthnow suggests in the previous chapter, "social vitality needs to be assessed partly in terms of citizens' willingness to consider higher-order questions, such as the meaning and purpose of life, the characteristics of a good society, . . . and making the world a better place." Only when civic engagement is coupled with reflection about these broader, more normative matters will the renewal of democratic life and democratic communities likely occur.

RELIGION AND SOCIAL CAPITAL

To what extent, then, is there something distinctive about religious social capital that serves to differentiate it from other kinds of social capital? Is the nature of the social capital generated within religious contexts qualitatively different from that generated outside its domain? Or is all social capital basically similar in nature, regardless of its origins?

In some ways, all social capital is alike. What may differentiate one kind of social capital from another is simply its particular source, but if its effects are the same regardless of its origins, then it likely does not matter whether or not associational memberships are with religious organizations.

Nevertheless, there are particular qualities about religious social capital that help to differentiate it from other forms of social capital and that serve to make it distinctive in nature, whether qualitatively or quantitatively.

First, religious social capital is distinctive in terms of its "quantity." The social capital generated in American society through religious means far exceeds the level of social capital produced through other means. This is evident by the fact that "As a rough rule of thumb, . . . nearly half of all associational memberships in America are church related, half of all personal philanthropy is religious in character, and half of all volunteering occurs in a religious context" (Putnam 2000, 66).

Second, the social capital generated through religious means may well be more durable than the social capital generated through other means. For example, assessments with regard to whether or not to continue to serve food at a soup kitchen (or other forms of civic engagement) may be based on different criteria of evaluation for religious than for more secular people. Rational or pragmatic considerations may foster assessments of one's civic engagement in terms of criteria of efficiency or effectiveness. Thus, if one perceives one's actions to have little effect or that one's endeavors could be accomplished more easily through different means, then one might be prone, given such criteria, to abandon such efforts. On the other hand, religious values often call for a different standard of evaluation. Success, or the lack of it, is not necessarily the standard employed by religious people; rather, being faithful to one's values, to one's commitments, or to one's calling is frequently employed as the standard by which to assess one's endeavors. Because frequency of church attendance can be viewed as a reflection of one's level of religious commitment, it is not surprising that church attendance, rather than religious affiliation, was more strongly related to volunteering (Chapter 6), charitable contributions (Chapter 7), and civic engagement (Chapter 10). Thus, the social capital generated through religious means may well have a more durable quality to it, because the motivation to remain faithful may well sustain such efforts.

Third, religious social capital is likely distinctive in terms of its range. Social relationships for religiously involved people are frequently based on different considerations than for those who are not so religiously involved. Religions often encourage their adherents to deal positively with others, regardless of the particular benefits that may or may not be derived from such relationships. In fact, religion often seeks to give "voice to the voiceless," to speak on behalf of others when other voices are silent, and to express values that cannot always be reduced to logic or simple calculations of self-interest. And membership in religious groups rather than any other type of foluntary association is "most closely associated with other forms of civic involvement, like voting, jury service, community projects, talking with neighbors, and giving to charity" (Putnam 2000, 66–67).

Fourth, religion also has a distinctive capacity to nourish social capital. According to Harris (Chapter 8), a unique feature of religion's contribution to the formation of social capital is its ability to nurture and sustain reciprocity among actors. Religiously endowed social capital may well provide stronger bases for group cooperation than social capital generated from more secular sources. Whereas group cooperation outside religious contexts may rest on material incentives to foster cooperation with others, collective action among religiously oriented groups may occur through non-material incentives (such as the desire to do good works), which are often rooted in the religious beliefs of such communities. In addition, the presence of transcendent values can foster stronger norms of reciprocity among those actors who expect that rewards for choosing to cooperate with others (or punishments for not so choosing) will occur—even if such rewards and punishments may only occur after one's death.

Finally, religious social capital is distinctive, in part, because of the disproportional benefits it wields within particular segments of American society. Citizen participation in the process of political decision-making and political equality stemming from such participation (e.g., one person, one vote) are values that democratic political systems promote. However, not all citizens participate, and those who do generally exercise disproportional political voice and influence. There are various reasons why some do and others do not become politically engaged (e.g., differences in personal resources, motivations, and recruitment), and certain resources closely linked to political participation are unequally distributed within democratic society (e.g., educational attainment). But churches play an important role in "enhancing the political resources available to citizens who would, otherwise, be resource-poor" (Verba et al. 1995, 320). Religious institutions tend to distribute opportunities for the exercise of civic skills in a relatively democratic fashion. Religiously active men and women, regardless of their levels of educational attainment, learn to run meetings, discuss and assess different proposals, manage disputes, and shoulder administrative responsibilities. As a result, religious institutions serve as an "important incubator for civic skills" (Verba et al. 1995, ch. 11; Putnam 2000, 66), and religion rivals education as the most powerful variable related to most forms of civic engagement (Smidt et al., Chapter 10 of this volume; Putnam 2000, 67).

Certainly, there may be other ways in which religious social capital is distinctive in nature; this volume represents an initial, but limited, inquiry into the topic. Future studies may reveal additional ways in which religious social capital is distinctive as well as refine some of the initial contentions made here.

RELIGION AND DEMOCRATIC LIFE

The role of religion in democratic life remains a controversial and debated topic. From the campaign trail to the courthouse, from television talk shows to the halls of Congress, the role of religion in American politics is discussed and debated with regard to both the role it currently plays and the role it should play. The issues are real and the emotions generated are frequently intense.

However, the public role of religion, especially its role in democratic life, is not necessarily confined to the political arena—whether in electoral politics, interest group politics, the policy-making or the policy-implementation process.

In fact, religion's role in democratic life is generally much broader and deeper than its presence within the political arena, as this volume has shown by examining religion's role in fostering involvement in civic associations and in generating social capital. Accordingly, religion serves public, and not just political, life in several different ways. First, religion contributes to the foundation of democratic society. In fact, one might argue that the absence of religious faith from public life is far more dangerous than an excess of religious passion. Religion in America, particularly in its institutional manifestations, is an important "vehicle for the kind of participation essential to the definition of public life" (Cochran 1990, 55). While despotic or totalitarian governments rule by coercion, a free republic is dependent on mass moral restraint. Democratic governments value internalized order (self-restraint) over external compulsion.

Religion importantly serves public life through its serving to shape individual character and virtue. The Founding Founders viewed religion as an indispensable prop to republican virtue. For them, religion and public life are intertwined in that "moral virtue underpins civic virtue, and religion fosters moral virtue" (Cochran 1990, 56). As Washington noted in his farewell address to the American people: "Of all the dispositions and habits which lead to political prosperity, religion and morality are indispensable supports. In vain would that man claim the tribute of patriotism, who should labor to subvert these great pillars of human happiness, these firmest props of the duties of men and citizens."

As Tocqueville examined American life in the early nineteenth century, he saw one of the dangers associated with democratic equality and freedom to be that of isolated individualism, where self-interest was no longer tempered, in part, by concerns for the common good. But Tocqueville noted a number of institutions in American life that served to dampen the effects of excessive individualism—that pulled people out of their isolated selves and drew them to interact with others, and, in so doing, enabled them to see other points of view that differed from their isolated, self-interested one. Among such institutions were voluntary associations, especially those related to religion. Thus, religious life and institutions were, for Tocqueville as well, of crucial importance for American civic and political life.

Washington and Tocqueville are not alone. Contemporary scholars too have maintained that rational self-interest is not a sufficient basis for social order and that religion can serve as that basis. For example, sociologist Robert Bellah has contended:

> any coherent and viable society rests on a common set of moral under-
> standings about good and bad, right and wrong, in the realm of individu-
> al and social action. It is almost as widely held that these common moral
> understandings must also rest in turn upon a common set of religious
> understandings that provide a picture of the universe in terms of which the

moral understandings make sense. Such moral and religious understandings produce both a basic cultural legitimation for a society which is
viewed as at least approximately in accord with them, and a standard of
judgment for the criticism of a society that is seen as deviating too far from
them (Bellah 1975, ix).

Thus, from this perspective, religious life, located within civil society, both
enables public moral choices to be made and fosters basic forms of civility and
social restraint which, in turn, promote the common, and not just one's individual good.

The second way in which religion contributes to public and not just political life is through the public and participatory activities of religious life.
Religion certainly has private components to it; an individual's relationship
with the sacred is a personal and relatively private matter. But religion does have
public aspects and occasions to it as well. Corporate worship is a public occa-
sion, and interaction with other believers occurs in a public space. Participation
in these public spaces and occasions transpires in order to shape the common,
public life of a group of believers. Relatively well-institutionalized religions general display a wide variety of such public occasions; members participate in
church governance, lead worship, education, and personnel committees, and
organize liturgies, celebrations, and church-sponsored community service or
civic projects. All are opportunities for participation with others in taking
responsibility, making collective decisions, compromising, expressing one's
views, and acknowledging the contrasting views of others.

Thus, the second way in which religions can legitimately affect democratic
life is through its associational activity. Churches are by far the most prevalent
form of voluntary association in American society. Through these associational
activities—whether by attending church with others, volunteering in a faith-
based soup kitchen, or learning organizational and negotiating skills through
participation in congregational committee structures—religion serves to shape
and color civic life. In so doing, religion, in turn, undergirds political life. It
does so through the moral and civic virtues inculcated, through the civic skills
imparted, and through the public engagement encouraged.

Public life is limited neither to the realm of the state nor to the realm of politics. Religion is a form of public life, and its private and public aspects serve to
"reinforce one another and correct each other's extreme tendencies" (Cochran
1990, 57). The public role that religion plays can be particularly important
when the state, the dominant public institution, become simply a "large, impersonal, distant provider of goods and services." Under such circumstances, if
public life is to be renewed and a basis for communal life is to be established,
then it likely will be "found outside those great impersonal abstractions of society and state" (Bernstein 1986, 47). Religion certainly provides one basis for a
renewed public life because it can be a space in which opportunity and responsibility for many kinds of public participation are made available (Cochran
1990, ch. 3).

Finally, a third way in which religion contributes to public life is through being a "voice."[2] The first amendment of the U.S. Constitution protects the expression of religious thoughts and values by allowing for freedom of speech and the free exercise of religion. Many religious traditions call adherents to engage in "prophetic politics"—to speak out against evil in all its forms, including its political forms, and to live out models of social life that better reflect the kingdom of God.

In its public role, religion may serve as one of the voices to which political power should be responsive in the formulation of public policy. A democratic polity cannot restrict and, in fact, should welcome moral insights into debates over issues involving important ethical questions. Such moral perspectives act as a counterweight to necessary but demoralizing pragmatism.[3] By reminding the state of its ethical obligations, religion can play an important public role in democratic life.

Religion can also help protect democratic society from movement toward greater statism and potential totalitarianism. Democratic governments are based on the principle of limited government, and religion serves as a major bulwark that can challenge the authority of the state when it exceeds its rightful boundaries. Totalitarian states generally attack institutional or corporate religious expression rather than individual religious belief because such institutions express and "promulgate belief in a transcendent reality by which the state can be called to judgment," and, in so doing, "such institutions threaten the totalitarian proposition that everything is to be within the state, nothing is to be outside the state" (Neuhaus 1984, 82). By seeking to reduce religion simply to privatized conscience, the totalitarian state attempts to restrict the public square to only two actors—the state and the individual. And, by such means, "religion as a mediating structure—a community that generates and transmits moral values—is no longer available" (Neuhaus 1984, 82).

From the beginning of American history, therefore, religion and the practice of democracy have been closely intertwined. The institutional separation of church and state mandated by the establishment clause stands alongside the free exercise of religion clause in the first amendment. While it may be desirable that church and state be separated within democratic life, it is impossible to separate religion from politics. All public policies embody particular moral values, and, in this sense, all governments "legislate morality." Whether or not they are derived from a particular religious faith, one's values affect the way one views the ends and purposes of government, the policy goals it should pursue, and the kinds of procedures to be employed. In this sense, religious values, like all other values, help to shape political life.

This volume, however, analyzes various ways in which religion relates to public life—a domain broader than political life—and it does so through the analytical lens of social capital analysis. When analyzing the relationship between religion and the generation of social capital, one becomes aware of the ways in which religion serves to undergird civic life, and, as a result, the chapters of this volume reveal different ways in which religion is intertwined with public as well as democratic life.

The analyses presented here on the interplay between religion, social capital, and democratic life are far from "definitive" in nature. Certainly, much more can and will be said about the ways in which the three are intertwined. It is hoped that this volume will serve to stimulate more, and deeper, thought and work on the topic. Should that occur, then both our scholarly understanding and our public life are likely to be the better for it.

Notes

Introduction

1. Actually, there have been a variety of factors that have contributed to this re-examination of associational life. This scholarly attention given to both "civil society" and "social capital" reflects an effort to construct "new paradigms with which to confront the problems of contemporary societies" (Foley & Edwards 1997, 550). Several factors and events have converged to spawn this effort. First, there have been, in the face of the apparent growth in egoistic and atomistic tendencies in American society, increasing calls for more communitarian values and concerns. Second, in the face of the devolution of state power both in the United States and elsewhere, there has been a growing emphasis placed on the role civil organizations play in public life. And, finally, in the face of the collapse of communism, the efforts of various Central and East European countries to forge democratic polities from the rubble of abandoned social structures have prompted an examination of how civil society shapes political life.

2. In his more recent book, Putnam (2000) has sought to address his critics and has marshaled a vast array of evidence which, taken together, paints a picture that points towards decline and not just simply change.

3. Still, there are two different, and conflicting, versions of civil society that have emerged in the recent revival of attention given to it (Foley & Edwards 1996). For some, a "healthy" civil society serves as a mediating institution between the individual and the state, providing protection against the potential totalitarian influences of the state. For others, a "healthy" civil society fosters social

223

connectedness and social trust and thereby facilitates and enables more effective government.

Chapter 2

1. Coleman (1990, 242) explained that norms "specify what actions are regarded by a set of persons as proper or correct, or improper or incorrect. They are purposively generated, in that those persons who initiated or help maintain a norm see themselves as benefiting from its being observed or harmed by its being violated. Norms are ordinarily enforced by sanctions, which are either rewards for carrying out those actions regarded as correct or punishments for carrying out those actions regarded as incorrect." Norms are dictated by others who have the power to provide rewards and punishments, but reach full capacity when they are internalized by the members of the group who are to carry out the specific action.
2. How norms are perpetuated and become an internalized expectation of people is a complex process. But certainly one facet of this process with regard to the fostering of such congregational norms is the socialization of religious leaders so that they are able to provide congregants with the skills for carrying out these expected tasks. Not only do most theological seminaries in the U.S. have, as part of their curriculum, a course on social ministry, but they often require seminarians to undertake a project that will prepare them to carry out such tasks in the future. In fact, one of the distinguishing factors differentiating those congregations that are involved in community affairs from those that are not is whether or not their pastor graduated from a theological seminary (Thomas, Quinn, Billingsley, & Caldwell 1994).
3. Local religious leaders also tend to be perceived favorably. As a result, when a crisis occurs within a community, religious leaders may be called upon to advise politicians, lend credibility to public action, or simply solve the crisis (Orr, Miller, Roof, & Melton 1994). For example, when racial tension recently broke out in the Grays Ferry section of Philadelphia, the mayor recruited local religious leaders to assist in calming down the residents and leading the campaign for tolerance and racial harmony. The reason the mayor did so was because he recognized that religious leaders are respected and that residents may be more willing to trust them than politicians.
4. Social and human capital are important because they enable people to achieve goals: e.g., overcoming social or political barriers; enhancing social prestige; increasing safety, security and freedom; and enabling economic success. The personal gains that result from being involved in extensive networks can be as simple as finding a reliable babysitter at the last minute, obtaining referrals for possible sources of support, or finding vendors who sell products at wholesale prices. Simply put, the more one is embedded in the network of exchange the more one can benefit from the experience and information of others.
5. These numbers are also supported by a census of congregations in Philadelphia (Cnaan 2000).
6. One example is the coalition of East Brooklyn Churches (EBC). Its goal was to redevelop a deteriorating neighborhood in Brooklyn, New York, that exhibited little financial stability, many abandoned properties, and an out-migration of most working-class families. The first campaigns were well organized and chosen to ensure success. As a result, street signs were replaced, food quality and sanitary conditions in local supermarkets improved, long-abandoned buildings were demolished, smokeshops (places for selling illegal nar-

cotics) were closed, and a voter registration campaign boasted an increase of 10,000 new voters in 1984. When EBC wanted to build 1,000 new homes in Brooklyn, it was estimated that the cost would be $7.5 million. Support for the plan, named the "Nehemiah Project," came from the Missouri Synod Lutherans ($1 million), the Episcopalians of Long Island ($1 million), and the Catholic Bishop of New York who became an avid supporter of the coalition ($2.5 million). Pressured to support the "Nehemiah Project," the city of New York donated the land, paid for landfill removal, and provided $10,000 in interest-free loans to new homeowners. In his review of EBC, Gittings (1987, 10) noted the success of this advocacy and housing coalition: "In an area bereft of banks, civic clubs, industry, and professionals, the churches were the only organizations—apart from the rackets—that remained alive amid the wreckage of the community."

7. Over the past several years, we have been involved in two separate studies of congregational life. The first study was carried out from 1996 to 1998 and included 251 congregations in seven cities (Chicago, Houston, Indianapolis, New York, Philadelphia, and San Francisco) and one small town (Council Grove, Kansas). The findings from this study are presented in Cnaan, with Brody, Handy, Yancy, and Schneider (in press, Rutgers University Press). The second project relates to a congregational census carried out in Philadelphia based 887 congregations. For an interim report on this study, see Cnaan (2000).

8. From a "rational choice" perspective, a major barrier to group participation is the "free rider" problem. This problem relates to the fact that individuals who share important common interests may not choose to join organizations that attempt to address their common concerns. According to such a perspective, "rational" individuals could well choose not to bear the costs of participation associated with organizational membership (time, membership dues) because they could still enjoy group benefits (e.g., favorable legislation) whether or not they are formal members of the organization.

9. In brief, Jesus tells a parable of a man traveling to Jericho who was attacked by thieves, stripped, robbed, wounded, and left for dead. A nobleman, a priest, and a Samaritan passed by, but only the Samaritan stopped to help. Jesus then said that it was he who showed mercy, that he was the man's true neighbor, and he commanded his followers to do likewise.

Chapter 3

1. This is one weakness in the recent National Congregation Study headed by Mark Chaves. At the American Sociological Association meeting in San Francisco in 1998, Chaves, the principal investigator for The National Congregation Study, did not, in any way, allude to para-church groups or their connections with congregations in his oral presentation of the initial findings from the study.

2. Habit for Humanity is a special-interest religious group that builds low-cost housing for the poor and engages on building sites volunteers who are quite divergent racially, religiously, and socially (Fuller 1994).

3. Bread for the World is a Washington, D.C.-based hunger lobby with 44,000 members in grassroots affiliates (Simon 1975; Beckmann & Hoehn 1992).

4. Focus on the Family is an evangelical ministry that has galvanized individuals and local congregations to greater political involvement around family-related legislation and policy (Dobson 1992; Rozell & Wilcox 1995, 1996).

5. Pax Christi USA is a Roman Catholic peace education and activist organization that works for the conversion of weapons industries to peaceful purposes and educates broadly on domestic and other forms of violence (McNeal 1992, 211–49).

6. PICO is an Oakland, California-based national network of church-based community organizations to renew neighborhoods, empower grassroots leadership, hold elected officials responsible to the neighborhoods, and gain essential services (Rogers 1990).

7. Participants at the 1995 PAX CHRISTI national assembly in Portland, Maine applauded President Richard Pateenaude of the University of Southern Maine for abolishing ROTC on his campus.

8. An interesting effort that addresses whether religiously generated social capital is somehow special was undertaken in the Chicago public school systems. One of the authors of an important study of social capital in the Catholic school systems, *Catholic Schools and the Common Good,* was hired to replicate in public schools the same kind of social capital found in the Catholic schools. He was unable to do so—absent were the religious motivation and a religious sense of community, some religio-ideological sense of common purpose, and the common sacrifice made in paying tuition, taking lower salaries to teach in schools, or raising funds for the schools by parents and students. As a result, he was totally unable to translate for the public school systems either the network of support of parents, students, faculty, and administrators, or the sense of trust and mutuality (in short, the social capital) that were found to be the major ingredients of success of Catholic schools in educating minority students toward achievement. Perhaps the flaw stemmed from a fundamental assumption of the project that religious social capital was, *tout court,* the same as any other kind of social capital. The purported "Catholic Lessons for America's Schools" of *Catholic Schools and the Common Good* did not, however, translate into a more secular context (Bryk, Lee, & Holland 1993, 297-327).

Chapter 4

1. The following account is based upon personal observation, May 29, 1994, San Antonio, TX. Research for the study of the Industrial Areas Foundation was supported by the American Academy of Arts and Sciences Project on Social Capital, the Louisville Institute of the Lilly Endowment and the Ford Foundation. I would like to thank the Mellon Foundation's Sawyer Program on the Performance of Democracies at the Center for International Affairs at Harvard University as well as Fordham University for fellowship support in completing the analysis of research data. I would also like to thank Ernesto Cortes, Jr., and the Southwest IAF network for their assistance in conducting the research and analysis presented here. And I would like to thank Richard L. Wood, Frank Pierson, Corwin Smidt and several anonymous reviewers for helpful comments on earlier versions of this chapter. Please direct correspondence to Mark R. Warren, Department of Sociology and Anthropology, Fordham University, Bronx, NY 10458; e-mail: warren@murray.fordham.edu.

2. See Appleman (1996) for a description of the different networks, and some data from a survey of three of them. For a discussion of a variety of church-based efforts in the inner city, see Clemetson & Coates (1992).

3. The IAF network has had many significant campaign successes outside of Texas as well. The IAF's affiliate in East Brooklyn developed the Nehemiah

Homes affordable housing project, which became a model for federal legisla-tion of that name (Ross 1995). BUILD in Baltimore initiated a "common-wealth" pact to supply college and work opportunities to high school gradu-ates. It also won city council passage of legislation requiring private contrac-tors for public services to pay a "union wage" (Orr 1992), a campaign repli-cated with success by the IAF's Metro New York network . The IAF's California network pushed the state legislature to pass a "moral minimum wage" that substantially increased the pay of low-wage workers.

4. I conducted field research between 1993 and 1999, employing a combination of in-depth interviews, participation observation, and analysis of organization documents and newspapers articles. For further discussion of some of the state-wide political campaigns of the Texas IAF, see Warren (2001), Wong (1997), Wilson and Menzies (1997), and Shirley (1997).

5. The authors also note that church membership increases political participa-tion among African-American Protestants more than Hispanic Catholics because Protestant congregations provide greater opportunities for skill devel-opment by lay members—in committees, ministries, and governing boards—than the more hierarchically organized Catholic parishes.

6. Edwards and Foley (1998) discuss this issue at greater length, but offer a somewhat different argument. They suggest that Putnam diverged from James Coleman's (1990) more structural approach to social capital, particularly in his work on the United States (Putnam 1995a). In my view, Putnam does treat social capital as a community-level phenomenon, with community defined geographically at potentially different levels—local, regional, and national. My concern is to demonstrate the importance of how social capital is structured in the different institutions that mediate these communities.

7. For a more detailed analysis of the IAF's relational organizing and nonparti-san political strategy, see Warren (1998; 2001).

8. Based on an analysis of data collected on turn-out figures to large actions in 1992 and 1993, most COPS parishes, and most Catholic parishes in other IAF affiliates like Metro Alliance and ACT in Fort Worth, can turn out 75-100 parishioners to large actions. The strongest can reach 200. Protestant churches in Metro Alliance and ACT, by contrast, turn out only 25-50 par-ticipants, with the strongest reaching 100 parishioners. COPS reaches 50,000 families through 27 parishes. It attracted 3400 members from 27 parishes to its 20th anniversary convention, an average of almost 125 per parish (person-al observation, May 29, 1994, San Antonio, Texas). Meanwhile, the mainly Protestant ACT reaches 25,000 families through 22 congregations. It drew 1500 members from the 22 congregations to its 10th anniversary convention, an average of about 75 per church (interview with the lead organizer, Perry Perkins, August 25, 1993, Fort Worth, Texas). Observations and reports from other network organizations show a similar pattern.

9. Exactly how to defend those rights has often been controversial, especially in Latin America, where the Pope opposed liberation theology. For a more thor-ough discussion of Catholic social thought, see Dorr (1983). On the influence of Vatican II, see Burns 1992). McGreevy (1996) discusses the impact of Vatican II on the American church's approach to issues of race and poverty.

10. On liberation theology, see Levine (1992). For a further discussion compar-ing the IAF to base communities, see Rogers (1990, 136–39).

11. *Gaudium et Spes: Pastoral Constitution of the Church in the Modern World, 1965,* reprinted in O'Brien and Shannon (1977, 200).

12. Author's interview with Reverend Mike Haney, July 19, 1993, San Antonio,

Texas. The pastoral obligation to respond to the social and economic needs was expressed in many interviews conducted with IAF-affiliated priests, including Father Al Jost, July 8, 1993; Father James Janish, May 27, 1994; Father Ed Pavlicek, July 9, 1993; Father Mike Haney, July 19, 1993; all in San Antonio, Texas; and Father Ignacio Cizur, June 4, 1993, in Dallas, Texas.

13. For a broader discussion of the changing role of the laity in the church, see D'Antonio et al. (1989).

14. The encouragement and support of bishops was mentioned in many interviews with priests, including, for example, the author's interview with Father James Janish, May 27, 1994, San Antonio, Texas.

15. Author's interview with Reverend Rosendo Urrabazo, July 19, 1993, San Antonio, Texas.

16. Author's interview with Beatrice Cortez, July 12, 1993, San Antonio, Texas.

17. There are several sources for this conclusion: personal observation, examination of active committee member lists of the organizations; and interviews with several Catholic pastors, for example Father James Janish, May 27, 1994, San Antonio, Texas.

18. For a related, but somewhat different, treatment of these institutional issues, see Skerry (1993, 166–73). In discussing the organizational affinity between the IAF and the Catholic church, Skerry emphasizes, one-sidedly in my view, the hierarchical nature of the two organizations.

19. Interview with Pauline Cabello, July21, 1993,San Antonio, Texas. Emphasis made by Cabello.

20. Author's interview with Patricia Ozuna, July 20, 1993, San Antonio, Texas.

21. Author's interview with Beatrice Cortez, July 12, 1993, San Antonio, Texas.

22. Author's interview with Ernesto Cortes, May 23, 1996, San Antonio, Texas.

23. Author's interview with Reverend Claude Black, July 21, 1993, San Antonio, Texas. Reverend Black, frustrated with the difficulty of founding a black organization, later joined the IAF affiliate Metro Alliance.

24. Author's interview with Revered Barry Jackson, March 4, 1997, Dallas, Texas.

25. For a treatment of the social and political activist traditions in COGIC, see Franklin (1996). Omar McRoberts (1999) discusses the more recent entry of black Pentecostal churches into social and political action in Boston.

26. Author's interview with Reverend Gerald Britt, June 4, 1993, Dallas, Texas. Baptists, which represent the largest African-American religious tradition, make up the vast majority of black churches in the Texas IAF. Some African Methodist Episcopal churches are also involved. Black Methodist congregations are not quite as fiercely independent as Baptist ones.

27. There are a couple of exceptions where the black minister is not involved in the IAF organization. But in these cases the church as a whole is currently inactive in the IAF, although officially still a member.

28. For a related discussion of African-American Protestant participation in the IAF, see Skerry (1993, 166–68). Skerry argues that the entrepreneurial nature of black pastorship makes the minister fiercely independent and generally difficult to organize into any collective process.

29. Author's interview with Reverend Gerald Britt, March 2, 1997, Dallas, Texas.

30. Author's interview with Reverend Barry Jackson, March 4, 1997, Dallas, Texas.

31. Based upon the author's analysis of membership data supplied by COPS. Metro Alliance, and ACT.

32. Author's interview with Maurice Simpson, August 28, 1993, Fort Worth, Texas.

33. Author's interview with Reverend Barry Jackson, March 4, 1997, Dallas, Texas.
34. I restrict my discussion of the weaknesses here to the IAF's organizing within communities of color. I have analyzed the Texas IAF's experience with white congregations elsewhere (Warren 2001). While the IAF has had some important success in involving white congregations, both Catholic and Protestant, it has not had much success in involving white Southern Baptists, the single largest Protestant denomination in the state.
35. Although this study did not collect systematic data on this issue, observations and interviews with over one hundred IAF leaders in the Texas IAF support this conclusion.
36. For a discussion of political participation amongst the poorest African Americans, see Cohen & Dawson (1993).

Chapter 5

1. Elsewhere, I analyze how various forms of religious participation can either foster or undermine such democratic participation (Wood 1995). The current chapter focuses on the constructive contribution to democracy made via religious social capital.
2. At the same time, this analysis sidesteps two other key debates regarding Putnam's work. The first concerns whether Putnam overly narrows the concept of social capital as articulated by Coleman (1988, 1990). This issue does not affect the present analysis because its focus on democratic success not only makes appropriate the attention given to trust and horizontal networks as key forms of social capital; but also because it does not assume that these are the only key forms. The second debate concerns the weakness of Putnam's 1995 data on the U.S. The present analysis does not use Putnam's U.S. data or assume that social capital has eroded in the U.S. as a whole (though see next note on Putnam's more recent work). For an excellent discussion of the first debate, see Foley and Edwards (1997). Putnam's key interlocutor in the second debate has been Skocpol (1996); see also Tarrow (1996).
3. Note, however, that Putnam's recent work (2000) presents strong empirical evidence that social capital has eroded systematically in the United States over the last thirty years. These critics now must contend with this much stronger evidence.
4. Church-based community organizing is quite distinct from the more familiar model of Christian political mobilization adopted by groups such as the Christian Coalition, Focus on the Family, and the Traditional Values Coalition over the last three decades. See the following accounts of community organizing: Boyte (1989), Greider (1992), and more recent work focusing primarily on faith-based organizing by Hart (2001), Warren (2001), Wood (1997, 1999, and forthcoming), Coleman and Wood (2001).
5. In this volume, Chapter 4 by Mark Warren focuses on the work of the Industrial Areas Foundation in Texas and the present chapter focuses on the work of PICO in California. Although all four networks can claim distinctive characteristics to their work—differences that matter but are beyond my purposes here—overall their strongest federations are far more alike than they are different. In this sense, the four networks plus a handful of independent efforts make up a coherent organizational field called "church-based community organizing," and this study focuses on PICO as a case study of this wider field. Generally, the dynamics analyzed here for a strong PICO federation

would apply also to the stronger federations in the other faith-based organiz-ing networks.

6. See *Beyond Identity Politics,* edited by John Anner (South End Press, 1996) for the only available book-length account of multiracial organizing.

7. In using the phrase "promoting democracy," I mean both halves of what Verba et al. (1995) call "voice" and "equality": the promotion of civic participation among those previously excluded from substantial participation, and the pur-suit of public policies that further egalitarian outcomes in society.

8. See the author's forthcoming book *Faith in Action* for a fuller discussion of the fieldwork underlying this study. Ethnographic data were collected during monthly meetings of the core citywide leadership of both organizations, as well as smaller weekly meetings in CTWO and at individual churches in PICO. I also observed both organizations' high-profile political events and lower-profile prayer vigils and fundraising events, their background research meetings with political officials, academics, and corporate leaders, and their participation at government-sponsored public hearings. I attended training workshops led by PICO organizers, political education and study groups led by CTWO organizers, the five-day "national training" run by PICO, and some parts of the summer-long training institute for minority organizers run by CTWO. The interviews in Oakland and five other cities lasted from 45 minutes to 2 hours, and included organizing staff, local leaders, and religious pastors, as well as political leaders the organizations have targeted.

9. They do not have any significant level of influence nationally, though PICO, the IAF, and perhaps Gamaliel now can claim to be national organizing efforts. Any real national-level influence will almost certainly require the four organizing networks to collaborate—which appears to be a distant possibility. Some efforts in this regard have been initiated, but it remains a very real Achilles heel of this movement.

10. Recently (Summer 2000), the PICO California Project was a primary force in transforming political dynamics surrounding healthcare reform in the state. This important story is beyond the purposes of this chapter, but told in detail in the author's forthcoming book *Faith in Action.*

11. But this legitimacy is not pure, because some sectors of American political cul-ture (and, in particular, many political elites) see religion as a dubious partic-ipant in the public realm (Carter 1993). Also, some neighborhood residents see the local church as an alienating presence rather than as a source of legit-imate authority

12. Different federations vary in this last regard, however. The Oakland federa-tion collaborated significantly with elected officials, but also specifically dis-tanced itself from them both in order to sustain its autonomy. In contrast, some observers saw the New Orleans federation as closely identified with the reformist mayor there. If accurate—and my own fieldwork in New Orleans was too brief to reliably assess this issue—this no doubt carries with it oppor-tunities for implementing the organization's agenda but also very real risks of losing autonomy and credibility.

Chapter 6

1. Social capital developed out of James Coleman's explanation for the impact on academic achievement of the social networks—what he called a value com-munity—surrounding urban Catholic schools (Coleman & Hoffer 1987; Coleman 1990). From there, the concept traveled to Italy, where Robert

Putnam has used it to explain the varying performance of Italy's regional governments. In Italy, religion—or at least Catholicism—dampens the formation of social capital. Putnam notes that among Italians, "organized religion . . . is an alternative to the civic community, not a part of it" (1993, 107). He does not suggest that this finding generalizes to all religious involvement, however, but rather that the Catholic Church's unique role in Italian society saps its members' civic initiative. Indeed Putnam (1995) himself, in bringing the concept of social capital back to the U.S., expresses concern over what his evidence suggests is a decline in Americans' rates of church attendance and membership in church-related groups.

2. The precise wording of the question, unfortunately, does not allow us to differentiate between volunteering for a church per se and a religiously oriented group not attached to a church.

3. This can be determined by dividing the second column (those who have volunteered in the previous month) by the first column (those who have volunteered in the last year). The resulting number can be considered a rough measure of the dedication to that type of voluntary activity. Religious volunteering has the highest quotient, almost 75 percent, of all forms of volunteering.

4. There is a relatively extensive literature on how to classify Protestant denominations. In drawing from that literature, denominations have been coded as recommended by Kellstedt and Green (1993). *Evangelical Protestant:* Southern Baptist Convention, American Baptist Convention, National Baptist Convention of America, National Baptist Convention USA, other Baptist, Baptist (not further specified), Missouri Synod Lutheran. *Mainline Protestant:* Episcopalian, Lutheran Church in America, other Lutheran, Lutheran (not further specified), United Methodist Church, other Methodist, Methodist (not further specified), Presbyterian Church in the US, United Presbyterian Church in the US, other Presbyterians, Presbyterians (not further specified), United Church of Christ, Disciples of Christ, other Protestant, Protestant (not further specified). *Black Protestant:* all blacks who belong to a Protestant denomination. Because of the imprecision of the denominational categories on the Giving and Volunteering questionnaire, we opted to include more than just those blacks who belong to predominantly African-American denominations.

5. This table weights the data to reflect the sociodemographic composition of the United States, a practice followed for all figures and tables.

6. The analysis reported here is restricted to a measure of whether respondents report volunteering in the last year, rather than the last month. In doing so, some accuracy is sacrificed, as experience has shown that the more recent the behavior measured, the more accurate the measure will be (Brady 1999). However, the slight loss in accuracy is warranted for two reasons. First, political volunteering constitutes one of the types of voluntarism, and is thus subject to an obvious temporal cycle (Rosenstone & Hansen 1993). Since the Giving and Volunteering surveys were conducted in the spring, a question about political volunteering in the past month would not include the bulk of campaign work done in the United States, which occurs in the fall. The second reason for using the question about volunteering in the last year is simply that most of the other literature on this subject employs the same measure. The reader should note that, almost invariably, any result reported is even more striking when volunteering in the last month is substituted.

7. This is consistent with previous research (Wuthnow 1997; Wilson & Jonoski 1995).

8. The complete list of organizations included in the nonreligious category is as follows: health (including mental health); education/instruction (formal and informal); human services; recreation (for adults); arts, culture, and humanities; work-related; youth development; private and community foundations, international/foreign (in U.S. and abroad).

9. These categories, while mutually exclusive, are not truly exhaustive. The category "other" has been excluded from the analysis, since there is no way of knowing what sort of volunteering this entails. This category constitutes only a tiny fraction of responses to the various volunteering questions, however.

10. More specifically, these three categories themselves are made up of the following types of groups: political party clubs (Democratic, Republican, other); nonpartisan political or community groups; other political causes; environmental quality protection; beautification; animal-related activities (exhibitions, public education, animal population control); animal protection and welfare (humane societies, wildlife and animal sanctuaries); civil rights; community and social action; advocacy (includes minority and women's equity issues); community improvement; community capacity planning; science; technology; technical assistance; voluntarism; philanthropy; charity; consumers organizations; advocacy organizations such as nuclear freeze, antipoverty boards.

11. This analysis has rested on the assumption that religious involvement has an exogenous effect on volunteering. In other words, the analysis has assumed that the causal arrow runs *from* church *to* the voluntary sector, and not the other way around. It is likely that this is not entirely the case. Sociologists of religion have noted that people are increasingly likely to shop around for a religious denomination to attend. It is not improbable that one of the criteria used by church-shoppers would be opportunities for voluntary activity. If this is so, then these results are slightly biased. But even with an awareness of this possibility, it seems reasonable to assume that the primary causal relationship runs from church attendance to volunteering. Using intuitive language, it seems more probable that people go to church and are invited to volunteer than that they go to volunteer and are invited to attend church.

12. We are aware of the controversy surrounding self-reporting of church attendance. See, for example, Hadaway, Marler, and Chaves 1993, 1998; Caplow 1998; Hout and Greeley 1998; Woodberry 1998; Smith 1998. Many scholars would question these numbers because they were collected by Gallup, whose surveys critics claim overestimate church attendance. These numbers may be inflated, we admit, but our interest is in comparing church attendance across denominations. As long as whatever bias is contained in these self-reports does not differ according to denomination—and we have no reason to think that it does—then our conclusion that the voluntary community is not disproportionately composed of one religious tradition holds.

13. A warning about the interpretation of this table is in order. Note that the various types of volunteering are not mutually exclusive but instead overlap. That is, someone who volunteers for a religious group might also volunteer for an advocacy group. Because people who volunteer for one thing are likely to volunteer for another, this is unavoidable. Likewise, the vehicles by which people are recruited are also not mutually exclusive. This too is unavoidable because this question on the survey asks respondents to indicate *all* the vehicles of recruitment that apply. Thus, this table *cannot* tell us that, say, people who are mobilized into advocacy volunteering are specifically recruited through their churches. It only says that people who volunteer for advocacy

causes (and who may volunteer for other things), are more likely to have been asked by someone at their church to participate in some type of volunteering than people who do not volunteer for advocacy causes (and who may volunteer for other things).

14. Including age squared allows the model to account for a possible curvilinear effect of age. It is probable that while there is a generally monotonic increase in volunteering as someone ages, volunteering falls off sharply for the elderly as they become less physically able to perform volunteer work.

15. They are Mormons, Jews, and those who report identifying with an assortment of small faiths such as Eastern Orthodox, Islam, and Christian Science, which for the purposes of our model have been grouped together as the catch-all category of "other."

16. To be precise, the item about whether one's parents volunteered was contained in a separate question. Respondents could specify whether their mother, father, or both volunteered. This was recoded to be a dichotomous variable— either one or both parents volunteered or not.

17. The Giving and Volunteering data limit the conclusions that can to be drawn. First, they are obviously based on retrospective reports, which are somewhat unreliable. Admittedly, there is no independent confirmation that these respondents had the experiences they said they had. These results, however, meet the plausibility criterion outlined by Verba, Schlozman, and Brady (1995), who report the results from a similar question. For example, activity in a religious organization increases the probability of religious volunteering, but no other types of volunteering. Likewise, being active in student government increases the probability of volunteering in an advocacy group as an adult. Obviously, we do not know if these responses are endogenous, so that today's volunteers are more likely to "remember" volunteering when young. But the results are certainly not noise. Note also that in making this argument for the effect of church involvement over time, the independent variable has changed. The analysis to this point has focused on church attendance; here the only independent variable measured was activity in a religious group. These are not the same, but are presumably highly correlated.

18. When all respondents are considered, the Giving and Volunteering data show this same relationship. For example, the bivariate correlation coefficients for the variables measuring time spent last month volunteering in each of religious, secular, informal, and advocacy activities are all positive. The more time spent on one type of volunteering, the more time spent on another.

19. To interpret this result, it is important to remember that this analysis only includes volunteers, and so these are probabilities of performing *nonreligious* volunteer work given that the respondent performs *some type* of volunteer work. Recall that this is not a model predicting the decision to volunteer generally, but rather what the respondent decides to do once he has made that decision. With that in mind, however, the decline in the probability of non-religious volunteering as church attendance increases is nevertheless substantively significant, and it runs counter to the more general trend of religion serving to enhance voluntarism.

20. Wuthnow's discussion of the voluntary activity of Evangelicals on one hand and Mainline Protestants and Catholics on the other does not include Black Protestants.

21. The activities coded as being for church maintenance are: aide to clergy, choir member/director, church ushers, deacons/deaconesses, parish visitors, and Sunday School/Bible teachers. The only activity engaged in by religious vol-

unteers which is unambiguously to benefit the wider community is volunteering for a soup kitchen. We have assumed that of those respondents who chose "other" as an activity, half were participating in a church maintenance activity (a conservative assumption). Even if all of those who chose "other" volunteer for activities in the wider community, that would still leave 75 percent of religious volunteering squarely inside the church.

22. This question was only asked in the 1995 survey.

23. We realize that this model does not account for the fact that people might attend a few meetings of a lot of organizations and thus report that they spend a large amount of time "volunteering," when their voluntarism is limited to attendance at meetings only. To account for this possibility, we also ran these models with a variable for number of organizations with which one affiliates. The substantive results do not change.

Chapter 8

1. Although religion's capacity to nurture reciprocity contributes to the formation of social capital, religiously induced reciprocity may have negative consequences for group action because it potentially undermines leadership accountability in African-American politics and society (Harris 1999).

2. The 7.5 million-member National Baptist Convention, USA, the largest religious organization of African Americans in the United States, has over thirty thousand churches and is geographically organized around more than 120 state conventions and district associations, many of which were founded during the late nineteenth century (Payne 1991, 32–47). The other two major Baptist organizations, the 3.5 million-member National Baptist Convention of America, Inc. and the 1.2 million-member Progressive Baptist Convention, two organizations that broke from the National Baptist Convention, USA, are similarly organized. These African-American Baptists have complete organizational autonomy from national and state associations over the governance of their churches and are congregationally centered, with many having their own constitutions that dictate the duties of the pastor, deacons, trustees, and clerical and support staff (Mukenge 1983).

3. Founded in the late eighteenth century out of protest against the racial discriminatory practices of the Methodist Episcopal Church, the African Methodist Episcopal Church is the oldest organized religious denomination of African Americans. The denomination has 3.5 million members with over eight thousand churches in nineteen episcopal districts (Payne 1991, 54–64). The General Conference, the supreme body of the A.M.E. Church, meets every four years (coinciding with the U.S. presidential elections). Delegates are elected to represent their districts at the General Conference, and denominational officers, including bishops, are elected by convention delegates. District and quarterly meetings are held between the General Conferences. The 1.2 million-member African Methodist Episcopal Zion Church (1796) and the 1 million-member Christian Methodist Episcopal Church (1870) are similarly structured.

4. In the Civic Participation Study, nearly 70 percent of African Americans report attending church services at least once a month, while white (55 percent) and Latinos (60 percent) attend church at relatively lower rates. Similarly, while 72 percent of African Americans report contributing funds to religious institutions, only 63 percent of whites and 58 percent of Latinos make contributions to churches. See Verba, Schlozman, and Brady (1995), Table 15.7.

5. The survey asks: "Here is a list of things that people sometimes have to do as part of their (church/synagogue) activities. After I read each one, please tell me whether or not you have engaged in that activity in the last six months as part of your (church/synagogue) activities. Have you written a letter? Gone to a meeting where you took part in making decisions? Planned or chaired a meeting? Given a presentation or speech?"

6. See Thomas E. Cavanagh's *Inside Black America: The Message of the Black Vote in the 1984 Elections.* Washington, DC: Joint Center for Political and Economic Studies, 1985, Table 7, p. 24. Black men's reported church attendance by age mirrors their reported voter participation rates. In the 1993-1994 National Black Politics Study, 41 percent of black men in the 18–20 (N = 17) and 21–24 (N = 17) age groups reported attending church weekly, while 51 percent of black men in the 55–64 cohort (N = 37) and 60 percent of the black men in the 65–74 cohort (N = 27) attended weekly church services.

7. The following are the listed options for one's activism: (1) I find it exciting, (2) I want to learn about my religion, (3) The chance to work with people who share my ideals, (4) I want to affirm my religious faith, (5) The chance to meet important and influential people, (6) The chance to further the goals of my religion, (7) The chance to influence government policy, (8) The chance to lend a hand to people who need help, (9) The desire for religious education for my child, (10) My duty as a member of my religion, (11) The recreational activities offered by my church or synagogue, (12) I am the kind of person who does my share, (13) The chance to further my job and career, (14) The chance for recognition from people I respect, (15) The chance to be with people I enjoy, (16) I did not want to say no to someone who asked, (17) I might want to get help on a personal or family problem, (18) The direct services provided by members, and (19) The chance to make the community or nation a better place to live.

8. Three responses—feelings of excitement, the desire to influence government policy, and the social pressures of turning down a request—did not fit into any of the four categories.

Chapter 9

1. "Rent-seeking" refers to attempts by a person or special-interest group to influence public policy in order to obtain particular benefits at the expense of all others in a community. For example, rent-seeking behavior includes lobbying the government for particular taking, spending, or regulatory policies that would confer benefits or special advantages to the particular person or group at the expense of taxpayers or consumers generally.

2. Much of the social capital literature struggles with this distinction between communalism and associational involvement. Walzer depicts the free association of people for the sake of sociability itself, forming and reforming groups of all sorts, as leading to some communal sense (Walzer 1991, 298). Coleman (1990), on the other hand, saw nothing to suggest that voluntary association itself provided resources for individual or collective action. His definition of social capital required the presence of some form of action arising from the associational involvement (Edwards & Foley 1997, 552). Thus, one could envision much of what Walzer describes—free association of people for the sake of sociability itself—but no social capital. Minkoff goes a step further than Walzer, claiming that initial associational involvement develops one's self-concept and the organization of that self-concept that are necessary for the further development of group ties. Association involvement is a step along

the way to creating a larger communal sense. Minkoff (1997, 614) argues that such involvement promotes debate, enlarging the arena of political discourse. On the other hand, Newton (1997, 583) claims that the question remains open as to whether such individual involvement leads to high levels of trust and reciprocity. If trust and reciprocity, and a larger sense of public good, are inherent aspects of social capital, leading to some action, it remains unclear whether associational involvement alone creates social capital. This study attempts to shed further light on this debate.

3. The German Reformed-dominated township near Wellsburg, representative of the community as a whole, experienced a tremendous increase in farm size in the 1970s—55 percent (Iowa State Assessor). This high level of growth has continued (U.S. Department of Commerce 1984 and 1994). Farm population changes are consistent with farm size change. Grundy County (largely German Reformed) saw a large drop in farm population between 1980 and 1990 ("Iowa Farm Population Drop" 1992). Due to lack of other opportunities, and increasing farm size, the population of Wellsburg had continued to drop (Iowa Department of Economic Development 1994).

4. The lack of commitment to Catholic education may be explained by Stark and McCann's (1993) findings that a greater proportion of Catholic families do send their children to parochial schools in less Catholic environments. In the Catholic environment of Cascade, Catholic education may seem unnecessary. However, this does not explain the lack of initiative on the part of the community to form its own school district.

Chapter 10

1. These fourteen options with regard to group members were the following: professional or job-related groups; social service groups for the elderly, poor, or disabled; religious or church-related groups; environmental groups; youth groups (scouts, youth clubs); community-based or neighborhood associations; health-related groups; recreational groups; senior citizen groups; veterans' groups; women's groups; political groups; educational, arts, music, or cultural organizations; and/or a small group that "meets regularly and provides support or caring for those who participate in it."

2. Religious tradition is a concept used to designate a grouping of religious communities that share a distinctive worldview. It is typically measured by denominational affiliations (cf. Kellstedt, Green, Guth, & Smidt 1996), and scholars typically recognize six major traditions in the United States: evangelical Protestant, mainline Protestant, black Protestant, Roman Catholic, Jews, and the non-religious or secular population. In the analysis here, however, seculars, Jews, and all other remaining respondents are categorized together and simply labeled "other."

3. This percent of Roman Catholics in Canada and the United States may appear to be somewhat lower than what one might expect. For example, in Canada, census data in 1981 revealed slightly more that 40 percent were Roman Catholics (see, for example, Bibby, Hewitt, & Roof 1998, 239)) and the rough figure used in the United States is 25 percent. Two different factors may account for this lower level. First, the church affiliation data was last available in 1981, nearly two decades prior to this survey. And, second, those respondents who claimed religious affiliation but who did not report standard religious beliefs (e.g., belief in God) were removed from the category of religious affiliation they claimed. Thus, such "nominal" Catholics were removed

from the Roman Catholic category and placed in the "secular" category, a category incorporated within the "other" category of this paper.

4. Regularly is used here to denote "weekly," while frequently is used to denote "more than once a week."

5. Of course, it is possible that the connection between religion and culture is stronger in the United States than Canada so as to encourage Americans, given social influences, to provide a more "religious" answer. See, for example, Reimer (1995).

6. According to Lipset, the American Revolution served to sever American ties not only with Great Britain but with its more collective orientations as well, while the counter-revolutionary origins of Canada supposedly led Canadians to embrace this greater collective orientation.

7. Some may attend church on a periodic or regular basis, but their involvement in church activities may stop with such attendance. On the other hand, others may be involved in church activities (whether in terms of committee work, social ministries, or education) beyond simple attendance at worship services.

8. Responses of "not at all," "at least once a year," and "a few times a year" were coded as low levels of church attendance. Responses of "once a month" and "a few times a month" were coded as medium levels of church attendance, while responses of "once a week" or "more than once a week" were coded as high levels of church attendance.

9. The resultant Multiple R for this eight-variable model used to account for variation in the index tapping social engagement is .456. Accordingly, the model accounts for approximately 21 percent of the variation in the dependent variable (Multiple R squared).

10. The resultant Multiple R for this eight-variable model used to account for variation in the index tapping social engagement is .529. Accordingly, the model accounts for approximately 28 percent of the variation in the dependent variable (Multiple R squared).

Chapter 11

1. In other places I have compared and contrasted cultural and structural resources (Williams 1995, 1996; Williams & Demerath 1998). See also Kniss (1996) and Jasper (1997) for analyses of the two ideas.

2. The phrase "rhetoric of obedience" is my term interpreting Jasper's argument. Similarly, while Jasper does not put it in these terms, his distinction between instrumental and moralist plays on the ambiguous meaning of "right" in the American vernacular—whether right means "correct" rather than incorrect in an analytic and technical sense, discernable through empirical testing, or whether right means "morally approved" and normatively prescriptive, dependent upon unvarying principles.

3. There is an irony in the current situation that even as gender, race, and ethnicity are being increasingly understood as "socially constructed" categories, their status as sources of political authority remain ascriptive and in some cases become increasingly "essentialized."

4. One might also argue that religious language identified the national community in the North American colonies before liberal rights talk evolved here.

Chapter 12

1. On the meanings of civil society, see especially Alexander and Smith (1993),

Cohen and Arato (1992), Gellner (1994), J. Hall (1995), and Seligman (1992).

2. These are emphasized in Berger, Neuhaus, and Novak (1996).

3. On the definition of institutions, see Berger and Luckmann (1966) and Powell and DiMaggio (1991).

4. An alternative interpretation is presented in Ladd (1996).

5. Research in progress by Timothy Dowd and John Pollack.

6. On community service, see Walter (1990, 1996).

7. On religion as an institution, see Wuthnow (1994c).

8. Trends in religious participation and their relationships with civic participation are discussed in greater detail in Wuthnow (1996).

9. Religion's role in promoting civic skills among the poor is emphasized in Verba, Scholzman, and Brady (1995); see also Chapter 2 by Cnaan and associates in this volume.

Chapter 13

1. Since the specific dependent variable examined differs somewhat between these studies, it may also be simply a function of the particular dependent variable chosen.

2. There are various other ways in which religion can serve democratic life. The discussion here is simply limited to these three.

3. Pragmatism as a philosophical approach is amoral in nature; it is not necessarily immoral. But because it is amoral in nature, pragmatism tends to "ignore" moral considerations.

References

Aitchison, A. 1994. Personal communications. July 13.

Alexander, J., & P. Smith. 1993. The discourse of civil society: A new proposal for cultural studies. *Theory and Society* 22: 151–207.

Almond, G., & S. Verba. 1963. *The civic culture*. Boston: Little, Brown.

Ammerman, N. 1997. *Congregation and community*. New Brunswick, NJ: Rutgers University Press.

Anner, J. 1996. *Beyond identity politics*. Boston: South End Press.

Appleman, J. 1996. *Evaluation study of institution-based organizing*. Unpublished manuscript.

Beckmann, D., & R. Hoehn. 1992. *Transforming the politics of hunger*. Washington, DC: Bread for the World Institute, Occasional Paper # 2.

Bellah, R. 1975. *The broken covenant: American civil religion in time of trial*. New York: Seabury Press.

Bellah, R., R. Madsen, W. M. Sullivan, A. Swidler, & S. M. Tipton. 1985. *Habits of the heart*. Berkeley: University of California Press.

_____. 1991. *The good society*. New York: Knopf.

_____. 1996. *Habits of the heart: Individualism and commitment in American life* (2nd ed.). Berkeley: University of California Press.

Bennett, W. J. 1995. Moral corruption in America. *Commentary* (November): 29.

Berger, P. L., & T. Luckmann. 1966. *The social construction of reality*. Garden City, NY: Doubleday.

Berger, P. L., R. J. Neuhaus, & M. Novak, eds. 1996. *To empower people: From state to civil society*. Washington, DC: AEI Press.

239

Bergesen, A. 1984. Social control and corporate organization: A Durkheimian perspective. In D. Black, ed., *Toward a general theory of social control*. New York: Academic Press.

Bernstein. R. 1986. The meaning of public life. In R. Lovin, ed., *Religion and American public life: Interpretations and explorations*. Mahwah, NJ: Paulist Press.

Berry, J., K. Portney, & K. Thomson. 1993. *The rebirth of urban democracy*. Washington, DC: The Brookings Institution.

Bibby, R., W. E. Hewitt, & W. C. Roof. 1998. Religion and identity: The Canadian, American, and Brazilian cases. *International Journal of Comparative Sociology* 39 (June): 237–50.

Bjorklund, E. M. 1964. Ideology and culture exemplified in southwestern Michigan. *Annals of the Association of American Geographers* 54: 22741.

Blanshard, B. 1959. Inward light and outward darkness. In H. M. Lippincott, ed., *Through a Quaker archway*. NY: Thomas Yoseloff.

Booth, J., & P. B. Richard. 1998. Civil society, political capital, and democraticization in Central America. *Journal of Politics* 60 (August): 780–800.

Borchert, J.R. 1987. *America's northern heartland: An economic and historical geography of the Upper Midwest*. Minneapolis: University of Minnesota Press.

Borkman, T., & M. Parisi. 1995. The role of self-help groups in fostering a caring society. In P. G. Schervish, V. A. Hodgkinson, & M. Gates, eds., *Care and community in modern society: Passing on the tradition of service to future generations*. San Francisco: Jossey-Bass.

Bound, J., & R. B. Freeman. 1992. What went wrong? The erosion of the relative earnings of young black men in the 1980s. *Quarterly Journal of Economics* 107: 201–33.

Boyte, H. C. 1989. *Commonwealth: A return to citizen politics*. New York: Free Press.

Boyte, H. C., & N. N. Kari. 1996. *Building America: The democratic promise of public work*. Philadelphia: Temple University Press.

Bradley, B. 1995. National Press Club luncheon speaker. *Federal News Service* (February 9), n.p.

Brady, H. E. 1999. Political participation. In J. Robinson, ed., *Measures of political attitudes*. New York: Academic Press.

Brady, H. E., S. Verba, & K. Schlozman. 1995. Beyond SES: A resource model of political participation. *American Political Science Review* 89: 271–94.

Brehm, J., & W. Rahn. 1997. Individual-level evidence for the causes and consequences of social capital. *American Journal of Political Science* 41 (3): 999–1023.

Brint, S. G. 1994. *In an age of experts: The changing role of professional in politics and public life*. Princeton, NJ: Princeton University Press.

Brinton, H. H. 1953. Education. In J. Kavanaugh, ed., *The Quaker approach*. New York: G. P. Putnams's Sons.

Bromley, D. G., & B. C. Busching. 1988. Understanding the structure of contractual and covenantal social relations: Implication for the sociology of religion. *Sociological Analysis* 49 (S): 15–32.

Brown, C. 1995. Cakes, cards, and candles. *American Demographics* (March), online.

Browning, D., B. J. Miller-McLemore, P. Couture, K. B. Lyon, & R. M. Franklin. 1997. *From culture wars to common ground: Religion and the family debate*. Louisville, KY: Westminster/John Knox.

Bryk, A., V. Lee, & P. Holland. 1993. *Catholic schools and the common good*. Cambridge, MA: Harvard University Press.

Burns, G. 1992. *The frontiers of Catholicism: The politics of ideology in a liberal world*. Berkeley: University of California Press.

Byrne, J. A. 1994. The pain of downsizing. *Business Week* (May 9): 61.

Caplow, T. 1998. The case of the phantom Episcopalians. *American Sociological Review* 63: 112–13.

Caplow, T., H. M. Bahr, J. Modell, & B. A. Chadwick. 1991. *Recent social trends in the United States, 1960–1990*. Montreal: McGill-Queen's University Press.

Capps, D. 1993. *The depleted self*. Minneapolis: Fortress.

Carter, S. 1993. *The culture of disbelief: How American law and politics trivialize religious devotion*. New York: Basic Books.

Casanova, J. 1994. *Public religions in the modern world*. Chicago: University of Chicago Press.

Case, A., & L. Katze. 1991. *The company you keep: Effects of family and neighborhood on disadvantaged youths*. Cambridge, MA: National Bureau of Economic Research, Working Paper 3705.

Castells, M. 1983. *The city and the grassroots: A cross-cultural theory of urban social movements*. Berkeley: University of California Press.

Cavanagh, T. E. 1985. *Inside black America: The message of the black vote in the 1984 elections*. Washington, DC: Joint Center for Political and Economic Studies.

Cavendish, J. 2000. Church-based community activism: A comparison of black and white Catholic congregations. *Journal for the Scientific Study of Religion* 39 (September): 371–84.

Charles, J. A. 1993. *Service clubs in American society: Rotary, Kiwanis, and Lions*. Urbana: University of Illinois Press.

Chaves, M. 1994. Secularization as declining religious authority. *Social Forces* 72: 749–74.

——————. 1999. *Religious organizations and welfare reform: Who will take advantage of "charitable choice?"* Washington, DC: The Aspen Institute.

Chaves, M., & L. Higgins. 1992. Comparing the community involvement of black and white congregations. *Journal for the Scientific Study of Religion* 31 (4): 425–40.

Cherlin, A. J. 1992. *Marriage, divorce, remarriage* (rev. ed.). Cambridge, MA: Harvard University Press.

Chesler, M. 1991. Mobilizing consumer activism in health care: The role of self-help groups. *Research in Social Movements, Conflicts, and Change* 13: 275–305.

Cisneros, H. G. 1996. *Higher ground: Faith communities and community building*. Washington, DC: Department of Housing and Urban Development.

Clemeston, R., & R. Coates. 1992. *Restoring broken places and rebuilding communities: A casebook of African-American church involvement in community economic development*. Washington, DC: National Congress for Community Economic Development.

Clouser, R. A. 1991. *The myth of religious neutrality: An essay on the hidden role of religious belief in theories*. Notre Dame, IN: University of Notre Dame Press.

Cnaan, R. A. 1997. *Social and community involvement of religious congregations housed in historic religious properties: Findings from a six-city study*. Philadelphia: University of Pennsylvania School of Social Work—Program for the Study of Organized Religion and Social Work.

——————. 2000. *Keeping faith in the city: Survey results on 887 congregations*. Philadelphia: Center for Research on Religion and Urban Civic Society, University of Pennsylvania.

Cnaan, R. A., with S. C. Boddie, F. Handy, G. Yancey, & R. Schneider. In press. *The invisible caring hand: American congregations and the provision of welfare*. New Brunswick, NJ: Rutgers University Press.

Cnaan, R. A., with R. J. Wineburg, & S. C. Boddie. 1999. *The newer deal: Social work and religion in partnership*. New York: Columbia University Press.

Cochran, C. E. 1990. *Religion in public and private life*. New York: Routledge.

Cohen, C. J., & M. C. Dawson. 1993. Neighborhood poverty and African American politics. *American Political Science Review* 87: 286–302.

Cohen, J. L., & A. Arato. 1992. *Civil society and political theory*. Cambridge, MA: MIT Press.

Coleman, James S. 1988. Social capital in the creation of human capital. *The American Journal of Sociology* 94: S95–S119.

———. 1990. *Foundations of social theory*. Cambridge, MA: Harvard University Press.

Coleman, James S., & T. B. Hoffer. 1987. *Public and private high schools: The impact of communities*. New York: Basic Books.

Coleman, John A. 1996. Under the cross and the flag. *America* (May 11): 6–14.

———. 1997. Exploding spiritualities: Their social causes, social location and social divide. *Christian Spirituality Bulletin* 5 (Spring): 9–13.

———. 1998. Religion and public life: Some American cases. *Religion* 28 (Spring): 155–69.

Coleman, John A., & R. L. Wood. 2001. PICO: Church-based community organizing. In J. A. Coleman, ed., *Public discipleship and modern citizenship*. Champaign: University of Illinois Press.

Collins, P. H. 1998. *Fighting words: Black women and the search for justice*. Contradictions of Modernity, volume 7. Minneapolis: University of Minnesota Press.

Comfort, W. W. 1959. Four essentials of Quakerism. In H. M. Lippincott, ed., *Through a Quaker archway*. New York: Thomas Yoseloff.

Cone, J. H. 1969. *Black theology and black power*. New York: Seabury.

Cortes, E. 1991. Reflections on the Catholic tradition of family rights. In J. Coleman, ed., *One hundred years of Catholic social thought*. Maryknoll, NY: Orbis Books.

Culhane, D. P., E. F. Dejowski, J. Ibanez, E. Needham, & I. Macchia. 1994. Public shelter admission rates in Philadelphia and New York City: The implications of turnover for sheltered population counts. *Housing Policy Debates* 5: 107–40.

Cunningham, H. 1995. *God and Caesar at the Rio Grande*. Minneapolis: University of Minnesota Press.

Curry-Roper, J. M. 1998a. Worldview and agriculture: A study of two Reformed communities in Iowa. In D. Luidens, C. Smidt, & H. Stoffels, eds., *Signs of vitality in Reformed communities*. Lanham, MD: University Press of America.

———. 1998b. Christian worldview and geography: Positivism, covenantal relations, and the importance of place. In H. Aay & S. Griffioen, eds., *Geography and worldview: A Christian reconnaissance*. Lanham, MD: University Press of America.

Curtis, J. 1971. Voluntary association joining: A cross-national comparative note. *American Sociological Review* 36: 872–80.

Curtis, J., E. Grabb, & D. Baer. 1992. Voluntary association memberships in fifteen countries. *American Sociological Review* 57: 139–52.

Curtis, J., R. Lambert, S. Brown, & B. Kay. 1989. Affiliating with voluntary associations: Canadian-American comparisons. *Canadian Journal of Sociology* 14 (2): 143–61.

D'Antonio, W. et al. 1989. *American Catholic laity in a changing church*. Kansas City, MO: Sheed & Ward.

D'Antonio, W., J. Davidson, D. Hoge, & R. A. Wallace. 1996. *Laity: American and Catholic*. Kansas City, MO: Sheed & Ward.

Delgado, G. n.d. *Beyond the politics of place: New directions in community organizing in the 1990s*. Oakland, CA: Applied Research Center.

Demerath, N. J. III. 1994. The moth and the flame: Religion and politics in comparative blur. *Sociology of Religion* 55: 105–17.

Demerath, N. J. III, & K. S. Straight. 1997. Lambs among the lions: America's culture war in cross-cultural perspective. In R. H. Williams, ed., *Cultural wars in American politics: Critical reviews of a popular myth.* Hawthorne, NY: Aldine de Gruyter.

Demerath, N. J. III, & R. H. Williams. 1992. *A bridging of faiths: Religion and politics in a New England city.* Princeton, NJ: Princeton University Press.

Dobson, J. 1992. *Dare to discipline.* Wheaton, IL: Tyndale House.

Dolan, J. 1985. *The American Catholic experience.* Garden City, NY: Doubleday.

Dorr, D. 1983. *Option for the poor: A hundred years of Vatican social teaching.* Maryknoll, NY: Orbis Books.

Dynes, R., & E. L. Quarantelli. 1980. Helping behavior in large-scale disasters. In D. H. Smith, J. Macauley, and associates, eds., *Participation in social and political activities.* San Francisco: Jossey-Bass.

Eaton, L. 1999. Banks put their faith in building churches. *New York Times,* 10 January, The Metro Section, pp. 19–20.

Eberly, D. 1998. Civic renewal vs. moral renewal. *Policy Review* (September-October): 44–47.

Edelman, J. M. 1977. *Political language.* New York: Academic Press.

Edwards, B., & M. W. Foley, eds. 1997. Social capital, civil society, and contemporary democracy. Special issue of *American Behavioral Scientist* 40 (5).

_____. 1998. Civil society and social capital beyond Putnam. *American Behavioral Scientist* 42 (1): 124–39.

Egerstrom, L. 1994. *Make no small plans: A cooperative revival for rural America.* Rochester, MN: Lone Oak Press.

Elshtain, J. B. 1995. *Democracy on trial.* New York: Basic Books.

Emerging Trends. 1990. Churches rated best able to deal with local community problems. (December): 3–4.

Etzioni, A. 1993. *The spirit of community: Rights, responsibilities, and the communitarian agenda.* New York: Crown.

Fantasia, R. 1988. *Cultures of solidarity: Consciousness, action, and contemporary American workers.* Berkeley: University of California Press.

Fenn, R. K. 1982. *Liturgies and trials: The secularization of religious language.* Oxford: Basil Blackwell.

Finke, R., & R. Stark. 1992. *The churching of America 1776–1990: Winners and losers in our religious economy.* New Brunswick, NJ: Rutgers University Press.

Fischer, C S. 1982. *To dwell among friends: Personal networks in town and city.* Chicago: University of Chicago Press.

Foley, M. W., & B. Edwards. 1996. The paradox of civil society. *Journal of Democracy* 7 (3): 38–52.

_____. 1997. Escape from politics? Social theory and the social capital debate. *American Behavioral Scientist* 40 (5): 550–61.

_____. 1998. Beyond Tocqueville: Civil society and social capital in comparative perspective. *American Behavioral Scientist* 42 (1): 5–20.

Foley, M. W., B. Edwards, & M. Diani. 2001. Social capital reconsidered. In B. Edwards, M. W. Foley, & M. Diani, eds., *Beyond Tocqueville: Civil society and the social capital debate in comparative perspective.* Hanover, NH: University Press of New England

Foner, E. 1988. *Reconstruction: America's unfinished revolution, 1863–1877.* New York: Harper and Row.

Frankl, V. E. 1963. *Man's search for meaning: An introduction to logotherapy* (rev. ed.). Boston: Beacon Press.

Franklin, J. H. 1980. *From slavery to freedom: The history of Negro Americans* (5th ed.). New York: Alfred A. Knopf.

Franklin, R. 1996. "My soul says yes": The urban ministry of the Church of God in Christ. In C. Green, ed., *Churches, cities, and human community: Urban ministry in the United States 1945–1985*. Grand Rapids, MI: Eerdmans.

Fukuyama, F. 1995. *Trust: The social virtues and the creation of prosperity*. New York: Free Press.

Fuller, M. 1994. *The theology of the hammer*. Macon, GA: Smyth & Helwys.

Furstenberg, F. F. 1996. The future of marriage. *American Demographics* (June): 34–40.

Gardner, J. W. 1994. *Building community for leadership studies program*. Washington, DC: Independent Sector.

Gellner, E. 1994. *Conditions of liberty: Civil society and its rivals*. London: Penguin.

Gingerich, B. N. 1985. Property and the gospel: Two reformation perspectives. *Mennonite Quarterly Review* 59: 248–67.

Gittell, R., & A. Vidal. 1998. *Community organizing: Building social capital as a development strategy*. Thousand Oaks, CA: Sage Publications.

Gittings, J. 1987. East Brooklyn churches and the Nehemiah Project: Churches in communities: A place to stand. *Christianity and Crisis* (February 2): 5–11.

Glasser, W. 1965. *Reality therapy: A new approach to psychiatry*. New York: Harper & Row.

Glendon, M. A. 1991. *Rights talk: The impoverishment of political discourse*. New York: Free Press.

Goodwyn, L. 1978. *The populist movement: A short history of the agrarian revolt in America*. Oxford: Oxford University Press.

Gramlich, E., D. Laren, & N. Sealand. 1992. Moving into and out of poor urban areas. *Journal of Policy Analysis and Management* 11: 273–87.

Granovetter, M. 1973. The strength of weak ties. *American Journal of Sociology* 78 (May): 1360–80.

_____. 1974. *Getting a job: A study of contacts and careers*. Cambridge, MA: Harvard University Press.

Greeley, A. 1997a. Coleman revisited: Religious structures as a source of social capital. *American Behavioral Scientist* 40 (5): 587–94.

_____. 1997b. The other civic America: Religion and social capital. *American Prospect* 32 (May-June): 68–73.

Greider, W. 1992. *Who will tell the people? The betrayal of American democracy*. New York: Simon & Schuster.

Grettenberger, S., & P. Hovmand. 1997. The role of churches in human services: United Methodist Churches in Michigan. Paper presented at the 26th annual meeting of the Association for Research on Nonprofit Organizations and Voluntary Action, Indianapolis, December.

Guterbock, T., & J. C. Fries. 1997. *Maintaining America's social fabric: The AARP survey of civic involvement*. Washington, DC: American Association of Retired Persons.

Habermas, J. 1984. *The theory of communicative action, vol. 1: Reason and the rationalization of society*, trans. by T. McCarthy. Boston: Beacon Press.

_____. 1989. *The structural transformation of the public sphere: An inquiry into a category of bourgeois society*, trans. by T. Burger with the assistance of F. Lawrence. Cambridge, MA: MIT Press.

Hadaway, C. K., P. L. Marler, & M. Chaves. 1993. What the polls don't show: A closer look at U.S. church attendance. *American Sociological Review* 58: 741–52.

_____. 1998. Overreporting church attendance in America: Evidence that demands the same verdict. *American Sociological Review* 63: 122–30.

Hall, J. A., ed. 1995. *Civil society: Theory, history, comparison*. London: Polity Press.

Hall, P. D. 1990. The history of religious philanthropy in America. In R. Wuthnow, V. A. Hodgkinson, and associates, eds., *Faith and philanthropy in America: Exploring the role of religion in the voluntary sector*. San Francisco: Jossey-Bass.

_____. 1992. *Inventing the nonprofit sector: And other essays on philanthropy, voluntarism, and nonprofit organizations*. Baltimore: Johns Hopkins University Press.

_____. 1996. Founded on the rock, built upon shifting sands: Churches, voluntary associations and nonprofit organizations in public life, 1850–1990. Unpublished manuscript. Yale University, PONPO, New Haven, CT.

Hamilton, C. V. 1972. *The black preacher in America*. New York: William Morrow.

Hammond, P. E. 1992. *Religion and personal autonomy*. Columbia: University of South Carolina Press.

Harris, F. C. 1994. Something within: Religion as a mobilizer of African-American political activism. *Journal of Politics* 56: 42–68.

_____. 1999. *Something within: Religion in African-American political activism*. New York: Oxford University Press.

Hart, S. 1992. *What does the Lord require? How American Christians think about economic justice*. New York: Oxford University Press.

_____. 2001. *Cultural dilemmas of progressive politics: Styles of engagement among grassroots activists*. Chicago: University of Chicago Press.

Hatch, N. O. 1989. *The democratization of American Christianity*. New Haven: Yale University Press.

Hertzke, A. 1988. *Representing God in Washington*. Knoxville: University of Tennessee Press.

Hill, R. B. 1998. *Report on study of church-based human services*. Baltimore: Associated Black Charities.

A history of Cascade, Iowa, 1843 thru 1977. n.d.

Hodgkinson, V. 1990a. The future of individual giving and volunteering: The inseparable link between religious community and individual generosity. In R. Wuthnow, V. Hodgkinson, and associates, eds., *Faith and philanthropy in America*. San Francisco: Jossey-Bass.

_____. 1990b. From commitment to action: How religious involvement affects giving and volunteering. In R. Wuthnow, V. Hodgkinson, and associates, eds., *Faith and philanthropy in America*. San Francisco: Jossey-Bass.

Hodgkinson, V. A., H. A. Gorski, S. M. Noga, & E. B. Knauft. 1995. *Giving and volunteering in the United States, 1994, volume II: Trends in giving and volunteering by type of charity*. Washington, DC: Independent Sector.

Hodgkinson, V. A., & M. S. Weitzman. 1993. *From belief to commitment: The community service activities and finances of religious congregations in the United States*. Washington, DC: Independent Sector.

_____. 1994. *Giving and volunteering in the United States, 1994*. Washington, DC: Independent Sector.

Hodgkinson, V., M. Weitzman, & A. Kirsh. 1990. From commitment to action: How religious involvement affects giving and volunteering. In R. Wuthnow, V. A. Hodgkinson, and associates, eds., *Faith and philanthropy in America*. San Francisco: Jossey-Bass.

Hoge, D., ed. 1994. Special issue: Patterns of financial contributions to churches. *Review of Religious Research* 36.

Hoge, D., C. Zech, P. McNamara, & M. Donahue. 1996. *Money matters: Personal giving in American churches*. Louisville, KY: Westminster/John Knox.

Houghland, J. G., & J. A. Christenson. 1983. Religion and politics: The relationship of religious participation to political efficacy and involvement. *Sociology and Social Research* 67: 405–20.

Hout, M., & A. Greeley. 1998. What church officials' reports don't show: Another look at church attendance data. *American Sociological Review* 63: 113–19.

Huckfeldt, R., & J. Sprague. 1995. *Citizens, politics, and social communication:*

Information and influence in an election campaign. New York: Cambridge University Press.

Hunter, J. D. 1991. *Culture wars.* New York: Basic Books.

Independent Sector. 1996. *Giving and volunteering in the United States.* Washington, DC: Independent Sector.

Inglehart R. et al. 1990. *World value survey, 1981–1983: Computer file and codebook* (2nd ed.). Ann Arbor, MI: Inter-University Consortium for Political and Social Research.

Iowa Department of Economic Development. 1994. *Community Quick Reference: Wellsburg, Iowa.* Des Moines, IA: May.

Iowa farm population drop. 1992. *Des Moines Register.* July 19: J1–2.

Iowa State Assessor. 1917–1980. *Annual Farm Census: Township data.* Ames: Iowa State University.

Jackson-Beeck, M., & J. Sobal. 1980. The social world of heavy television viewers. *Journal of Broadcasting* 24: 5–11.

Jasper, J. M. 1992. The politics of abstractions: Instrumental and moralist rhetorics in public debate. *Social Research* 59 (2): 315–44.

_____. 1997. *The art of moral protest.* Chicago: University of Chicago Press.

Jenkins, J. C. 1987. Nonprofit organizations and policy advocacy. In W. Powell, ed., *The nonprofit sector.* New Haven, CT: Yale University Press.

Joseph, M. V. 1987. The religious and spiritual aspects of clinical practice: A neglected dimension of social work. *Social Thought* 13 (1): 12–23.

Judis, J. B. 1992. The pressure elite: Inside the narrow world of advocacy group politics. *American Prospect* 9: 15–30.

Kanter. R. 1972. *Commitment and community: Communes and utopias in sociological perspective.* Cambridge, MA: Harvard University Press.

Keith-Lucas, A. 1972. *Giving and taking help.* Chapel Hill: University of North Carolina Press.

Kellstedt, L. A., & J. C. Green. 1993. Knowing God's many people: Denominational preference and political behavior. In D. C. Leege & L. A. Kellstedt, eds., *Rediscovering the religious factor in American politics.* Armonk, NY: M. E. Sharpe.

Kellstedt, L. A., J. Green, J. Guth, & C. Smidt. 1996. Grasping the essentials: The social embodiment of religion and political behavior. In J. C. Green, J. Guth, L. A. Kellstedt, & C. Smidt, eds., *Religion and the culture wars: Dispatches from the front.* Lanham, MD: Rowman & Littlefield.

King, G. 1989. *Unifying political methodology: The likelihood theory of statistical inference.* New York: Cambridge University Press.

Kluegal, J., & R. E. Smith. 1986. *Beliefs about inequality: Americans' view of what is and what ought to be.* New York: Aldine de Gruyter.

Kniss, F. 1996. Ideas and symbols as resources in intrareligious conflict: The case of American Mennonites. *Sociology of Religion* 57: 7–23.

Kunjufu, J. 1994. *Where are you Adam? Why black men don't go to church.* Chicago: African-American Images.

Ladd, E. C. 1996. The data just don't show erosion of America's "social capital." *The Public Perspective* 7 (1): 5–6.

Lamont, M., & M. Fournier, eds. 1992. *Cultivating differences.* Chicago: University of Chicago Press.

Lasch, Christopher. 1979. *The culture of narcissism: American life in an age of diminishing expectations.* New York: Norton.

Launius, R. D. 1986. Quest for Zion: Joseph Smith III and community-building in the reorganization, 1860–1900. In M. L. Draper, ed., *Restoration Studies.* Independence, MO: Herald.

Leege, D. C. 1988. Catholics and the civil order: Parish participation, politics, and civil participation. *The Review of Politics* 50(4): 704–36.

Leege, D. C., & T. A. Trozzolo. 1985. Religious values and parish participation: The paradox of individual needs in a communitarian church. *Notre Dame Study of Catholic Parish Life* 4:1–8.

Leinberger, P., & B. Tucker. 1991. *The new individualists: The generation after* The Organization Man. New York: Harper Collins.

Levi, M. 1996. Social and unsocial capital: A review essay of Robert Putnam's *Making Democracy Work*. *Politics and Society* 24: 45–55.

Levine, D. 1992. *Popular voices in Latin American Catholicism*. Princeton, NJ: Princeton University Press.

Lichterman, P. 1996. *The search for political community*. New York: Cambridge University Press.

Lienisch, Michael. 1994. *Redeeming America: Piety and politics in the new Christian right*. Chapel Hill: University of North Carolina Press.

Lincoln, C. E., & L. H. Mamiya. 1990. *The black church in the African American experience*. Durham, NC: Duke University Press.

Lipset, S. M. 1986. Historical traditions and national characteristics: A comparative analysis of Canada and the United States. *Canadian Journal of Sociology* 11: 113–55.

_____. 1990. *Continental divide*. London: Routledge.

Logan, R. W. 1968. *The betrayal of the Negro: From Rutherford B. Hayes to Woodrow Wilson*. New York: Collier Books.

Luloff, A. E. 1990. Community and social change: How do small communities act? In A. E. Luloff & L. Swanson, eds., *American Rural Communities*. Boulder, CO: Westview.

McLanahan, S., & G. Sandefur. 1994. *Growing up with a single parent*. Cambridge, MA: Harvard University Press.

Mamiya, L. 1994. A social history of the Bethel A.M.E. Church in Baltimore. In J. Wind & J. Lewis, eds., *American congregations*. Chicago: University of Chicago Press.

Mansbridge, J. J. 1991. On the relation of altruism and self-interest. In J. J. Mansbridge, ed., *Beyond self interest*. Chicago: University of Chicago Press.

Marulo, S., & J. Lofland, eds. 1990. *Peace Action in the 80's*. New Brunswick, NJ: Rutgers University Press.

Massey, D. S., & M. L. Eggers. 1990. The ecology of inequality: Minorities and the concentration of poverty, 1970–1980. *American Journal of Sociology* 95: 1153–88.

McDonnell, M. 1994. Personal communications. July 13.

McGreevy, J. 1996. *Parish boundaries: The Catholic encounter with race in the twentieth century*. Chicago: University of Chicago Press.

McLoughlin, W. A. 1978. *Revivals, awakenings, and reform*. Chicago: University of Chicago Press.

McNeal, P. 1992. *Harder than war: Catholic peacemaking in the twentieth century*. New Brunswick, NJ: Rutgers University Press.

McRoberts, O. 1999. Understanding the "new" black Pentecostal activism: Lessons from ecumenical urban ministries in Boston." *Sociology of Religion* 60 (Spring): 47–70.

Merry, S. E. 1988. Legal pluralism. *Law and Society Review* 22(5): 869–96.

Midgley, J., & M. Livermore. 1998. Social capital and local economic development: Implications for community social work practice. *Journal of Community Practice* 5: 29–40.

Miller, D. 1998. Religion, privatization, and civic life: The nature of civic engagement in a changing religious environment. Paper presented at the Calvin College Conference on Religion, Social Capital, and Democratic Life. Grand Rapids, Michigan, October 16–17.

Milofsky, C. 1997. Organization from the community: A case study of congregational renewal. *Nonprofit and Voluntary Sector Quarterly* 26: s139–s160.

Minkoff, D. C. 1997. Producing social capital. *American Behavioral Scientist* 40(5): 606–19.

Monroe, K. R. 1996. *The heart of altruism: Perceptions of a common humanity.* Princeton, NJ: Princeton University Press.

Monsma, S. V., & C. J. Soper. 1997. *The challenge of pluralism.* Lanham, MD: Rowman & Littlefield.

Morris, A. D. 1984. *The origins of the civil right movement: Black communities organizing for change.* New York: Free Press.

Mukenge, I. R. 1983. *The black church in urban America: A case study in political economy.* Lanham, MD: University Press of America.

Nafziger, E. W. 1965. The Mennonite ethic in the Weberian framework. *Explorations in Entrepreneurial History* 2: 187–204.

Nardulli, P. F., J. K. Dalager, & D. E. Greco. 1996. Voter turnout in U.S. presidential elections: An historical view and some speculation. *P.S.: Political Science and Politics* 29: 480–90.

National Congress for Community Economic Development (NCCED). 1999. *Community-based development organizations.* Washington, DC: National Congress for Community Economic Development.

Neuhaus, R. J. 1984. *The naked public square: Religion and democracy in America.* Grand Rapids, MI: Eerdmans.

Newton, K. 1997. Social capital and democracy. *American Behavioral Scientist* 40 (5): 575–86.

Nie, N. H., J. Junn, & K. Stehlik-Berry. 1996. *Education and democratic citizenship in America.* Chicago: University of Chicago Press.

Nolan, J. L., Jr. 1997. *The therapeutic state: Justifying government at century's end.* New York: New York University Press.

Norris, P. 1996. Does television erode social capital? A reply to Putnam. *P.S.: Political Science and Politics* 29: 474–79.

O'Brien, D., & T. Shannon, eds. 1977. *Renewing the earth: Catholic documents on peace, justice and liberation.* New York: Image Books.

Olson, D. 1989. Church friendships: Boon or barrier to church growth? *Journal for the Scientific Study of Religion* 28: 432–47.

————. 1993. Fellowship ties and the transmission of religious identity. In J. Carroll & W. C. Roof, eds., *Beyond establishment: Protestant identity in a post-Protestant age.* Louisville, KY: Westminster Press.

Olson, M. 1964. *The logic of collective action: Public goods and the theory of groups.* Cambridge, MA: Harvard University Press.

O'Neill, M. 1989. *The third America: The emergence of the nonprofit sector in the United States.* San Francisco: Jossey-Bass.

Orr, J. B. 1998. *Los Angeles religion: A civic profile.* Los Angeles: University of Southern California, Center for Religion and Civic Culture.

Orr, J. B., D. E. Miller, D. C. Roof, & J. G. Melton. 1994. *Politics of the spirit: Religion and multiethnicity in Los Angeles.* Los Angeles: University of Southern California.

Orr, M. 1992. Urban regimes and human capital policies: A study of Baltimore. *Journal of Urban Affairs* 14 (2): 173–87.

Park, J., & C. Smith. 2000. To whom much has been given . . . Religious capital and community voluntarism among church-going Protestants. *Journal for the Scientific Study of Religion* 39 (September): 272–86.

Paterson, J. L. 1987. Stewardship: Theory and practice in a Canadian Christian farmers organization. Expanded version of a paper presented at the annual meeting of the Association of American Geographers, Portland, Oregon, April.

Pattillo-McCoy, M. 1998. Church culture as a strategy of action in the black community. *American Sociological Review* 63: 767–84.

Payne, W. J., ed. 1991. *Directory of African American religious bodies*. Washington, DC: Howard University Press.

Peaslee, A. J. 1959. The Quakers and world conditions. In H. M. Lippincott, ed., *Through a Quaker archway*. New York: Thomas Yoseloff.

Peterson, S. 1992. Church participation and political participation: The spillover effect. *American Politics Quarterly* 20: 123–39.

Pew Research Center for the People & the Press. 1997. *Trust and citizen engagement in metropolitan Philadelphia: A case study*. Washington, DC: Pew Research Center for the People & the Press.

Potapchuk, W. R., J. P. Crocker, & W. H. Schechter. 1997. Building community with social capital: Chits and chums or chats with change. *National Civic Review* 86:129–40.

Powell, W. W., & P. J. DiMaggio, eds. 1991. *The new institutionalism in organizational analysis*. Chicago: University of Chicago Press.

Psacharopoulos, G. 1992. *Returns to investment in education: A global update*. Washington, DC: The World Bank.

Putnam, R. D. 1993a. *Making democracy work: Civic traditions in modern Italy*. Princeton, NJ: Princeton University Press.

_____. 1993b. The prosperous community: Social capital and public life. *The American Prospect* 13 (Spring): 35–42.

_____. 1995a. Bowling alone: America's declining social capital. *Journal of Democracy* 6 (January): 65–78.

_____. 1995b. Tuning in, tuning out: The strange disappearance of social capital in America. *PS: Political Science and Politics* 28 (December): 664–83.

_____. 1996. The strange disappearance of civic America. *American Prospect* (Winter): 34–48.

_____. 1998. Foreword. *Housing Policy Debate* 9 (1): v–viii.

_____. 2000. *Bowling alone: The collapse and Revival of American community*. New York: Simon and Schuster.

Queen, E. L. 1996. *The religious roots of philanthropy in the west: Judaism, Christianity, and Islam*. Indianapolis: Indiana University Center on Philanthropy, Working Paper # 96-4.

Reimer, S. 1995. A look at cultural effects on religiosity: A comparison between the United States and Canada. *Journal for the Scientific Study of Religion* 34 (4): 445–57.

Rogers, D., G. Bultena, & K. Barb. 1975. Voluntary association membership and political participation: An exploration of the mobilization hypothesis. *The Sociological Quarterly* 16 (Summer): 305–18.

Rogers, M. 1990. *In cold anger: A story of faith and power politics*. Denton, TX: University of North Texas Press.

Rogers, S. C., & S. Salamon. 1983. Inheritance and social organization among family farmers. *American Ethnologist* 10: 529–48.

Ronsvalle, J., & S. Ronsvalle. 1992. *The state of church giving through 1992*. Champaign, IL: Empty Tomb.

Roof, W. C.. 1979. Concepts and indicators of religious commitment: A critical review. In R. Wuthnow, ed., *The religious dimension*. New York: Academic Press.

_____. 1993. *A generation of seekers*. San Francisco: HarperSanFrancisco.

Roof, W. C. & W. McKinney. 1987. *American mainline religion.* New Brunswick, NJ: Rutgers University Press.

Roozen, D. A., W. McKinney, & J. W. Carroll. 1984. *Varieties of religious presence: Mission in public life.* New York: Pilgrim Press.

Rosenstone, S. J., & J. M. Hansen. 1993. *Mobilization, participation, and democracy in America.* New York: Macmillan.

Ross, T. 1995. *The impact of Industrial Areas Foundation community organizing on East Brooklyn: A study of East Brooklyn congregations, 1978–1995.* Ph.D. dissertation, University of Maryland, College Park.

Rozell, M., & C. Wilcox, eds. 1995. *God at the grassroots.* Lanham, MD: Rowman & Littlefield.

_____. 1996. *Second coming: The new Christian right in Virginia politics.* Baltimore: Johns Hopkins University Press.

Salamon, L. M. 1992. *America's nonprofit sector.* New York: The Foundation Center.

Sandel, M. J. 1996. *Democracy's discontent: America in search of a public philosophy.* Cambridge, MA: Harvard University Press.

Schambra, W. 1994. The old values and the new citizenship. *Policy Review* (Summer): 25–41.

Schlozman, K. L., H. Brady, & N. Nie. 1997. The big tilt: Participatory inequality in America. *The American Prospect* 32 (May-June): 74–80 (http://epn.org/prospect/32/32verbfs.html).

Schlozman, K. L., & J. T. Tierney. 1986. *Organized interests and American democracy.* New York: Harper & Row.

Schnucker, G. 1986. *The East Friesens in America: An illustrated history of their colonies to the present time.* Trans. by K. De Wall of 1917 German edition. Topeka, KS: Jostens.

Schor, J. 1992. *The overworked American.* New York: Basic Books.

Schudson, M. 1998. *The good citizen.* New York: Free Press.

Seligman, A. 1992. *The idea of civil society.* New York: Free Press.

_____. 1997. *The problem of trust.* Princeton: Princeton University Press.

Shirley, D. 1997. *Community organizing for urban school reform.* Austin: University of Texas Press.

Silverman, C. 2000. *Faith-based communities and welfare reform: California religious community capacity study.* San Francisco: Institute for Nonprofit Organization Management, University of San Francisco.

Simon, A. 1975. *Bread for the world.* New York: Paulist Press.

Sinopoli, R. C. 1992. *The foundations of American citizenship: Liberalism, the constitution, and civic virtue.* New York: Oxford University Press.

Skerry, P. 1993. *Mexican Americans: The ambivalent minority.* New York: Free Press.

Skocpol, T. 1996. *The Tocqueville problem: Civic engagement in American democracy.* Presidential address for the annual meeting of the Social Science History Association, New Orleans, Louisiana, October 12.

Skocpol, T., & M. Fiorina. 1999. Making sense of the civic engagement debate. In T. Skocpol & M. Fiorina, eds., *Civic engagement in American democracy.* Washington, DC: Brookings Institution Press / New York: Russell Sage Foundation.

Smidt, C. 1999. Religion and civic engagement: A comparative analysis. *The Annals of the American Academy of Political and Social Science* 565 (September 1999): 176–92.

Smith, T. W. 1996. Factors relating to misanthropy in contemporary American society. GSS Topical Report No. 29. Chicago: NORC.

_____. 1998. A review of church attendance measures. *American Sociological Review* 63: 131–45.

Sochen, J. 1980. Jewish women as volunteer activists. *American Jewish History* 70: 23–34.

Stark, R., & J. C. McCann. 1993. Market forces and Catholic commitment: Exploring the new paradigm. *Journal for the Scientific Study of Religion* 32 (2): 111–24.

Steere, D. V., ed. 1984 *Quaker spirituality: Selected writings*. New York: Paulist Press.

Stepan, A. 1988. *Rethinking military politics*. Princeton, NJ: Princeton University Press.

Stob, H. 1983. Observations on the concept of antithesis. In P. De Klerk & R. R. De Ridder, eds., *Perspectives on the Christian Reformed Church*. Grand Rapids, MI: Baker Book House.

Stolle, D., & T. R. Rochon. 1998. Are all associations alike? Member diversity, associational type, and the creation of social capital. *American Behavioral Scientist* 42 (September): 47–65.

Sugar Creek Mennonite Church, Wayland, Iowa: 1871–1971. 1971. n. p.

Sugar Creek Mennonite Church, Wayland, Iowa: 1972–1986. 1986. n. p.

Sweetser, T. 1983. *Successful parishes*. Minneapolis: Winston Press.

Tarrow, S. 1996. Making social science work across space and time: A critical reflection on Robert Putnam's *Making Democracy Work*. *American Political Science Review* 90 (June): 389–97.

Tate, K. 1991. *From protest to politics: The new black voters in American elections*. New York: Russell Sage Foundation.

Taylor, C. 1995. Liberal politics and the public sphere. In A. Etzioni, ed., *New communitarian thinking: Persons, virtues, institutions, and communities*. Charlottesville: University of Virginia Press.

Taylor, H. 1996. Americans more alienated than at any time in last 30 years. *The Harris Poll* (January 15).

Teachman, J., K. Paasch, & K. Carver. 1997. Social capital and the generation of human capital. *Social Forces* 75 (June): 1343–59.

Thomas, G. M. 1989. *Revivalism and American culture*. Chicago: University of Chicago Press.

Thomas, S. B., S. C. Quinn, A. Billingsley, & C. Caldwell. 1994. The characteristics of northern black churches with community health outreach programs. *American Journal of Public Health* 84: 575–79.

Tipton, S. M. 1993. An American paradox: The place of religion in an ambiguous polity. In S. Arjomand, ed., *The political dimensions of religion*. Albany: SUNY Press.

de Tocqueville, A. 1969. *Democracy in America*. J. P. Mayer, ed., G. Lawrence, trans. Garden City, NY: Doubleday.

United States Department of Commerce. Bureau of the Census. 1984. *1982 Census of Agriculture*. Volume 1, geographic areas series. Part 15: Iowa: state and county data. Table 4.

United States Department of Commerce. Bureau of the Census. 1994. *1992 Census of Agriculture*. Volume 1, geographic areas series. Part 15: Iowa: state and county data.

United States Department of Commerce. Bureau of the Census. 1995. *Statistical Abstract of the United States, 1995–1996*. Washington, DC: Government Printing Office.

Verba, S., & N. Nie. 1972. *Participation in America: Political democracy and social equality*. New York; Harper & Row.

Verba, S., K. L. Schlozman, & H. E. Brady. 1995. *Voice and equality: Civic voluntarism in American politics*. Cambridge, MA: Harvard University Press.

_____. 1997. The big tilt: Participatory inequality in America. *The American Prospect* 32 (May-June): 74–80 (http://epn.org/prospect/32/32verbfs.html).

Verba, S., K. L. Schlozman, H. E. Brady, & N. Nie. 1993. Race. ethnicity and political resources: Participation in the United States. *British Journal of Political Science* 23, 453–97.

Walker, C. E. 1982. *A rock in a weary land: The African Methodist Episcopal Church during the Civil War and Reconstruction.* Baton Rouge: Louisiana State University Press.

Walker, J. L., Jr. 1991. *Mobilizing interest groups in America: Patrons, professions, and social movements.* Ann Arbor: University of Michigan Press.

Wald, K., L. Kellstedt, & D. Leege. 1993. Civic involvement and political behavior. In D. Leege & L. Kellstedt, eds., *Rediscovering the religious factor in American politics.* Armonk, NY: M. E. Sharpe.

Wall, E., G. Ferrazzi, & F. Schryer. 1998. Getting the goods on social capital. *Rural Sociology* 63(2): 300–22.

Walter, V. A. 1990. Children as citizens in training: Political socialization for a strong democracy. *Nonprofit and Voluntary Sector Quarterly* 19: 7–20.

_____. 1995. Children as volunteers: Learning by doing. In P. G. Schervish, V. A. Hodgkinson, & M. Gates, eds., *Care and community in modern society: Passing on the tradition of service to future generations.* San Francisco: Jossey-Bass.

Walton, H., Jr. 1975. *Black Republicans: The politics of the black and tan.* Metuchen, NJ: Scarecrow Press.

Walzer, M. 1991. The idea of civil society. *Dissent* (Spring): 293–304.

Warner, S. R. 1993. Work in progress toward a new paradigm for the sociological study of religion in the United States. *American Journal of Sociology* 98: 1044–93.

Warren, M. 1998. Community building and political power: A community organizing approach to democratic renewal. *American Behavioral Scientist* 42 (1), 78–92.

_____. 2001. *Dry bones rattling: Community building to revitalize American democracy.* Princeton, NJ: Princeton University Press.

Warren, M. R., & R. L. Wood. 2001. *Faith-based community organizing: An interfaith funders report.* New York: Interfaith Funders.

Wattenberg, M. P. 1990. *The decline of American political parties 1952–1988.* Cambridge, MA: Harvard University Press.

Weisbrod, B. A. 1988. *The nonprofit economy.* Cambridge, MA: Harvard University Press.

West, C. 1982. *Prophecy deliverance! An Afro-American revolutionary Christianity.* Philadelphia: Westminster.

Western, B. 1995. A comparative study of working-class disorganization: Union decline in eighteen advanced capitalist countries. *American Sociological Review* 60 (April): 179–92.

Williams, B. 1988. Formal structures and social reality. In D. Gambetta, ed., *Trust: Making and breaking cooperative relations.* Oxford: Basil Blackwell.

Williams, R. H. 1995. Constructing the public good: Cultural resources and social movements. *Social Problems* 42 (1): 124–44.

_____. 1996. Religion as political resource: Culture or ideology? *Journal for the Scientific Study of Religion* 35 (4): 368–78.

_____. 1997. Afterword: Culture wars, social movements, and institutional politics. In R. H. Williams, ed., *Cultural wars in American politics: Critical review of a popular myth.* Hawthorne, NY: Aldine de Gruyter.

_____. 1998. Voluntarism. In R. Wuthnow, ed., *The encyclopedia of politics and religion*, volume II. Washington, DC: Congressional Quarterly Books.

_____. 1999a. Visions of the good society and the religious roots of American political culture. *Sociology of Religion* 60 (Spring): 1–34.

_____. 1999b. Public religion and hegemony: Contesting the language of the common good. In W. H. Swatos & J. Wellman, eds., *The power of religious publics*. Westport, CT: Praeger.

Williams, R. H., & N. J. Demerath III. 1991. Religion and political process in an American city. *American Sociological Review* 56: 417–31.

_____. 1998. Cultural power: How underdog religious and nonreligious movements triumph over structural odds. In N. J. Demerath III, P. Hall, T. Schmitt, & R. H. Williams, *Sacred companies: Organizational aspects of religion and religious aspects of organizations*. New York: Oxford University Press.

Willmer, W., J. D. Schmidt, & M. Smith. 1999. *The prospering para-church*. San Francisco: Jossey-Bass.

Wilson, J., & T. Janoski. 1995. The contribution of religion to volunteer work. *Sociology of Religion* 56 (Summer): 137–52.

Wilson, R. H., & P. Menzies. 1997. The colonias water bill: Communities demanding change. In R. H. Wilson, ed., *Public policy and community: Activism and governance in Texas*. Austin: University of Texas Press.

Wilson, W. Julius. 1987. *The truly disadvantaged: The inner city, the underclass, and public policy*. Chicago: University of Chicago Press.

_____. 1996. *When work disappears: The world of the new urban poor*. New York: Alfred A. Knopf.

Wind, J. P., & J. M. Lewis, eds. 1994. *American congregations*, 2 vols. Chicago: University of Chicago Press.

Wolfe, A. 1998. *One nation, after all*. New York: Viking.

Wong, P. 1997. The indigent health care package. In R. H. Wilson, ed., *Public policy and community: Activism and governance in Texas*. Austin: University of Texas Press.

Wood, R. L. 1995. *Faith in action: Religion, race, and the future of democracy*. Ph.D. dissertation, University of California, Berkeley.

_____. 1997. Social capital and political culture: God meet politics in the inner city. *American Behavioral Scientist* 40(5): 595–605.

_____. 1999. Religious culture and political action. *Sociological Theory* 17 (November): 307–32.

Woodberry, R. D. 1998. When surveys lie and people tell the truth: How surveys oversample church attenders. *American Sociological Review* 63: 119–22.

Wuthnow, R. 1981. Two traditions in the study of religion. *Journal for the Scientific Study of Religion* 20:16–32.

_____. 1988. *The restructuring of American religion: Society and faith since World War II*. Princeton, NJ: Princeton University Press.

_____. 1991. *Acts of compassion: Caring for others and helping ourselves*. Princeton, NJ: Princeton University Press.

_____. 1994a. *God and Mammon in America*. New York: Free Press.

_____. 1994b. *Producing the sacred: An essay in public religion*. Urbana: University of Illinois Press.

_____. 1994c. *Sharing the journey: Support groups and America's new quest for community*. New York: Free Press.

_____. 1996a. *Christianity and civil society: The contemporary debate*. Valley Forge, PA: Trinity International Press.

_____. 1996b. *Learning to care*. New York: Oxford University Press.

_____. 1997. *The crisis in the church: Spiritual malaise, fiscal woe*. New York: Oxford University Press.

_____. 1998. *Loose connections: Joining together in America's fragmented communities*. Cambridge, MA: Harvard University Press.

_____. 1999. Mobilizing civic engagement: The changing impact of religious involvement. In T. Skocpol & M. P. Fiorina, eds., *Civic engagement in American democracy*. Washington, DC: Brookings Institution Press / Russell Sage Foundation.

Yinger, J. M. 1969. A structural examination of religion. *Journal for the Scientific Study of Religion* 8: 88–99.

Zald, M., & J. McCarthy. 1987. Religious groups as crucibles of social movements. In M. Zald & J. McCarthy, eds., *Social movements in an organizational society*. New Brunswick, NJ: Transaction Books.

Zeff, J., & P. Lyons. 1996. *The downsizing of America*. New York: Times Books.

About the Contributors

Stephanie Clintonia Boddie is an Assistant Professor at the George Warren Brown School of Social Work at Washington University in St. Louis. Her areas of interest are community development and community health with a particular focus on faith-based organizations. She has co-authored two books and several book chapters and articles in the areas of faith based social services.

David Campbell is an Assistant Professor of Political Science at the University of Notre Dame. His research has explored how religion, politics, and public policy intersect in America. He is the editor (along with Paul E. Peterson) of *Charters, Vouchers, and Public Education* (Brookings 2001), to which he has contributed a chapter on the civic education offered by America's public and private schools. He is also a co-author of *The Education Gap: Vouchers and Urban Schools* (Brookings 2002).

John A. Coleman S.J. is Casassa Professor of Social Values at Loyola Marymount University in Los Angeles. Among his sixteen books is *Religion and Nationalism* (Orbis Press, 1995). He has recently published "Christianity and Civil Society" in Robert Post and Nancy Rosenblum, *Civil Society and Government* (Princeton University Press 2001) and "Selling God in America" in Richard Madsen, Ann Swidler, William Sullivan, and Stephen Tipton, eds, *Meaning and Modernity* (University of California Press 2001).

Ram A. Cnaan is a Professor and Director of the Program for the Study of Organized Religion and Social Work at the University of Pennsylvania, School of Social Work. He is the author of *The Newer Deal* (Columbia University 1999) and *The Invisible Caring Hand* (NYU Press 2002). Dr. Cnaan studies the role organized religion plays in helping those in need.

Janel Curry is the Dean for Research and Scholarship and Professor of Geography and Environmental Studies at Calvin College. Her area of research interest is in societal paradigms and natural resource management. She has recently published a book with Steven McGuire titled *Community on Land: Community, Ecology, and the Public Interest* (Rowman and Littlefield 2002).

John C. Green is Professor of Political Science and Director of the Ray C. Bliss Institute of Applied Politics at the University of Akron. He has written extensively on religion and politics in the United States. He is co-author of *The Bully Pulpit, Religion and the Culture Wars*, and co-editor of *Prayers in the Precincts*.

James. L. Guth is William R. Kenan, Jr. Professor of Political Science at Furman University. He has written extensively on the role of religion in American and European politics. He is co-author of *The Bully Pulpit, Religion and the Culture Wars* and is currently engaged in a study of the impact of religious belief and practices on public support for the European Union.

Fredrick C. Harris is Associate Professor of Political Science and Director of the Center for the Study of African-American Politics at the University of Rochester. His areas of interest are political participation, social movements, and African-American politics. He is the author of *Something Within: Religion in African-American Political Activism* (Oxford University Press 1999), which won the best book award by the National Conference of Black Political Scientists, the V.O. Key Award by the Southern Political Science Association, and the Outstanding Book Award by the Society for the Scientific Study of Religion.

Lyman Kellstedt has recently retired from teaching at Wheaton College but continues to engage in research on religion and American politics. He has written extensively on the topic and is co-author of *The Bully Pulpit, Religion and the Culture Wars*.

Donald A. Luidens is Professor of Sociology at Hope College. His research interests have been in the sociology of religion with particular focus on mainline Protestants. Among his publications is the co-authored book *Vanishing Boundaries: The Religion of Mainline Protestant Baby Boomers*.

Roger J. Nemeth is a Professor of Sociology at Hope College in Holland, Michigan. He has long-standing research interests in the changing nature of congregations in American religious life.

Corwin Smidt holds the Paul B. Henry Chair in Christianity and Politics and serves as the director of The Henry Institute for the Study of Christianity and Politics at Calvin College. He has written extensively on the role of religion in American politics. He is co-author of *The Bully Pulpit, Religion and the Culture Wars*, and *Evangelicalism: The Next Generation*.

Mark R. Warren is Associate Professor in the Program on Communities and Schools at the Harvard University Graduate School of Education. He is the author of a book on the Texas/Southwest Industrial Areas Foundation, the nation's most prominent faith-based community organizing network, entitled *Dry Bones Rattling* (Princeton University Press 2001), and is co-editor of *Social Capital and Poor Communities* (Russell Sage Foundation 2001). Mark is currently studying the relationship between community building and school improvement in urban areas, and has begun a research project on white Americans who are active in working for racial justice.

Rhys Williams is Professor and Head of the Department of Sociology at the University of Cincinnati. His research interests focus on the intersection of religion, politics, and social movements, particularly in the United States. His publications include *A Bridging of Faiths: Religion and Politics in a New England City* (with Jay Demerath; 1992) and *Cultural Wars in American Politics: Critical Reviews of a Popular Myth* (editor; 1997). He is currently working on a book about the religious roots of American political language.

Richard Wood is the author of *Faith in Action: Religion, Race, and Democratic Organizing in America* (Chicago University Press 2002), a study of the political culture of faith-based and race-based models of democratic engagement. He holds an M.A. in theology from the Graduate Theological Union and a Ph.D. in sociology from the University of California at Berkeley. He now serves as an Associate Professor in the University of New Mexico's Department of Sociology.

Robert Wuthnow is the Gerhard R. Andlinger Professor of Social Sciences and director of the Center for the Study of American Religion, Princeton University. His numerous books include: *The Restructuring of American Religion; Rediscovering the Sacred; Christianity and Civil Society: The Contemporary Debate;* and *Loose Connections: Joining Together in America's Fragmented Communities.*

Gaynor Yancey is Assistant Professor of Social Work at Baylor University in Waco, Texas. Her research interests include studying faith-based organizations and their practices related to helping address the needs of underserved, urban populations. She is currently involved in a study of effective practices of faith-based organizations and the public/private sector.

Steve Yonish did his graduate studies in political science at the University of Wisconsin. He is currently working for Forrester Research in the Boston area.

Index

Page numbers in *italics* refer to tables.

259